The Psychology of Managerial Incompetence:

A Sceptic's Dictionary of Modern Organizational Issues

Adrian Furnham
Professor of Psychology
University College London

Whurr Publishers Ltd
London

© 1998 Whurr Publishers

First published 1998 by
Whurr Publishers Ltd
19b Compton Terrace, London N1 2UN, England

Reprinted 1998, 2000

British Library Cataloguing in Publication Data
A catalogue record for this book is available from the British Library.

ISBN 01 86156 063 X

Every effort has been made to obtain permission to use copyright material used within this book.

Photoset by Stephen Cary
Printed and bound in the UK by Publish on Demand Ltd, London

Dedication

For Alison, naturally

Adrian Furnham is author of:

The Economic Mind
The Protestant Work Ethic
Personality at Work
Consumer Profiles
Biodata
Corporate Assessment
Business Watching
Why Psychology?
The New Economic Mind
The Myths of Management
The Psychology of Behaviour at Work
Children as Consumers
The Psychology of Money
All in the Mind, The Essence of Psychology

Contents

Introduction	1
A.	Alienated workers	15
	Amnesic organizations	17
	Appraisal and its problems	18
	Assessing potential	23
B.	Benchmarking	27
	Biodata	29
	Blaming the victim	32
	Book reviews	33
	Bureaucracy	34
	Business books	36
	Business ethics	37
	Business and pleasure	39
C.	Career development: counselling for the future	41
	Carrot and stick	43
	CC index	44
	Change checklist	45
	Complaints	46
	Compliments and customer feedback	48
	Conspicuous consumption	50
	Consumer boycotts	51
	Corporate culture	53
	Creativity cannot be taught	55
	Cross-functional teams	58
	Culture shock	58
D.	Definitions	63
	Desks	65
	Diversity in business	67
	Doubletalk	70
	Drafting reports	71
	Dressing down	72

E.   Economic success   75
      Electronic mail   76
      Entertrainment   78
      Eponymous fame   79
      Equity at work   80
      Expert scientists   83
      Explaining away lack of ability   84

F.   Fear of giving feedback   87
      File thickness   89
      Filthy lucre   89
      Financial year   90
      Focus groups   91

G.   Graphology   95
      Group think   97
      Gurus ideas   99

H.   Hairiness   103
      Haloes   104
      Headhunters   104
      High flyers   105
      Human resources   106

I.   Impostor syndrome   109
      In-house trainers   111
      Interview questions   113
      Intrinsic motivation   113

J.   Job-ad speak   117
      Job hobbyist   118
      Job satisfaction   119
      Job title inflation   120

K.   Keeping people waiting   123
      Knowledge of people   123

L.   Leadership   127
      Left brain and right brain   129

M.   Managing your boss   133
      Mapping values   135
      Marketing speak   137
      Measuring performance   137

	Mission statements	139
	Money madness	140
	Money as a motivator	144
	Monitoring workers	145
	Multiple feedback	146
	Music while you work	148
N.	National differences	151
	Need for power	152
	Negotiating the Pacific Rim	156
	Nepotism	158
	Newsletter begging	158
	Norms: knowing what is average	159
O.	Opportunism	163
	Opposing innovations	163
P.	Pay	167
	Performance-related pay (PRP)	168
	Place dropping	169
	Power ordering	170
	Procrastination	171
	Public relations	174
	Punishing the punctual	176
Q.	Quantum mechanics and administration	179
R.	Rating staff	181
	References	183
	Reinventing one's discipline	186
S.	Selecting selectors	187
	Selection fallacies	190
	Selection versus training	192
	Slogans	192
	Successful sales staff	193
T.	Teaching thinking	197
	Teamwork	198
	Telecentres	200
	Time-filling strategies	203
	Time types	205
	Tips	205
	Training: Is it measurable?	206
	TV ads	208

U.   Understanding potential problems   211
     Upward ratings   213

V.   Verbification   217
     Vitae   217

W.   Word rationing   219
     Workplace deviants   220

Introduction

Why is it that all the jokes about management style are derogatory? *Seagull* management involves 'flying' into an organizational outpost, dumping all over the employees and flying out again. *Mushroom* management, too, has scatological and coprological images for it involves keeping employees in the dark and periodically covering them with manure.

Another theme is pusillanimity or management cowardice. The *kipper* style of management refers to the filleted fish that we find in shops, which is two-faced and has no guts like some managers. The *juggler* management style refers to the fact that these experts are keeping many balls in the air at the same time while protecting their own.

Other styles refer to the non-existent management style, sometimes called *absentee landlord* or *golf-club* style. Here the boss is too often 'out' doing other things (or hiding) to manage. This style, however, often leads the staff to do likewise and one soon finds the whole outfit becomes the *Marie Celeste* organization.

This book is about the things managers do and believe. It is about the myths they hold and why so many managers are, in effect, incompetent. It aims to educate and amuse as well as provide advice about what to do, as well as what not to do, in managing others. It is arranged in alphabetical order and hopefully covers most areas where managerial incompetence manifests itself most strongly.

My predecessor, in whose chair I sit, upon whose desk I write, and whose title I share, wrote a superb book called *On the Psychology of Military Incompetence*. An ex-military man, *sans* both an eye and arm to prove it, a perspicacious historian, but uniquely also a trained and celebrated psychologist, Dixon (1976) documented innumerable incidences of folly on the battlefield.

He described, analysed and explained what, with hindsight, seemed extraordinary stupidity of people in the armed forces over the past century. In many incidents, if not most, the arrogance and ignorance of military managers led to manifold deaths. The examples outlined are comically tragic. It is difficult to comprehend how unbelievably stupid individuals can be in times of stress. The result for many ordinary people is literally catastrophic: loss of life, limb and livelihood.

This book is not about military incompetence but managerial incompetence. The two are, of course, closely related, as military officers are no more than the managers in a specialist field. The military has strong traditions: accepted codes of behaviour and unique tasks but battalions, regiments and smaller units can be seen as organizations like any other.

It may, at first, appear as if the consequences of military incompetence are more dire than those of simple managerial incompetence. A battlefield of corpses hardly ranks with the collapse of, and resultant lay-offs at, the local widget factory. The long-term effects of psychological and physical stress resulting from incompetent management can be equally great, however; as can the spin-off effects on the family and associates of the badly managed employee.

Dixon claimed that military incompetence is preventable, tragically expensive and predictable. Military disasters, he argued, followed a pattern that makes psychological sense. He notes that incompetence in the military is fundamentally no different from that in commerce, politics or state service except:

- military organizations may attract a minority of people who are particularly prone to failure at high levels of command;
- the nature of militarism serves to accentuate less adaptive traits in leaders;
- the military are not democratically elected and few are sacked, dismissed or demoted for their incompetence;
- the pay-off or consequences of bad military decisions are often incredibly high.

The idea that military incompetence is simply a function of low intelligence is rigorously rejected. Dixon's explanation lies in militarism, which he sees as the development of rules and conventions designed to control hostility and reduce anxiety. The anti-intellectualism and anti-effeminacy, codes of honour, sensitivity to criticism and intolerance of ambiguity, above average aggression and low self-esteem are military values and are closely associated with incompetence. All of these values can be found in certain companies that rejoice in the quasi-military management style and values. Alas, these authoritarian and dogmatic traits are those that lead many 'military managers' to find it easy to 'fit in' and, in time, rise to positions of power. Dixon notes that the military personality is one who is drawn to, and seems to have an emotional investment in, using force to solve problems. Dixon's work, and that of others, has revealed that the incompetent military leader is emotionally dependent, socially conformist, religiously orthodox with a distrust of the new and strange. Traits particularly associated with the military incompetent include lack of creativity and imagination and very little evidence of aesthetic appreciation, cognitive complexity, independence, self-expression and altruism. The lethal combination of high anxiety and low self-esteem in part makes the behaviour of the incompetent simultaneously bizarre, but unpredictable, with awful consequences. The urge to simply order, control and follow rigid but ineffectual codes of conduct epitomizes the failed military manager. The opposite traits of tact, flexibility and imagination seem to be the best predictors of managerial success.

Dixon's view is that authoritarian people are attracted to military organizations and will presumably be more likely to succeed in them. Just as we are all attracted to organizations (work, educational, recreational) because of the values they stand for, and the way they 'go about things', so people seek out jobs that fit their personalities. Military fiascos based on the blunders of senior officers clearly follow a pattern. There is a tendency to underestimate the capabilities of the enemy relative to one's own; an inability to admit mistakes, which motivates attempts to blame others and makes it difficult to learn from experience; a fundamental conservatism that inhibits change and ignores technical advances; a failure adequately to use reconnaissance; a tendency to discount warning signals that indicate things are going wrong; passivity and procrastination; failure to take the initiative and exploit advantages gained; and finally, a predisposition to use frontal assaults, often against the enemy's main line of defence.

It is difficult to 'prove' retrospectively that the personalities of classic failure in the world of the military were all authoritarians. Nevertheless, Dixon's analysis is important and gives an insight into all types of managerial incompetence.

The work on military incompetence in part explains managerial incompetence. Of course most armies share a similar structure and culture, which is fairly instantly recognizable. Certain individuals are attracted to the military corporate culture, which is particularly strong and enduring. There are many organizations that share military values but there are others that are almost the precise opposite. This does not mean they are necessarily immune from incompetence but rather that they are simply prone to different types of incompetence.

Paradoxically, incompetent managers are often good at avoiding changes and avoiding making decisions. The incompetent manager is often change averse and cunning at undermining those who are genuinely forward looking. Dim, challenged or under par executives often attempt to undermine the ideas of brighter, more change-oriented specialists.

Although incompetent managers have stylistic preferences for each of these change- and risk-avoidance tactics, it is likely that many have used quite a number in their time. There are other, similar tactics used by managers to avoid decisions and reject change:

- The temper-tantrum method. The manager regresses, calls the decision requester names, stamps his or her foot, appears outraged or insulted, or even apoplectic. If possible the manager should weep with indignation.
- The hush-hush method. The manager might call the specialist change agent to one side and in a conspiratorial stage whisper point out that he/she is rushing in where angels fear to tread. He/she may suggest that the specialist clearly does not understand the latest company figures, the real wishes of the CEO, the contents of the secret corporate plan, etc. and that requesting such a decision will make the specialist look naïve – even mean possible sacking.
- The clarification method. This is the 'more details please' approach. This analysis–paralysis method is aimed at exhausting the decision requester because it is potentially endless and has nothing to do with actually gaining information. Most requesters eventually give up and thus no decisions are made.
- The double-talk method. The use of in-house management jargon can easily confuse those not fully conversant with this ambiguous language. Try: 'but that's against the delayering, re-engineering ethos of this company' or 'how does that square with empowerment quality circles?'
- The denial method. Denying that a decision has to be made or change made and that a situation requires change can be very effective.
- The 'that's your problem, shorty' method. This method involves handing the problem straight back to the change

agent. The idea is to make him or her feel weak, selfish, even demanding, but this requires skill in developing the appropriate degree of hauteur.

- The 'haven't got time/tear jerker' method. Here the decision maker will state plainly that he/she hasn't got time to consider the problem but cleverly manages to come up with a reason that makes the requester feel very uncomfortable. Absence or resignation of a key member of staff also works as an excuse. A close relation just admitted to intensive care is usually a winner.
- The 'pass the buck' method. For example, a change resister might say: 'Do ask John, he has the latest figures' or 'That will have to go before the board. Pity you've just missed the last meeting; the next one is in a couple of months.'
- The 'I'm glad you called' method. This is followed by a swift change of subject, ending with the requester being given something different to investigate.

Some managers are not only incompetent – they are pathologically deranged and mentally unstable. Their style and decisions are often based more on gratifying neurotic needs than making reasoned decisions. Neurotic, paranoid and with delusions of grandeur, they can easily lead an organization to destruction.

A trained psychoanalyst interested in organizational behaviour has in fact described whole organizations in terms of individual pathology. Thus, instead of the neurotic or paranoid patient we have the neurotic and paranoid organization. The argument is not that managers become neurotic because their firms fail but rather that companies fail because their managers are neurotic. It is assumed that corporate culture, structure and strategy, if powerfully shaped by a neurotic CEO, reflect his or her personal pathology.

Kets De Vries and Miller (1985) believe that the intrapsychic functioning of key organization members is a major factor influencing shared organizational fantasies. It permeates all levels of functioning, shapes the organizational culture and makes for a dominant organizational adaptive style. This style influences decisions about strategy, structure, selection and self-perception. To the extent that the key organizational member (i.e. managing director) functions neurotically, the organization may also exhibit similar tendencies. In an organization in which power is highly centralized in a leader with paranoid tendencies ('everybody is out to get me') there is likely to be a good deal of vigilance caused by distrust of subordinates and competitors alike. This may lead to the development of many control and information systems and a 'secret service'-type fascination with gathering intelligence from inside and outside the firm. Paranoid thinking will also lead to much centralization of power as the top executive tries to control everything himself (nobody can be completely trusted). The strategy is likely to emphasize 'protection' and reducing dependency on particular consultants, sources of data, markets or customers. There is likely to be a good deal of diversification with tight control over divisions and much analytical activity. The personality of the leader driven by intrapsychic fantasies centring on distrust can set the tone for strategy, structure, and organizational culture.

Kets De Vries and Miller (1985) identified five very common neurotic styles, well established in the psychoanalytic and psychiatric literature: paranoid, compulsive, dramatic, depressive, and schizoid. Each style has its specific characteristics, its predominant motivating fantasy and its associated dangers. In addition to the paranoid organization discussed above, consider the following.

The *compulsive organization* emphasizes ritual; it plans every detail in advance and carries out its activities in a routine, pre-programmed style. Thoroughness and conformity are valued. These organizations are hierarchical and generally have elaborate policies, rules, and procedures. The strategies of compulsive firms reflect their preoccupation with detail and established procedures. Each compulsive organization has a distinctive area of competence and specializes in this area, not in the area that is a response to the marketplace.

The *dramatic organization* is hyperactive, impulsive, dramatically venturesome, and dangerously uninhibited. In such an organization, decision makers act only on hunches and impressions, taking on widely diverse projects. Top managers reserve the right to start bold ventures independently; subordinates have limited power.

The *depressive organization* lacks confidence, is inactive, conservative, insular, and has an entrenched bureaucracy. The only things that get done are activities that have been made routine. Depressive organizations are well established and serve a single mature market.

The *schizoid organization* lacks leadership. Its top executive discourages interaction. Sometimes the second level of executives makes up for the leader's lack of involvement but often they simply fight to fill the leadership vacuum. In such organizations strategy more often reflects individual goals and internal politics rather than external threats or opportunities the organization needs to take into account.

The style of each organization is set out in Table 1. The strengths and weaknesses of each firm are described in Table 2.

Table 1: Summary of the five neurotic styles

Key factor	Neurotic style				
	Paranoid	Compulsive	Dramatic	Depressive	Schizoid
Characteristics	Suspiciousness and mistrust of others; hypersensitivity and hyperalertness; readiness to counter perceived threats; overconcern with hidden motives and special meanings; intense attention span; cold, rational, unemotional	Perfectionism; preoccupation with trivial details; insistence that others submit to own way of doing things; relationships seen in terms of dominance and submission; lack of spontaneity; inability to relax; meticulousness, dogmatism, obstinacy	Self-dramatization, excessive expression of emotions; incessant drawing of attention to self; narcissistic preoccupation; a craving for activity and excitement; alternating between idealization and devaluation of others; exploitativeness; incapacity for concentration or sharply focused attention	Feelings of guilt, worthlessness, self-reproach, inadequacy; sense of helplessness and hopelessness – of being at the mercy of events; diminished ability to think clearly; loss of interest and motivation; inability to experience pleasure	Detachment, non-involvement, withdrawal; sense of estrangement; lack of excitement or enthusiasm; indifference to praise or criticism; lack of interest in present or future; appearance cold, unemotional
Fantasy	I cannot really trust anybody; a menacing superior force exists that is out to get me; I had better be on my guard	I don't want to be at the mercy of events; I have to master and control all the things affecting me	I want to get attention from and impress the people who count in my life	It is hopeless to change the course of events in my life; I am just not good enough	The world of reality does not offer any satisfaction to me; my interactions with others will eventually fail and cause harm, so it is safer to remain distant
Dangers	Distortion of reality due to a preoccupation with confirmation of suspicions; loss of capacity for spontaneous action because of defensive attitudes	Inward orientation; indecisiveness and postponement; avoidance due to the fear of making mistakes; inability to deviate from planned activity; excessive reliance on rules and regulations; difficulties in seeing 'the big picture'	Superficiality; suggestibility; the risk of operating in a non-factual world – action based on 'hunches'; overreaction to minor events; others may feel used and abused	Overly pessimistic outlook; difficulties in concentration and performance; inhibition of action, indecisiveness	Emotional isolation causes frustration of dependency needs of others; bewilderment and aggressiveness may result

From The Neurotic Organization by Kets De Vries and Miller (1984). Reproduced with the permission of Jossey-Bass Publishers.

Table 2: Strengths and weaknesses of the five organizational styles

Style	Potential strengths	Potential weaknesses
Paranoid	Good knowledge of threats and opportunities inside and outside the firm.	Lack of concerted and consistent energy – few distinctive competencies.
	Reduced market risk from diversification.	Insecurity and disenchantment among second-tier managers and their subordinates because of the atmosphere of distrust.
Compulsive	Fine internal controls and efficient co-operation.	Traditions embraced so firmly that strategy and structure become anachronistic.
	Well-integrated and focused product-market strategy.	Things so programmed that bureaucratic dysfunctions, inflexibility, and inappropriate responses become common.
	lack of influence and discretion;	Managers discontented owing to their stifling of initiative.
Dramatic	Creates the momentum for passing through the start-up phase of a firm.	Inconsistent strategies that have a very high element of risk and cause resources to be needlessly squandered.
	Some good ideas for revitalizing tired firms.	Problems in controlling widespread operations and in restoring their profitability.
		Rash and dangerous expansion policies.
		Inadequate role played by second tier of managers.
Depressive	Efficiency of internal processes.	Anachronistic strategies and organizational stagnation.
	Focused strategy.	Confinement to dying markets.
		Weak competitive posture due to poor product lines.
		Apathetic and inactive managers.
Schizoid	Second-tier managers share in strategy formulation; a variety of points of view may be brought to bear.	Inconsistent or vacillating strategy.
		Issues decided by political negotiations more than facts.
		Lack of leadership.
		Climate of suspicion and distrust, which prevents collaboration.

From The Neurotic Organization by Kets De Vries and Miller (1984). Reproduced with the permission of Jossey-Bass Publishers.

The bottom line of a lot of this work is that certain dysfunctional aspects of the performance of business people and organizations may be resistant to change because they are based on powerful unconscious motivation. Most of us have met the paranoid manager and the compulsive CEO. What is surprising is how quickly they are able to shape the department, section or organization as a whole to fit their personal delusions, fantasies and personal needs.

Observations suggest that neurotic managers choose, create and maintain dysfunctional work groups that have shared fantasies and organizational myths, and these myths often distract them from primary tasks. Their neuroticism means they transfer their anxieties and misperceptions onto their staff (superiors, subordinates, peers and even shareholders and customers) and this frustrates and angers staff who may be stranglingly bound or cursorily abandoned by a neurotic manager.

Psychologists believe that much managerial neuroticism is a legacy of frustrating interpersonal experiences at earlier life stages. Pathological symptoms are seen as basically the outcome of defensive reactions needed for the preservation of the self. The rigidity, apathy, and defensiveness of some managers are, it is argued, all defensive strategies devised to circumvent unknown or threatening situations. They are often unsuccessful, however, and lead whole companies to become neurotic.

Adaptation to the world of work can lead to a profound sense of inadequacy for some, which is associated with frustration, disappointment, and apathy. Frustrated aggression in the workplace can be turned either inward or outward. The former leads to inner doubt, anxiety and guilt; the latter to extreme stress. Organizations must learn to expect and channel aggression because survival and adaptation is determined, in part, by the balance between inward- and outward-directed aggression. Inward aggression is associated with narcissism, rivalry, and dependence.

The desire to be exceptional and the virtual impossibility of achieving perfection often lead to narcissism and the all-or-nothing character. Inevitably these types are anxious, over-aroused and vigilant. They may never finish tasks, may be overly forgetful or unwilling to follow up promises precisely because they fear negative feedback. It can also lead to 'workaholism' where work provides a structure that seemingly prevents emotional breakdown and self-fragmentation.

A neurotic manager may be exceptionally rivalrous and competitive with hidden fears of retaliation dating back to early childhood. On the other hand the unstable manager may become dependent, identifying with, and overzealously internalizing the values of, power over others, even gurus. The dependent manager may take refuge in idleness, ignorance, helplessness or irresponsible acts.

Managers who turn their aggression outward are often highly rebellious: many are job hoppers because of a history of being quickly lured and fired. For them, work often unconsciously assumes the form of a symbolic struggle for obedience and control and they drift through organizational life troubled by frustrations and disappointments.

There is one more major reason for managerial incompetence. It is what Shapiro calls fad surfing – the practice of riding the crest of the latest management wave and then paddling out again just in time to ride the next one. She notes that fad surfing is always absorbing for managers, lucrative for consultants, but disastrous for organizations. She is critical of the 'vision thing' and mission statements. She argues that rather than be concerned with just flattening or delayering organizations managers must organize for their people in their own particular situation, rather than just doing 'what the theory says'. Corporate culture is used as an excuse for not making desperately needed changes in the way a company conducts its business.

She asks us to consider the myth of the open environment, the continuous improving or learning organization or loyalty based management. Somewhat cynically, but totally accurately, she defines the open (work) environment as 'A place where you can say anything you want as long as you don't rock the boat and where you can find out anything you want as long as you discover it by using the internal grapevine'. Despite the way in which the organization trumpets its open communication philosophy, all employees find out that there is nothing to gain and much to lose by actually contributing ideas and observations, let alone criticisms. Further, gossip on the unofficial grapevine is seen (and proved) to be more reliable than official statements.

Empowerment is a new form of delegation that terrifies senior managers when done well. Customer satisfaction is a new job-creation programme for consultants. Shapiro argues that neither the new management techniques nor the problems they are meant to solve are new. Managers need to be more courageous in resisting fads and making decisions that inevitably have no guarantees. She offers some wickedly funny but disarmingly accurate definitions:

> **benchmarking** 1: Comparison of operations against best in class; a superb way of sparking new ideas and significant insights when the examples are selected with thought and imagination; 2: The basis for great jobs in which the incumbents have no substantive responsibilities other than to gallivant around the world, meet all sorts of interesting people, make occasional proclamations about all the neat things other companies do, and submit appropriately lavish expense reports.

> **customer satisfaction** 1: New name for the oldest premise in business – that unless customers are more satisfied with your product than they are with their next best alternative, they won't be your customers for

long; 2: New name for one type of standard market research, often designed in rote compliance with guidelines, thereby limiting actual thinking about how to provide customers with a better deal than the competition offers; 3: New job-creation program, leading to legions of new experts within companies and consulting firms.

empowerment 1: The result that ensues when employees understand what 'doing a good job' means for their position, are motivated to do so, and are given the tools and autonomy for using their hundred decisions a day toward this purpose; 2: New name for what used to be known as 'delegation'; 3: A process now also sometimes called 'employee involvement' or 'employee satisfaction' (but never 'delegation'), that when done well can scare the living daylights out of corporate chiefs and union executives alike.

flat organization 1: The process of reducing the number of levels that make up an organization's structure in order to increase its ability to respond quickly and effectively to changes in customer needs and competitive dynamics; 2: A set of actions once known as 'decentralization,' that historically has in turn a precipitate and equal and opposite set of reactions – namely recentralization; 3: An organizational concept that aims to abolish all hierarchy and thereby produces new organizations with slower decision-making and greater focus on internal politicking than ever before.

mission statement 1: A short, specific statement of purpose, intended to serve as a loose musical score that motivates everyone to play the same tune without strict supervision; 2: Frequently, an assertion of undying commitment to some amalgam of 'total quality,' 'low-cost producer,' 'empowered workforce,' 'excellence,' 'continuous improvement,' and other bizbus shibboleths that, although written for a specific organization, is equally applicable to an aircraft manufacturer, a software development firm, a community hospital, a department store chain, or the local dry cleaner; 3: In some companies, a talisman, hung in public spaces, to ward off evil spirits.

total quality management (TQM) 1: A management philosophy based on the idea that quality is a prerequisite for improving the competitive position of any company rather than a cost-burden that only some companies can afford; 2: A set of tools that mostly predate the TQM label and that, when practised as part of a TQM program, so totally absorb management in 'process' that the process becomes an end in itself; 3: A process import thought by some to be an integral tactic in Japan Inc.'s secret strategy for destroying American enterprise.

(Shapiro, 1996)

Davis (1997), too, suggests that many managers become incompetent, or are incompetent, because they believe in too many myths. He lists 23 myths and argues that all managers need to abandon the idea that gurus know everything, that numbers should always be respected, that the Pacific Rim always gets things right or that age and sex (gender) are important to success. He is particularly scathing about management consultants and managers who use them. Their desire for repeat business, he believes, prevents them from doing good work and delivering tough messages and is too concerned with image and not content. He argues that myths do more harm than good. These myths are generated and perpetrated by teachers in business schools, consultants, governments and business organizations.

Furnham (1996) has argued that so many incompetent managers hold and follow management myths for five reasons:

1. They don't get clear, specific, feedback on their actual style so they cannot learn from experience.
2. They are superstitious and it takes careful and honest analysis and experimentation to dispose superstition.
3. Most have had a pretty erratic (often poor) formal management education.
4. Many are simply desperate for answers and will follow anyone or any theory that has sufficient self-proclaimed confidence.
5. Many managers hate, and are frightened by, ambiguity and uncertainty and conform to myths simply to avoid these.

Managers hold and follow myths for many reasons. One is that the gurus of 'management science' often do not help. As Micklethwaite and Wooldridge (1996) point out: 'In few other academic disciplines do personal peccadillos play such a large part. In writing about management, many of the gurus are simply writing about themselves – and their own decidedly abnormal lives' (p. 365). They point out that management theory is a mishmash, an essentially immature discipline. This partly ties in with the fact that it attracts charlatans but also that its audience demands instant solution.

> Anxious managers grasp at management literature as a panacea for all their worries. Many firms turn to management theory only when they are desperate. Their minds clouded by panic, they start out with exaggerated expectations, put the theory into practice for a few months, start to despair when it fails to produce results, and then turn to a new theory. Two years and twenty theories later, their business may well be bankrupt. But who is to blame: the theorists who failed to save the firm or the managers who got it into trouble in the first place? (p. 369)

Micklethwaite and Wooldridge (1996) warn the incompetent or simply unsure manager how to select good consultants:

- If you suspect any advice, theory or fad is bunk it nearly always is.
- Beware of authors and consultants who overdo and emphasize their academic honours.
- Beware those who argue entirely by analogy.
- Beware of internal contradictions – of strategies done at the same time that have opposite effects.
- Criticize sloppy writing and pseudo scientific jargon that is often meaningless.
- Note whether the gurus are interested or knowledgeable about wider social, economic, and political issues that must impact on organizations.

The lesson is simple: bad consultants exacerbate rather than solve problems. They magnify incompetence.

It takes a couple of decades to 'grow' a general manager. But time alone is not sufficient: one needs raw talent (ability) and emotional stability, and the manager must have had (and learnt from) particular experiences. To a large extent what makes a good manager is the recognition about personal shortcomings (rather than avoiding them), accepting responsibility for those deficits (rather than denying them), and then struggling to do something about it (rather than ignoring their faults) (McCall, Lombardo and Morrison, 1990). Managers also need to be courageous.

This book is not about the deep-seated emotional problems of many managers. Rather it is about the day-to-day decisions that they have to make and issues they have to deal with. It is not easy being a manager: few have any systematic education or much support. For this reason, perhaps, so many fall victims to stress, office politics and ignominious firing. Worse, many of the things they do have been shown to be short sighted or wrong. Many managers are fashion victims who follow the self-appointed gurus to destruction.

This short book arrays a series of essays in alphabetical form. Each aims to be both controversial and helpful, dispelling myth and offering advice. The tone is sceptical not cynical; the aim is to educate and entertain.

References

Davis W (1997) Great Myths of Business. London: Kogan Page.
Dixon N (1976) On the Psychology of Military Incompetence. London: Jonathan Cape.
Furnham A. (1996) The Myths of Management. London: Whurr.

Kets De Vries M and Miller D (1985) The Neurotic Organization. San Francisco: Jossey-Bass.

McCall M, Lombardo M and Morrison A (1990) The Lessons of Experience. New York: Lexington Books.

Micklethwaite J and Wooldridge A (1996) The Witch Doctors: What the management gurus are saying, why it matters, and how to make sense of it. London: Heinemann.

Pettigrew A (1974) The influence process between specialists and executives. Personnel Review 3, 24–30.

Shapiro E, (1996) Fad Surfing in the Boardroom. Oxford: Capstone.

Alienated workers

You find them in all organizations: the passed over and the pissed off (POPOs). They are frequently in late middle age, of limited education and qualifications, and have an 'impressive' service record.

They have been led to believe, or in a self-deluded way expect, that they should be steadily promoted. However, this has not occurred and they remain middle management for two reasons. Either someone has decided that they are 'Peter Principled' (already promoted to their level of incompetence) or else the organization has been downsized or rightsized (but not capsized) and there is nowhere for them to be (except somewhere else). It may be they were poorly selected in the first place or badly managed for years.

One stunning factor associated with POPOs is that they have *never* been given any significant, serious feedback on their performance – *ever*. Ask disgruntled, alienated POPOs when last they had a 30-minute conversation about their performance and they usually say never in their working career. If people are neither praised (stroked) for good work, nor punished for bad, it is not surprising that they become alienated.

So we find angry, alienated POPOs sniping at everything in sight. They are extremely negative about every initiative and often jealous of the more successful and competent. They are 'work-to-rule' types, not in terms of union rules but personal style. They become the 'quit-but-stay' worker who quit their enthusiasm, their commitment to the organization and their dedication but do not leave. They have torn up their emotional or psychological contract but not their legal contract, doing the minimum required to stay in work.

Alienated workers seek each other out. They form the disgruntled cohort of workers whose memory is as long as their enthusiasm is short. They dwell over past 'injustices'; resent young people and are deeply cynical about all initiatives made by companies. Many are happy to park their brain with the car in the car park in the early morning, only bothering to refit it after knocking off exactly at the allotted time. So what should be done with the POPO? What are the options? Three seem reasonably successful:

- *Buy them out.* It may seem costly in the short term but it may be the most cost-effective solution. Everyone has their price, and if the company is prepared to throw in some outplacement counselling and other services, even the most security-minded employee might be prepared to leap into the job pool of life. Most are frightened of what they perceive to be the icy-cold, shark-infested waters of the commercial world. The company environment, however much it has changed, still looks warm and protective. To sell the concept of a leaving package one needs to reverse these perceptions, pointing out how cold and competitive the company must become and how warm and cosy the opportunities are out there in the real world.

- *Raise the game.* Quit-but-stayers need to know that there are significant changes in the way things are done in the new organization. The talk of 'revenue up, cost down', 'lean-and-mean' organizations needs to be supported by tougher targets for individual workers. There are various ways to raise the game which include changing equipment to that new technology which has to be mastered; removing or reducing support staff and functions; or more simply, demanding more productivity. The thought of having to perpetually put in more effort frequently frightens off alienated individuals or they change into productive and committed workers.

- *Introducing new blood.* This more risky strategy involves bringing in new (mostly young) people with no memory of the past. Forward-looking, enthusiastic and manageable, new people show up the alienated workers. They prove that the new system can work and provide excellent models if carefully selected. As long as they outnumber and can outperform the alienated workers, the poisonous cynicism of the latter will not have a debilitating effect on the former. The POPOs often appear more pathetic than wise and the ostracism from the young and upwardly mobile may succeed in either scaring them off or changing them.

Alienated workers are a menace to the organization and themselves. They need either to learn to adapt to new conditions, recognize the new world as it is, or quit the workplace.

Amnesic organizations

It is usually only on some anniversary that organizations look back. It may be the death of a founder, the millionth product or customer, or the fiftieth year since the business was formed that encourages the historical overview. Usually these anniversaries are simply used as a PR opportunity. The glance back is cursory and more associated with nostalgia than analysis. A cursory, somewhat rosy-glowed history of organization may be written, but all too often these are short 500–2000 word stories for customers or inductees.

Consultants who work with the same organization over any period of time notice the extent to which the cry of, and supposed need for, change simply leads to the repackaging of old ideas, processes and procedures. When new managers come into an organization they often feel the need to make their presence felt. They do so by one of two behaviours observable in the big cat family. Lions, when taking over a pride, kill the young of all females so that they quickly come into fertility and bear their young, so perpetuating their genes. They seem to care little about the species (read the organization) but only about their own survival and that of their offspring (read department). Their ideal is to destroy all that went before and, of course, if there are no records of the past, then nothing is remembered of the previous processes or structures.

A second method associated with big or small cats is less dramatic but can be equally unpleasant. It is associated with spraying urine around one's territory to indicate where one is boss. The incoming manager, the power-broker, the organo-politician all enjoy the idea of having a big department, a big territory, a big budget. And they will fight to keep it, constantly spraying their authority. Over time strange anomalies arise in departments because of the spraying of the zealous feline bosses. But because no records are kept it becomes unclear why this odd, unusual, and inefficient state-of-affairs ever arose in the first place.

However, some organizations employ business historians to write their story. Unfortunately this is rarely done at the departmental level so the history of numerous campaigns, thrusts and initiatives is forgotten. It is particularly striking if high turnover in senior positions means there is no record of previous attempts to solve major problems. 'Old-hand' cynics might point out to the newcomer that previous similar attempts had derailed but, without details, it is not easy fully to understand the issues.

One simple way to look at history concerns the focus of the organization: external versus internal. Consider a T on its side. The straight line represents a state where the company seems clearly focused on both the external (customers, competition) and the internal (structure, processes) equally. Over time the focus may change – concern with being taken over, or increasing market share, or introducing a new performance management system may mean that the whole organization becomes externally or internally focused. This may be healthy and adaptive . . . or it may not. The question is: what are the consequences, and what can people learn from the exercise?

Those who are concerned about fads and fashions that ultimately do little good and cost vast sums of money need, like all others, to justify their cynicism with proof. Logging and recording the history does that. This is a ship's log approach – a system-wide, total organization record. Not the glossy annual report for shareholders but a record, like a set of committee minutes, of what was decided, what occurred and what the consequence was. This is ultimately a very useful exercise because not only does it discourage managers from making the same mistake again and again but also it encourages all managers (especially in the softer disciplines) to monitor and measure what they manage.

Organizations are surprisingly amnesic. Many behave similarly to Alzheimer's patients who recall very little of their own intimate history. Sensibly kept records of the introduction of systems, initiatives and processes and how they worked provide invaluable evidence, not only for the historian but the manager at the coal face. The aphorism is equally true in business: those who know no history are condemned to repeat it.

Appraisal and its problems

'All appraisal systems interfere with teamwork, foster mediocrity, concentrate on short-term outcomes and focus on the product not the process.' Discuss.

It is almost universally true that performance appraisal is one of the most frequent sources of dissatisfaction in the entire human resource remit. Rarely does the boss or his/her subordinate look forward to it, and often neither is totally satisfied with the outcome of the system. It becomes a sterile paper chase. In short, many argue for the removal of the whole performance appraisal process – the pain is not worth it.

Even if an organization introduces a moderately successful appraisal system, in all probability, the enthusiasm will wane and it will soon look as bad (corrupt, inefficient, superficial) as any that went before. And when the cost of developing, implementing and maintaining the system is considered, some argue it is simply better jettisoned. Stories abound of organizations dropping quietly and shamefully a system they trumpeted as 'state-of-the-art', 'best prac-tice' or hailed with other neologisms. Many a human resources (HR) director has found that he has become an independent consultant as the organization out sourced its scapegoat for the ultimate failure of the appraisal process.

Yet it is hard to imagine an organization doing without some sort of appraisal system. All managers need to give their staff some sort of feedback on their performance. They have to make deci-sions about promotion, training, succession planning and possible performance-related pay, and they need to know and understand their staff. All good man-managers have their own systems, even if the organization does not require them. They regularly review their staff's performance and give them specific, explicit feedback on it and how to improve, and they reward the good and counsel the weak. In this sense they invent their own system. The difference is that individual practices are not organization-wide, are not linked to performance-related pay, do not always provide data comparable to that collected by other managers and do not rein-force the business strategy.

Some organizations may be bound by a contract or legal guide-lines to conduct appraisals, sometimes in a particular way. The liti-gious Americans have gone to court over performance appraisals. Nearly 100 cases have gone to court. Guidelines have therefore been developed to help people make sure they are conducting legally sound appraisals. They include:

- Performance ratings should be based on specific dimensions of job performance requirements.
- Ratings should be based on specific behavioural practices and must be shown to employees.
- Where possible there should be multiple raters to ensure relia-bility.
- Each individual should have the validity of his/her ratings assessed as regularly as possible.

- Extreme (negative) ratings should be accompanied with documentation about incidence, data, location and outcome.
- The system should have an appeal process.

Most organizations are not legally required to introduce any system, however. The HR department may be very eager to do so, but is it wise? Do the costs outweigh the benefits? Indeed, do appraisal systems ultimately help or hurt the organization?

- *The system can interfere with teamwork.* There are a number of issues involved here. First, performance appraisal is nearly always conducted on an individual basis but people do, and are constantly exhorted to, work in teams. Most are interdependent and it is not possible or desirable to separate the contribution of various individuals. Second, it is difficult to know whether the variability in work output is a function of the person's motivation and ability or the 'production process'. That is, whether the way the organization is structured and the processes ordained determine performance more powerfully than individual effort, or even the ability of individuals. Third, that the system overemphasizes individual differences in performance, seeking to look for differences that are not there. In this sense some say it seeks to be divisive, emphasizing diversity over homogeneity, 'we-feeling' and common goals. These arguments have some force when it comes to traditional assembly-line jobs, which are on the wane anyway. Job performance in service industries, however, depends heavily on the effort and ability of individuals because there are few rigorous dictates on how to behave. It is also quite possible to separate the performance of the individual from other environmental factors by asking raters to identify how specific 'other' factors (mechanical breakdowns, cuts in budget, chronic absenteeism of a staff member) might have affected an individual's performance. Man-managers are in fact highly individualistic in how they approach tasks and are given few guidelines on how to behave. Hence there are huge individual differences in conscientiousness and output of work. Finally, nothing prevents an appraisal system being conducted for teams as a whole with individuals each sharing the mean team rating. People are usually happy to enjoy the 'class average' if they feel the 'class' has been working together with equitable input. There is compelling and obvious evidence at the managerial level that there are individual differences in job performance. It must be foolish to ignore these, especially by failing to reward the best performers, whose efforts and abilities contribute the most. There is nothing as alienating and demotivating as having effort and good performance ignored, and seeing lazy and mediocre peers get equal rewards to the dutiful, diligent, deliverers.

- *Appraisal systems send mixed messages.* The gap between the rhetoric and reality of appraisal systems can be a serious problem. The rhetoric says the system is about communication and improving the quality of decisions. The reality is that often it is only about performance-related pay. Organizations say the appraisal process is crucial for all managers but rarely reward those who do it well and conscientiously, or punish those who don't do it, or do a poor job. The party line is that appraisal is crucial for providing the data on which administrative decisions are made. Yet, all too often, ratees have no clear idea of what is done with ratings, partly because few organizations have a clear and consistent policy on how they actually process, store or make decisions on the data arising from them – and even if they do, they do not communicate it effectively. This is not an inherent problem with the system. It is rather a reflection of the way it is introduced, used and abused. The objection is valid, however, because most appraisal systems are poorly introduced, administered and monitored. Send mixed messages and employees, like managers, are soon in two minds as to whether or not they want the system at all.

- *The appraisal system is a major cause of dissatisfaction and discontent.* There are commonly five reasons why the system is the most popular butt of complaints and ridicule in any organization. There are what has been described as a demoralizing trilogy; ranking, rating and forced distribution. The appraisal system, often driven by statistical necessity, forces raters to differentiate and make distinctions that are neither realistic nor functional. In fact, pointing out (minor) differences between employees can disturb team morale. Sometimes there is genuinely little difference between the enthusiasm and output of team members and drawing attention to minor differences can cause major problems. Ratees are more often disappointed by the appraisal because self-assessments are usually more favourable than others' assessments. In this sense most ratees feel their appraisal is insensitive and unfair (read average) even when it is completely accurate. This is more of a problem for some – particularly those with delusions of grandeur – than others and there may be no way of ever overcoming it if the self-deluded refuse to accept less than flattering feedback. The managers who do the rating have ambivalent and contradictory roles, for they are both judge and counsellor, evaluator and mentor. This ambiguity can be a cause of stress for managers more used to challenging their staff than supporting them and vice versa. Thus the raters end up being as unhappy as the ratees unless they are trained. Any good system should teach managers how to conduct progress reviews and annual appraisals: to be comfortable giving negative (challenging) feedback, or areas for improvement. Most importantly, the ratings are subjective. Even when thorough, fair and reliable in the sense that others agree because they are not objective, appraisals become a lightning conductor for generalized concerns over fairness and equity. In the personnel jargon, they violate the requirements of procedural justice because employees believe there are systematic biases at work. The best way around this ever-present issue is to have multiple raters; ideally superior, subordinates, peers and customers. Reliability does not ensure validity but it helps in the perception of bias problem. All raters need to be trained to use forms to differentiate confidently when appropriate. Finally, in some organizations there is a shared perception, fixed in the corporate culture and passed on to newcomers, that the whole system is both a joke and an imposition. Even if staff individually see its merits, because it takes so much time and is so widely despised, even the reasonable manager will eventually become dissatisfied with the system. It is no fun being the champion of the laughing stock and much easier to join the baying dogs.

In defence of appraisal systems, discontent is a self-fulfilling prophecy. Perhaps the best way to deal with the complaints is to encourage the disillusioned and desolate to point out not what is wrong with the current system, but how it can be fixed. Focus should be moved to alternatives or ways of correcting problems. Critics should be asked what alternatives they prefer: no appraisal system and pay being dependent on collective bargaining with promotions being linked predominantly to service or who you know, or an alternative system with managers each given a 'bung' of cash to be left to distribute at their own discretion. In short, 'what other approach can overcome the current problems without causing new or different ones?'

Of course it is possible to point out the ways in which appraisal systems help organizations. Most obviously they provide a rich and useful data bank to enhance the quality of HR decisions – promotions, pay, layoffs and transfers across the whole organization. They can also help individuals to think through their present and future roles in a better way and perhaps, most important of all, they help build a good relationship between manager and staff. At their best they can build and cement employee commitment and satisfaction. None of these benefits automatically follows from an appraisal system but it is difficult to imagine the first two without a well-devised, organization-wide system.

Any good appraisal system needs constant support and monitoring. Managers need to be trained to give feedback, in differentiating their ratings and being consistent. Senior managers need to model what they want from the system and the human resources department needs to present itself as a helpful coach, not a petulant school prefect. The military often runs tough, efficient and well-accepted systems through being systematic and consistent.

The disillusionment with appraisal systems is nearly always a function of implementation, not theory. We are appraised at school – at sport, in skilled extra-mural activities – but we are seldom angry or cynical about the process. It is only at work that adults become highly emotional about appraisal. Pusillanimous human resource managers, untrained raters and uncommitted senior staff are a recipe for disaster. Yet all organizations need to appraise – to estimate value or quality. One cannot manage what one doesn't measure, and that's especially true of people.

Assessing potential

Can one assess the potential of a person to succeed years ahead? This is even more problematic than selection because one is not selecting for a specific job. It is most likely that the workplace, the work tasks and the work styles of the future will be surprisingly different from that of today. One is thus attempting to select for a job that does not currently exist or that one cannot currently fully describe, or else the selector is attempting to assess the potential of any one individual for a number of different future, possible, 'virtual' jobs. So how could one go about it? There are perhaps only three important questions to ask and answer:

- *What characteristics change over the life span?* Despite the fact that self-help books and workshop presenters tell us that personal change is common, possible and desirable, most of the evidence is against them. Try going to a school reunion to see, apart from wrinkles, how little one's classmates have changed over the years. Certainly it is commonly agreed that once one has attained a certain age – say that 'of majority' – very little changes. Intelligence levels decline modestly but, in effect, change little over the working life. The same is true of abilities, be they with language, numbers, music or lateral thinking. Most people like to think that personality can change – particularly the more negative features like anxiety, low self-esteem, proneness to depression, impulsivity or a lack of emotional warmth. Data collected 50 years apart give the clear message 'still stable after all these years'. Extroverts become marginally less extroverted; the acutely shy appear a little less so, but the fundamentals remain much the same. Major personal crises can change our personal coping strategies – we might take up or drop drink, drugs, religion or relaxation techniques and this can have pretty dramatic effects. But the bottom line for those at about 30 is 'what you see is what you get'. Skills can be improved, certainly, and new ones introduced, but at rather different rates.

- *What is the cost of development?* People can be better groomed for a job. Just as politicians are carefully packaged and repackaged through dress, hair-stylists and speech therapists, so people can be sent on training courses, diplomas or experimental weekends. There is an organizational cost to this development that may be more than the upfront price of a course. Better to select for what you actually see than attempt to change it. So many brides who believe not 'Aisle, altar, hymn' but 'I'll alter him' become disappointed by their lack of success. Acquiring and retaining skills is expensive and difficult. The cost may simply not be worth it.

- *What are the fundamentals to look for?* The first is most simple: it's *intelligence* or *ability*. If you prefer to be politically correct, try capacity or cognitive potential. Since the turn of the century we have known about what psychologists call 'g' (it stands for general intelligence). Despite the attention paid to *idiots savants*, bright people are pretty good at most things and dim people pretty bad. On average, bright people learn faster and adapt more quickly . . . when they want to. Selectors and assessors are scared of giving IQ tests but they do use specific ability tests. School marks and university grades are only weak indicators of intelligence. Intelligence is a must; necessary but not sufficient. The second factor is *emotional stability*. Neuroticism or what the Americans call 'negative affectivity' is a powerful negative predictor of job success. The emotionally unstable are poor at consumer relations, become capricious and irascible managers and are prone to high levels of absenteeism, even accidents. Neuroticism is a 'select out' factor, a warning sign. There is a mountain of evidence that suggests both that neuroticism does not change much over the years and is related to career failure. Thus one selects for its opposite – the stable, the phlegmatic, the emotionally adjusted. Finally, the third factor is that old standby – *conscientiousness*. The work ethic – Protestant, Puritan, Jewish or Islamic – is a powerful predictor of job success. Often developed in childhood by ambitious, future-oriented, middle-class parents, the conscientious are – by definition – diligent, responsible, punctilious and dutiful. They are conscientious on and off the job and this attribute is therefore not too difficult to assess. They can be counted upon and their conscience is a powerful controller of their work style. Some may be a little risk averse, others a little too self-deprecating, but they can always be relied on. It is the reliability of the conscientious that, in part, makes them an asset. So that is all you need: bright, stable, conscientious people. Two out of three won't do. The full trio is a shorthand for the traits of fast trackers. Whilst some stars may ascend in the management firmament without some of these characteristics, those possessing all three are a safe bet.

Benchmarking

Although business performance can be measured objectively and as an absolute in any free enterprise situation, it is crucial to take the competition into consideration. Market share is, of course, a well-known business comparator. Organizations are now encouraged more and more to do extensive 'benchmarking' of their products, procedures and processes. Many hope to establish and maintain best practice through the benchmarking or comparison process.

The benefits of benchmarking are quite simply that all organizational functions are forced to investigate their industry's 'best practices' and compare these with their own operations. Remember that 'best practice' is a relative concept – 'best' may still be bad. There is, however, nothing new in the idea – Xerox introduced it formally less than 20 years ago.

There are a number of features central to benchmarking. First, it must be a continuous process because the competition constantly changes. Second, it aims at certain specific objective measures of comparison. Third, it can and should apply to all facets of business products, services and practices. Finally, perhaps the most important point is that benchmarking should not be aimed solely at direct product competitors, but those recognized as industry leaders.

Whether dignified with the handle 'benchmarking' or simply called 'competitor comparisons', the process has obvious benefits. It enables the better practices from any industry to be incorporated creatively into the practices of the benchmarked function. It can provide ideas and motivation to those who have to implement the benchmarked findings.

Benchmarking may break down much ingrained reluctance to accept certain operations. People seem more receptive to new ideas and their adoption when the ideas do not originate in their own industry, perhaps because they are already tried and tested, and have proved successful. Conversely, the 'not invented here' syndrome can undermine the benchmarking process. Many managers believe their own corporate circumstances to be unique, special and unlikely to respond to competitors' innovations.

Benchmarking may also identify technological breakthroughs and determine cost benefits that may be achieved if they are, or are not, incorporated in an organization's own operations. There are also 'networking' benefits for the benchmarkers who may broaden their professional contacts and interactions.

In theory benchmarking is not simply a mechanism for determining resources reduction. It is not a panacea or a programme – it is an ongoing process with a structured methodology. It is not a cookbook, although certain steps can be followed. It aims to focus on the competition and to compare internal actions against the external standards of the industry. It can promote cohesion and teamwork by directing attention towards business practices to remain competitive instead of towards personal individual interest.

Benchmarking is an ongoing comparison process that attempts to ensure that best industry practices are uncovered, analysed, adopted and implemented. The Japanese, master mimics and copiers, are well known for it. So why do not all companies do it routinely?

Like all business deals, benchmarking is sold by some consultants and business writers as an essential element in business success. Of course it has its limitations. Focusing on competitors' performance, if undisciplined, may simply divert attention from the ultimate purpose of the process. Benchmarking solely against competitors may also uncover practices that are not optimal or worthy of evaluation and hence a waste of effort. Furthermore, competitive benchmarking may lead to meeting the competitors' position, but it will not necessarily lead to creating practices superior to those of the competition. The questions need to be asked before the benchmarking bandwagon trundles off into the expense-laden sunset: 'Against whom should we benchmark and why?' What precise features are we benchmarking (process, structure, product)? Who is the best person for such a task? What is the output of the exercise (report, presentation)? Is it a cost-effective method and what are the alternatives?

Just as some organizations resist doing staff surveys (climate, culture audits, call them what you will) because they do not want to know what the state of morale is in their organization, so they resist the process of benchmarking for fear that it will highlight their own shortcomings. Others arrogantly believe they are already aware of the fundamental differences between their own and their competitors' operations and do not need to waste time and money in the process. They may be right, but whether one calls it benchmarking or something else, all managers need to be kept abreast of the competition and (real) developments in management techniques in other sections of their industry.

Biodata

Despite their widespread use, many managers are sceptical about the usefulness of ability and personality tests in selection. Supply (by psychometric consultants) and demand (by HR professionals trying to look sophisticated) has seen an impressive growth in the use of selection tests. Some believe that the best predictor of the future is the past. Life-history or biography is all you need. Early childhood experiences, the school you went to, whether or not you did military training; the age at which you married . . . these are biodata. But what in our past is the best predictor of our potential?

For most of this century, recruiters have existed who stressed the importance of biographical factors (or 'biodata') in predicting occupational success. Astute factual questions can reveal a great deal. Favourites include 'Are you a religious person?' and 'How far do you travel to work?'

There are some very clear advantages to the biodata approach. Biodata represent an alternative to the traditional selection or employment interview, with the advantage that every interviewee is asked the same question in exactly the same way and the value judgements made by the interviewer are standardized, relevant and of known validity.

There are distinct cost benefits as well. Although there may be fairly extensive research and development costs at the outset, once predictive questions have been identified, biodata are very cheap to use. Biodata forms can be developed in multiple-choice formats that are amenable to machine scoring, or direct entry to a computer terminal. Thus, processing large numbers of applicants can become a routine clerical activity, freeing up the valuable time of personnel professionals or line managers.

The standards set in using biodata are objective and consistent. Reading through application forms is an extremely tedious activity. It is often shared by a number of managers, who may not set precisely the same standards or use the same criteria. This is especially true where similar jobs are being filled across a number of locations or offices, or when recruitment takes place only at specific times of the year. The biodata approach allows for basic standards to be set objectively and with total consistency.

Minorities can be identified and treated fairly. In setting up a biodata form, the link between the information on the form and suitability for the job needs to be established. This, in itself, tends to ensure that irrelevant factors are excluded from the selection process. In addition, the research necessary to construct the application form can provide the basis for setting up and monitoring an equal-opportunities programme. Biodata forms, especially when computer scored, are completely blind to incidental items such as personal names that might indicate an ethnic background.

Although biodata application forms have not always delivered the same level of predictive accuracy in practical usage as has been obtained in academic experimentation, their track record is still good. Compared with the unstructured interview, which is a typical alternative, or to reading an application form in an unstructured way, they can produce increases in selection success rates of many orders of magnitude.

One study looked at simple biographical predictors of middle-aged middle managers. The list of factors thought to be predictive was long: which school they went to; position in the family; age of first mortgage; sport preferences and so on. These items can form an ideal 'ink-blot' projection game for personnel professionals. This study found that for these Britons more than 45 years old, the best predictor of managerial success was at what age they first went abroad: the younger, the better. Why? When travel was more expensive and more difficult, and when we Europeans were somewhat more xenophobic, it tended to be the more adventurous, curious and well-off parents who took their children abroad. It is possible that these characteristics associated with one's parents lead adults to be more successful later in life. The question does not work for younger people who travel abroad routinely, but remains an interesting marker for those interested in selection.

Before jumping overboard on this method, consider the following 10 limitations:

- If many biographical items are used in selection, the organization inevitably becomes more homogeneous, which has both advantages and disadvantages. Heterogeneity may occur across divisions (with different criteria) but not within them.

- Biodata work on the idea that past behaviour predicts current performance but if current criteria are very unstable (say in a rapidly changing market) one is perpetually out of date. Biodata may be best in stable organizations and environments.

- Biodata have been shown to be fakeable. One researcher checked information given by applicants for a nursing aide post with what previous employers said. Half the sample over-estimated how long they had worked for their previous employer. Overstating previous salary and describing part-time work as full-time were also common. More seriously, a quarter gave reasons for leaving their previous job with which the employer did not agree, and no fewer than 17% gave as their previous employer someone who had never heard of them.

- If biodata items show major biographical correlates such as sex, race, religion and age, one may want to select or reject particular individuals on those grounds, which is illegal. The courts may in fact challenge items such as age, sex and marital status if such items are included in inventories for the purpose of personnel selection. In that event, whatever gains in predictive power are to be derived through an inclusion of these items must be weighted against the possible expenses of legal defence.

- Many organizations have never really examined their selection in detail. The criteria have just grown up over time or reflect the personal preferences of recruiters. The process of diagnosing clear selection criteria in advance of setting up a biodata system will have considerable benefits for the whole of the selection process.

- In setting up a biodata form, the link between the information on the form and suitability for the job needs to be established. This in itself tends to ensure that any other elements are excluded from the selection process. In addition, the research necessary to set up the form can provide the basis of setting up and monitoring an equal opportunities programme. Because of the fear of litigation it is probably more the fact that biodata may be associated with illegal discrimination which has prevented managers using it.

- The same criteria do not have the same predictability across jobs, organizations, countries or time periods. As criteria have to be established every time, the development of biodata can be expensive.

- The major disadvantage of biodata being entirely empirical and non-theoretical is that one can never know which of myriad biographical factors to choose from. Because there is no theory, one cannot explain which features predict occupational success and why.

- In a predictive design, the questionnaire is intended to be used for applicants, hence it is developed using data from applicants. The disadvantage is that it is a very time-consuming process. For example, it might take at least 12 months to obtain reliable, meaningful, job-related data on new employees. If an organization does not have a regular intake of new staff, there could be two or three years' delay between sending the draft biodata form to applicants and obtaining a sample of employees large enough to warrant further development work.

- Biodata scoring keys do not appear to hold up indefinitely. There is evidence that the validity of biodata shrinks over time and periodic revalidation and reweighting may be necessary.

Blaming the victim

When one is young, arrogant, and believes oneself to be omniscient, it is common to despise those one perceives as being less fortunate than oneself. Being both gauche and bright, it is attractive to believe that technical skills (preferably one's own) are the solution to all problems.

One prominent business school professor reported on a striking pattern he had noticed. He taught on various courses: MBAs for aspirant, acquisitional entrepreneurs; six-week to six-month courses for mid-to-early career high flyers; and three- to 10-day courses for top chief executive officers (CEOs) wanting 'time out' for reflection and to recharge their batteries. He asked attendees which skills they thought were essential and most difficult to acquire; what parts of business had most ultimate impact on the bottom line (e.g. accounting systems, marketing, manufacturers); and to what extent their ideas about management had changed with experience.

The pattern he noticed was arresting – the older the business manager, the more he/she rated the importance of *human resource management*. It wasn't that they necessarily rated the department or director highly, but they recognized the intractable and complicated nature of human resource issues. The young Turks, particularly those from an information technology or engineering background, saw HR as nothing more than common sense, soft, flim-flam.

It may well be that age is as likely to bring confusion as wisdom, but whence my colleagues' observations? Is it a case of that old sociological phenomenon of blaming the victim? Managing people is difficult; they are coy, capricious, irascible and irresponsible. One often fails despite all sorts of efforts of compromise and diplomacy. There is no magic bullet in HR, despite what the gurus tell us, and the older we get, and the more secure we become, the more we are prepared to admit it and praise others who can do it.

Hubris is linked to lack of insight; humility to experience. Are HR managers like all other victims – not only being dealt a bad hand but being blamed for it? Is their job not much more taxing and complicated than the relative simplicity of (ever-advancing) accountancy, certainly marketing, possibly engineering? Is the low status of HR a case of 'kick the bastard when he's down', or a management equivalent of *schadenfreude*?

Book reviews

Most managers claim not to have the time to read management books. Fewer are prepared to admit that the effort is probably not worth the gain. But most would, in theory, like to sound erudite and well read by mentioning famous gurus and their latest concepts. The easiest way out seems to be not to read the book but the review, which might give the gist of a 50 000-word book in 500 words. There are, in fact, both abbreviated (condensed) versions of business books as well as, more interestingly, reviews of reviews or collections of reviews.

Do book reviews tell more about the author, the book or the reviewer? It is the last of these. Furthermore, regular reviewers are often gratuitously nasty. They have found it pays. They know that only pessimism sounds profound; that being a prophet of doom and gloom and biting criticism make them sound wise and insightful whereas optimism and praise are perceived as foolhardy and ignorant.

In a paper called 'Brilliant and Cruel', the American psychologist Teresa Amabile asked people to judge excerpts from matching negative and positive book reviews. She found that negative reviewers were perceived as more intelligent, competent and expert than positive reviewers, even when the content of the positive review was independently judged as being of higher quality and greater forcefulness.

She believes that most reviewers know this and that it is simply a self-presentation strategy by the intellectually insecure. Certainly, there is nothing inherently more intelligent in criticism than in praise. W.H. Auden pointed out that one cannot attack a bad book without showing off, but some reviewers apply the dictum to all books.

Management book reviews perhaps tell us most about the reviewer, something about the author, but frequently little about the book. Beware the short cut of trying to find out about a book by simply reading reviews.

Bureaucracy

A bureaucracy is a system of management or government character-ized by specialization of functions, adherence to fixed rules and a hierarchy of authority. Adherents say it brings logic, order, stability and systems. Protagonists believe it is an infuriating and inflexible system of administration, marked by rigid attention to rules and procedures. It has been said that the perfect bureaucrat is one who avoids decisions and escapes all responsibility. Bureaucracy tends to defend the status quo, long after the quo lost its status.

It is easy to attack bureaucracy, and the word now has an almost exclusively pejorative tone. Forbes, the eponymous publisher, said there were three problems to which there are no solutions: inflation, bureaucracy and dandruff. But faced with Third World-style corrup-tion and chaos, many people have longed for the predictable and regulated world of the bureaucrat. Indeed, one can make a reason-able case that the infrastructure without which no economy can flourish has to be bureaucratic in the original sense. Such a bureau-cracy has the following characteristics:

- specialization and logical division of labour;
- formalization with appropriate rules and documentation of regulations;
- chain of command that is logical and unitary;
- a manageable span of control;
- centralization of authority.

The popular view, reinforced so often by amazing 'case histories', is that obsessive, obstructive and obstinate types are naturally attracted to bureaucracies. Parkinson, famous for his law ('work expands to fill the time available'), believed the bureaucrat is devoted to paperwork and thus loses initiative. Indeed, the monetarist Friedman famously said 'there is little doubt that if you were going through every govern-ment bureau in the UK and fired every sixth man, the productivity of the other five would go up rather than down.' They appear to enjoy being inflexibly and procedurally driven, preventing ordinary mortals who have not correctly filled out the blue, green and red forms from doing the simplest things. Those concerned with regulation and control, however, point to Barings Bank and other well-known documented disasters to show how a breakdown in procedure can lead to chaos.

Are you suited to working in bureaucracies or not? Try the following quiz:

	Mostly agree	Mostly disagree
1. I value stability in my job most	...	...
2. I like a predictable organization	...	...
3. The best job for me would be one in which the future is exciting and unpredictable	...	...
4. The armed services would be a nice place to work	...	...
5. Rules, policies and procedures tend to frustrate me	...	...
6. I would enjoy working for a company that employed about 100 000 people worldwide	...	...
7. Being self-employed would involve more risk than I'm willing to take	...	...
8. Before accepting a job, I would like to see a detailed job description	...	...
9. I would prefer (given equal pay) a job as a freelance house painter to one as a clerk for the Department of Social Security	...	...
10. Seniority should be as important as performance in determining pay increases and promotion	...	...
11. It would give me a feeling of pride to work for the largest and most successful company in its field	...	...
12. Given a choice, I would prefer to make £25 000 per year as a deputy chairman in a small company than £30 000 as a specialist in a large company	...	...
13. I would regard wearing an employee uniform with a number on it as a degrading experience	...	...
14. Parking spaces in a company lot should be assigned on the basis of job status and service	...	...
15. If an accountant works for a large organization, he or she cannot be a true professional	...	...
16. Before accepting a job (given a choice), I would want to make sure that the company had a full package of employee benefits	...	...
17. A company will probably not be successful unless it establishes and follows a clear set of rules and procedures	...	...
18. Regular working hours and vacations are more important to me than the variable if exciting life of a consultant-type job	...	...
19. You should respect people of a higher rank	...	...
20. Rules are meant to be broken	...	...

One point for each of the following:
Mostly agree: 1-2, 4, 7-8, 10-11, 14, 16, 18-19. Mostly disagree: 3, 5-6, 9, 12-13, 15, 17, 20

A very high score (15 or over) would suggest that you would enjoy working in a bureaucracy. Perhaps with anal obsessive tendencies, you might thrive in a civil service role. A very low score (5 or lower) would suggest that you would be frustrated by working in a bureaucracy, especially a large one. Indeed, your profile means you would be likely to become frustrated with all bureaucracies with which you come into contact.

Business books

Bestselling books can make a lot of money. Not only are there impressive royalties but the fame that a book can bring means that authors can be invited onto the management conference and celebrity dinner circuit. It is not uncommon for a seriously famous guru to receive £5000–10 000 ($8000–15 000) for one hour's speech! Fame perpetuates itself and a book is an important part of the process.

So what are the secrets of success in the now fairly crowded and competitive market? The first problem for the potential bestseller business book writer is that not all the things the readers like to read are true. Consider the following list and the problems associated with writing a business book that sells. The book must be simple: plentifully peppered with memorable anecdotes, vignettes and stories. No problem here if you believe business life is simple. The book must underscore the point that human behaviour is changeable. Well it is, but only within certain limits and at great cost. Ask any dieter, stutterer or technophobe. In fact the major problem for all managers is that it is very difficult to change people's attitudes and/or their work-related behaviours.

The book must emphasize the individual as the unit of analysis and change. The successful business book must therefore be psychological in its focus on people and underplay organizational, economic and political factors that self-evidently shape organizational success. The book must stress the techniques that increase and improve a manager's control. Again, fair enough if you believe in hands-on autocratic management rather than empowering management. Next, the book should provide a list of steps and principles. A road map to management or a simple guide to how to achieve success is fine as long as one is encouraged to make judgements as well.

It is important that the book must suggest that its ideas have universal application and appeal. None of this multicultural, diversity nonsense in a bestseller – the idea is that the secret formula works everywhere for all groups. The book must claim or demonstrate some short-term payoff or benefit. The idea that one can manage better and more cost-efficiently has enormous appeal, but the immediacy of the benefits is probably an over-exaggeration.

Ideally the book should provide lists of happy customers and those who have successfully adopted the ideas. They are usually the author's friends or clients. The book must not be counterintuitive and self-confirming approaches endorsing prior ideas and beliefs are essential. Here is the rub: the book can't have radically new ideas if the readers already hold them. That is why so many repackage common sense and the things that people already know. The book must above all espouse a unitary perspective where boss and employee, management and union have ultimately shared goals and mutual benefits. If only! In fact unions are rarely mentioned.

Finally the book must stress the nature of business leadership as a romantic, heroic enterprise. This perhaps says it all – the more like a fairytale it is, the better readers like it. The dilemma for the would-be writer then is not a literary one but an ethical one. Bestsellers must be bullshit if they are to sell. Honest, practical books that do not oversimplify or promise the earth make only modest earnings. So there is a paradox – best sellers may be compulsory reading for the jargon but these are probably less helpful than a less well-known book that is more practical and honest about the problems that arise.

Business ethics

What is business ethics? Is the concern with business ethics (a) an ephemeral trend (b) a justifiable pursuit or (c) oxymoronic impossibility?

Business ethics is one of the darlings of the Politically Correct. Some organizations run in-house courses on the topic; others establish tell-tale telephone numbers so that employees can report on unethical activities. Hence a moralistic McCarthyism seems to be spreading around corporate bodies.

As a response to the current fascination with business ethics, academics have written thought-pieces in magazines, established learned journals, even chairs and fellowships at distinguished universities. They run seminars, debate case histories, even have tests of moral maturity. As a result, the so-called discipline appears to have achieved respectability and companies take it very seriously, setting up committees and groups to discuss these issues.

Ethics used to be mainly the concern of philosophers and theologians. Some ethicists now venture forth from their abstract, cobwebbed studies into the bright lights and generous-speaking-fee world of the business seminar. Applying Aristotelian ethics to mergers and acquisitions may be something of a problem, but it is none the less a growth industry.

But what is business ethics? It is essentially ethics applied to business issues; it isn't a particular brand of ethics. Medical ethics and research ethics already exist. All medical and behavioural scientists are regularly required to subject their research proposals to the scrutiny of the ethics committee, and the same might still be the lot of the entrepreneur, even the management consultant. Imagine taking every takeover bid, every merger and acquisition proposal, indeed each hiring-and-firing decision to the in-house ethics committee for approval. In a sense we do: many decisions have to be passed by various regulatory bodies, which have a quasi-ethical remit. Indeed, some business issues are so over-controlled, regulated and monitored that there hardly seems any point debating those topics further.

Why do we have ethics committees charged with making these decisions? Why can't individuals do it? What training skills or knowledge does one need to be on these committees?

If there are a set of agreed ethical principles to follow, why do we need a committee to puzzle them out? A job-creation scheme for the moral majority perhaps. There are various ethical codes: some absolutist, others relativist, some with general, others with abstract principles. Thus one could mention the radical relativist ethics, called situation ethics, of the American academic Fletcher, or the more austere, retributive or absolutist ethics of the Church Fathers or Muslim Clerics. One might ask a trained ethicist or philosopher to fathom out how to apply these abstract ethical principles to everyday business situations, instead of a jury-type collection of the great-and-the-good.

The real reason committees are used, of course, is to *diffuse responsibility*. No one person or perhaps one moral code can personally be held responsible. A second reason for an ethics committee concerns that bane of American social and corporate life: *litigation*. Many ethics committees are about 'cover-your-arse' to prevent, circumvent or mitigate legal suits. If this is true, the ethical committee should be replaced by (and renamed) a litigation inquiry.

Rather than waste time and simply getting 'feeling good' points, a company should first decide on a set of ethical principles (many exist), appoint an expert ethicist to decipher and apply them, and have him/her assisted by a sharp litigation lawyer. Large groups of well-meaning busybodies won't do.

It has been said that if you are guilty, choose to be judged by a jury (which is a committee of the untrained); if innocent, choose a judge and two assessors. The reason is obvious – juries are more likely to make mistakes and be swayed by sweet-talking but obfuscating lawyers but judges, who are trained and experienced, are more likely to dispense true justice. Hence, the guilty one has a better chance through the jury making a mistake; if innocent a judge is less likely to be wrong.

The amateur business ethics committee, rather than being the flavour of the month, has reached its sell-by date. Often an arena for time-wasting busybodies, it should be staffed by experts who bring ethical and/or legal knowledge to discussions. This is not to say that business people should not be ethical in their practices. But what is ethical is another story.

Business and pleasure

Mixing business and pleasure is inadvisable. Like the blur between tax avoidance and evasion it can, over time, be remarkably uncertain when a business cost is a personal cost and vice versa. Hotel dry-cleaning; company car petrol and the entertainment budget are all grey areas for many in business.

But what causes more pain and has much longer consequences is the office affair. There are so many reasons why they occur. The wealth and power of the highly successful middle-aged businessman makes them highly attractive to women of all ages. Equally the menopausal male frequently sees the bright eyes and firm limbs of a female half his age to be a way to totally reinvigorate all aspects of his life.

The one-night fling at the sales conference; the drunken fondle at the Christmas party; the illicit affair between unlikely colleagues is a frequent occurrence. They occur because of loneliness, avarice, lust as well as the simple desire to destroy an individual. But there is also the character who preys upon others . . . the lecherous lecturer; the slimy salesman; the debauched director can be fairly easily identified. The following three are the most common:

- *Mr Veneer.* Nobody is more delighted that large numbers of women are reaching senior business positions, for Mr Veneer is playing a numbers game. He invites a constant stream of women out on his expense account, knowing that he will strike it lucky sooner or later. A suave, practised, married womaniser, he is the archetypal salesman. His normal habitat is the discreet West End restaurant where he is addressed by name. He will get down to business straight away with such open tactics as 'my wife lives in the country and I have a flat in town', 'look into my eyes and tell me why you really asked me out to lunch' or even 'I fancied you from the first moment I saw you'. Naturally, his second wife doesn't understand him. Should the female decide to enter into negotiations she will be asked out to dinner and then back to his flat for a 'night-cap'.

- *Mr Invisible.* He is frequently part of the female's peer group, or perhaps a colleague whom she has known vaguely for years. More probably a gauche, balding, quiet, married man, the venue will be a City wine bar or bistro and he will expect his lunch partner to go Dutch. The meal will be uneventful until the bombshell: 'I have decided not to have an affair with you', 'I'd like to have you on my team, but I'm not sure you could handle it' or even 'I know you are available'. He likes to give the impression he has never done anything like this before and should his target succumb will choose a quiet country house hotel to act out his mid-life crisis. A middle-class trainspotter, he is able to remain invisible behind an anodyne, or innocuous personality.

- *Mr Flamboyant.* The professional bachelor/divorcé of a certain age who drives a red Porsche and is the 'Boss'. He would like everyone to think that he can pull endless women because he is so sexy, not because he is loaded. He will choose a suitably extravagant and trendy venue and will open negotiations sometime during the main course; he wouldn't like to look too keen. His opening gambit is 'What's so great about young men? I can give a girl five orgasms a night', 'My last girl friend was 22' or 'I always envisage you on top'. He has of course done this many times before and likes his target to know it. Should she decide to conclude the deal she will probably end up in Monte Carlo for the weekend. At least that is the promise, but Mr Flamboyant and reality are not close friends.

It is easy to say but not always to obey: don't mix business and pleasure. And beware the lady-killer or, indeed, the husband snatcher. The monetary and psychological cost of the almost-inevitable consequences of divorce is never compensated by the fleeting pleasure of the affair.

Career development: counselling for the future

The whole idea of career development in the new flat, middle-managementless organization may strike a sour, cynical note with many. 'What career?' they wonder. Managing career expectations is easy – quash them. You should be lucky to have a job let alone consider a career.

For those keen on 20:20 hindsight and the rosy-hued retrospective glance to 'the good old days' it seemed that ability and long service were rewarded by a steady climb up the corporate ladder. People were led to expect that the 'tea-boy to managing director' dream was possible. The speed and ultimate end-point in the career were defined only by ability and service (and perhaps a bit of politics).

The term 'career' has, for many, a very limited meaning that is usually confined to organizational chart descriptions. It has been estimated that people had about 100 000 working hours over a 47-year working period (18–65) to pursue their career. Now 47 years has been reduced to 30 years with many retiring at 50 and hence thinking of a 'second career'.

In the quiet pre-1980s, companies seemed to offer a *cradle-to-grave* option where they would protect, develop and encourage their staff with almost a guarantee of lifetime employment. The Reagan/Thatcher revolution and the reoriented 1980s changed the whole career emphasis of companies dramatically. Then it became 'all-up-to-you'. You, not the HR specialist nor your manager, were responsible for your career development. You were the sole captain of your ship and master of your fate and there was no company support for your endeavours to develop your career.

The 1990s seem to have settled down to a compromise between the two extreme positions. There is more of the sense of partnership between the individual and the organization, both with responsibilities.

The way people approach 'their career' is characterized by many rather different strategies. We have all known *drifters* who appear rather directionless and unambitious. They may appear not to be able to hold down a job for any period of time yet they had to learn to be flexible and adaptable as they took on new jobs every so often. Drifters could be seen to be capricious or fickle, even reckless or more positively as adventurous and experimental.

The very opposite of the drifters are the *lifers* whose first job/company is their last. Although they may have not chosen their first job very judiciously or with foresight, they soon settled down much as those imprisoned for life. Whereas this may be an excellent strategy if one is in a company on the move, it is more likely to be a trade-off of high risk/high gain over security. Lifers are loyal but they are risk averse and liable to be alienated as performance management systems replace seniority-based or service ideologies.

Hoppers look like snakes-and-ladders experts. They seem to go quite fast up short ladders perhaps in small companies or departments, but slide down slippery snakes as they change their jobs in the hope of betterment. They lack the long-term vision of the planner who has the whole journey mapped out. Planners have clear targets, sometimes over-ambitiously fantasized. They can articulate where they want to be at the major milestones of life (aged 40, 55 or 60). They may even cultivate headhunters, apply (whimsically) for jobs on a regular basis and update their CVs monthly. Planners are certainly committed to their career development, perhaps at the cost of their peers, employees and organization.

A final strategy is that of the *hobbyist*. Some are SOBOs (shoved out but better off) but many, often in their 40s, become concerned (even obsessed) with self-development. They echo the surprising observation of a minister who for years counselled the dying, heard their confessions and their regrets: not *one* said they wished they had spent more time at work. The hobbyist may take early retirement, turn to consultancy or simply define quality of life as more important than the rat race. This makes them interesting people but not always deeply committed to the company's interest.

Many big organizations are beginning to conceive of a *career contract*. The idea is simple but the implications are wide. Three groups have specific responsibilities for an individual's career development. First, the organization itself should provide training and developmental opportunities where possible. Courses, sabbaticals, job share, shadowing experiences and the like all help. They need to provide a variety of options – a career cafeteria – if they can. And, of course, they need to provide realistic and up-to-date career information.

Managers, too, have responsibilities to those they manage. They need to provide high quality and timely feedback on performance so that staff can appraise themselves realistically. They need to have regular, expectation-managing discussions about performance and to support their reports with their action plans. Again, where possible, they need to offer developmental assignments where they can acquire new skills.

Finally, every individual needs to accept responsibility for his or her own career. Individuals cannot expect to remain passive in the process. Individuals need to seek out salient information on careers within and outside the organization; they need to initiate talks with their manager about careers and be prepared to invest in assessing their strengths and weaknesses. An annual career 'strengths, weaknesses, opportunities and threats' (SWOT) analysis may be a good discipline. They need to be prepared to take up development opportunities, even if they are outside their particular comfort zone.

Everybody thinks about 'where they are going' at work, be it up, across, down or out. Some HR people prefer the term 'path' to 'career', in the hope that it reduces expectations and implies a set route. Not talking about it does not mean it goes away, however. All managers need to be prepared and able to talk to their direct subordinates about their hopes and aspirations and to manage their expectations appropriately . The responsible organization, often with some flim-flam talk about careers in its mission statement, accepts the contract concept for the betterment of all parties involved.

Carrot and stick

Managers, like parents, realize that you need both carrot and stick to motivate and persuade. The promise of reward and the threat of punishment are powerful weapons in the armoury of the average manager who needs both to discipline and encourage.

Some managers don't believe in punishment, preferring only to withdraw reward when displeased. Others, from 'the school of hard knocks', believe that birching – whether psychological, monetary or physical – never did anyone any harm.

Researchers in London, using pharmacological and brain lesion work as well as personality tests, have found impressive evidence of two quite different brain systems. One means that certain people are highly sensitive to cues of reward and are disposed towards them. The other means that people are especially responsive to punishment cues and experience great anxiety in situations where there is impending or possible punishment. Thus some people will do anything for reward and ignore the risk of failure, whereas others are cautious and will do anything to avoid punishment.

Are marketing people differentially sensitive to reward and accountants differentially sensitive to punishment? Marketing managers' offices are often festooned with awards and prizes. This seems to contrast starkly with the minimalism of accountants, whose offices lack all adornment.

Maybe it is true that extroverted, hail-fellow-well-met marketeers can best be managed by lots of promise of reward. Equally, the threat of public humiliation alone may be enough to deter the introverted, cautious accountants from misbehaving and cause them to work very hard. Note that neither the rewards nor the punishments have to be great. It is often enough merely that they are public. Some marketing people will work very hard for some relatively worthless trinkets as long as they are publicly awarded and displayed.

The message is clear – threats, even the enforcement of punishment, may be quite ineffective for some employees, whereas the promise of small, even significant, rewards may be quite unappealing for others. The trick, of course, is knowing which type of person is which.

CC index

Many of us still receive letters with the quaint term 'cc' on them, followed by a list of names of those who have also been sent the letter. The term stands for 'carbon copy' and the institutionalization of the process may be as old as the technology itself. The e-mail system has now become a very popular mechanism for the cc process.

What does the frequent use of the cc procedure tell us about organizations that use it? Observers of corporate culture have described various prototypes, including the bureaucratic organization. These risk-averse, procedural driven organizations are highly political and who sends what, and knows what, is a nice marker of their power. In the dreary merry-go-round of minutes, meetings and monitored minutiae, who gets sent information through the cc index is crucial. Even the rank order of the people cc-ed at the bottom of the last page is informative. Not to be cc-ed may be the first indication that one may be for the chop!

CC-ing is really about Covering your Competence. In the legal-istic world of documents, the cc is a vital weapon. It may indicate an organization in terminal decline where energy is wasted on internal politics rather than on production or pleasing the customer.

Change checklist

Many people still have scar tissue from organizational change. We have all probably been offered the Russian Front option – you change your behaviour as the organization requires or go to the Russian Front! Adapt or die! Accept the change or leave!

People dislike change because they have ingrained behavioural habits, have 'sussed-out' the system and sometimes are awaiting the rewards for time serving. The fear of failure and ridicule; the effort of acquiring new skills and the uncertainty that comes with change make it feared and resisted, particularly by those who have been with an organization for a long time.

For many middle and senior managers it has been difficult to avoid change-management seminars. Often these are heavy on diag-nosis and short on cure. Some describe the 'stages-of-change' and how to manage each one of these differently. After the prescription for managing change, there are always two depressing caveats – that we are in a period of constant change, and that in the future change will be more dramatic and more traumatic.

But how do you know whether a planned change strategy is work-ing? What valid and unobtrusive measures are available to know how you are doing? Has there been a noticeable increase in: graffiti (public graffiti on notice-boards and public places like toilets) or poor timekeeping (ostentatious lateness; absenteeism and physical sick-ness). Extravagant use of resources – from paper clips to telephone calls; theft, espionage, even arson. Damage to service facilities and products (machine abuse); damage to the symbols of management (cars, toilets); poor workmanship, low quality control, higher rejec-tion. Increase in the victimization of weak, minority groups. Public talk about low morale, apathy and so on.

There are, in addition, some more subtle and interesting features to the threat of radical corporate change. One may be a noticeable and measurable increase in efficiency. Some employees react to the threat of change by trying to prove that the old system can and did work. This is often true of middle managers threatened by downsiz-ing but it is not common.

Often there is a new silence around the organization. This may be indicative of fear, depression or, more likely, uncertainty. Most noticeably, there is the emergence of new social grouping. People who never sat, ate, or chatted with each other do so. Because people are 'not all in the same boat' with respect to change, those who spot new opportunities form new alliances.

Thus there are self-made mergers and acquisitions after the announcement of change. Different groups have different vested interests and they notice that cross-functional groups that previously hated and distrusted each other now find a cause for alliance. It can be surprising how sections of the organization previously indifferent and even hostile to each other team up in an alliance against the common enemy.

Change follows a fairly predictable pattern – a period of resistance; then confusion; after that integration and finally commitment. A wise manager realizes that you need to manage differently at each stage. Thus, during the first stage, management needs to be available, visible and open but managers need to be strict, directive and have constantly to push through the required change. In the second phase they need to develop a clear mission, to have clear achievable standards, to be good role models and to put training in place. In the easier third and fourth phases they need to keep focus, build up teams, recognize excellence and reward performance, and then, alas, prepare for the next change round.

Complaints

In a recent American survey of office-worker complaints a familiar list emerged. About half thought the office too hot, the other half too cold. There were, naturally, grumbles about space – small work areas, not enough filing space, too few meeting rooms and inadequate parking facilities. There were, as always, complaints about the toilets – too dirty, too small. Some disliked the slowness of the lifts; others felt that the chairs were uncomfortable. There were inevitably many jibes at the cafeteria and the coffee and tea facilities. And some were concerned about security arrangements.

To what extent are these realistic or accurate complaints and to what extent are they symptoms of something else? The warden of a university residence reported the seasonal pattern of complaints that occurred as well as the incidences of hooliganism, arson and calculated wilful destruction. All this peaked in April, with little or no incidence in November. Most common complaints were about the food and the bathroom/toilets. The pattern was the same every year and quite predictable. And it seemed the problem solved itself within months.

Freudians should express no surprise here. Oral characters or those who fixated at the breast-feeding stage and who still get satisfaction through the mouth tend to complain about the food. Law, dentistry, music (singers, brass/wind players) students tend to find the food too bland or too spicy, too hot or too cold, too much or too little. Whether oral-incorporative (wine tasters, opera singers) or eliminative (barristers, orators), those people experience their world through the mouth and become very sensitive to their mouth and stomach when unhappy.

Anal characters, on the other hand, have most difficulty with the cleanliness of toilets, showers and baths. Shaped by their experience of potty training, they are often attracted by disciplines like accountancy, librarianship and economics, which stress order, parsimony and timekeeping. They may also feel unhappy about the timing of meals and other meetings. For them, dirty toilets are the last straw and a primary source of complaint.

What should the warden do in the face of these complaints? He noted that in the early years he tried to do something about them. Cooks and cleaners were disciplined, even sacked. Exotic sauces were purchased and new, softer toilet rolls were introduced but the warden soon learned that these costly changes had little or no effect and that the problem healed itself. In the jargon of therapy, it's called spontaneous remission: the problem goes away of its own accord. By late June/July all the problems went away only to return with seasonal regularity.

The cause of the problem was, of course, the exams. Put under pressure the students externalized their anxiety and frustrations. The students became more sensitive about their environment and about noise, cleanliness, food and other facilities. Under stress they project their frustrations and difficulties onto their residence. They seemed to have no problems until exam pressures began to take their toll in April. Hence complaints are often a symptom of something else.

Clearly not all complaints about the features and facilities in an office are the symptoms of stress or other issues. Whilst it is true that neurotics complain much more than non-neurotics, there are, on occasion, perfectly legitimate causes to complain about. Ergonomists would be out of a job were it not the case. In fact some of these 'physical' problems may be on the increase because organizations are cutting costs. Open plan offices with small partitions reduce personal space; the cleaning budget is cut and old equipment repaired rather than replaced. But complaints may equally be a function of job insecurity in these unsettled times.

So how does one detect the genuine from the disingenuous complaint? The obvious means is to physically measure temperature, space, noise levels or whatever, but this simply states the point numerically – it does not explain how or why the problem arises. Perhaps the easiest way of looking is to look for patterns in complaints. Is it one group of complaining people? Do they only complain at one time of the year, month etc? To whom do they complain and are complaints always accompanied by a proposed solution?

Neurotic, stressed attention-seekers are notorious complainers. Yet even the most adjusted and stoical employees find it necessary to point out that their efficiency and comfort are being affected by environmental factors.

It may be unwise to attempt to remedy a complaint of an office worker by taking the problem at its face value. It may be equally imprudent to assume that all complaints are symptoms of some underlying psychological management or structural issue. But the latter certainly lead to the former.

Compliments and customer feedback

Organizations with performance management systems are ever eager to find 'objective' criteria upon which to evaluate their staff. Some businesses seek feedback frequently, through surveys and interviews. They sometimes attempt random, quota or even total sample interviews or simply rely on customers to fill out brief questionnaires placed in hotel rooms, shopping malls and restaurants.

But they often receive unsolicited letters, phone calls and faxes from various customers. They fall typically into two categories: letters of compliment, full of praise, and letters of complaint that detail a catalogue of unhappy experiences. Should these letters, particularly those which mention individuals by name, be used in their appraisals or assessment? Much depends on their representativeness and accuracy; and both of these criteria are seriously in doubt.

Who writes letters of complaint and compliment and why? Imagine you have just had a good flight or a terrible meal; a salesperson has given you genuinely helpful advice in your best interests; or you have experienced customer service reminiscent of state-run enterprises with a take-it-or-leave it philosophy! If you have been fired up by the experience and want to communicate your feelings, to whom do you write? What do you say? What details are relevant? How long after the event do you write?

Some letters, usually those from complainers, provide minuscule, blow-by-blow details of what went wrong and who was to blame, while praisers offer glib descriptions of their happy experience. Most people can't be bothered. They soon forget the experience; simply do not know whom or where to write to, or see little point in the exercise. But there is a small band who delight in this voluntary feedback exercise, doing it regularly. What motivates them? For some it can be a selfless vote of thanks or a repayment for a kind deed. For others it may be a genuinely altruistic act to help an organization change or maintain its service.

There are nearly always more complainers than complimenters, and the complainers have too often been reinforced for their activity. Some first-time complainers get serious replies from fairly senior managers or even have their letters printed in magazines. Others are rewarded by replacement products, free tickets or other compensatory offers. Professional complainers are a bit like those competition fanatics who are addicted to any and all prize-led competitions. The random reinforcement principle gets them addicted and so it does with complainers.

Hence one hears about the person who was once mildly hurt (a small bruise) on a flight, who was given first-class tickets by a litigation-phobic organization and who now spends all flights trying to have someone bump into him. Or the hotel guest who, having been lavishly and inappropriately rewarded for a minor complaint, now whinges about everything in the hope of repeat compensation.

Letters of compliment and complaint nearly always have an impact far greater than they deserve. They do so primarily because so many organizations do not proactively seek out customer feedback, relying on others to write in. If the only feedback a service business gets is from complaining-compensators or complimenting characters, they end up getting a very odd picture of their customer care.

Receive enough irate letters from the disgruntled customer and you can be pretty sure you have a problem but by then it is probably too late and you have lost too many customers. Ask them before a few feel obliged to have to tell you. All managers need to be proactive in soliciting feedback from customers. To get an accurate picture of how the customer feels about your product or service, you need to do a simple, random poll. Waiting for those odd few to contact you is lazy and stupid for it paints a very distorted picture of what customers really experience.

Conspicuous consumption

Nearly 100 years ago, Thorstein Veblen pointed out that many of the rich of his time engaged in conspicuous consumption. They bought and displayed products to show off their taste, wealth and refinement. All advertisers have exploited this fact and are able to distinguish between a product and an image.

Thus we have the company BMW. Its product is the motor car, but what does it really sell? An upmarket image. Louis Vuitton makes luggage but sells prestige. Disney owns and runs theme parks, but sells happiness, fun and an innocent view of the world. As we can see from advertisements, a variety of manufacturers of breakfast cereals are selling not muesli and cornflakes but fitness and health. What does Estée Lauder sell? The product is make-up, but hope is what it sells.

It is not a bad discipline for employees struggling with mission statements or 'who-is-your customer' quizzes to attempt to distinguish the product, tangible or intangible, from what is truly being sold to the consumer.

There is widespread agreement on the prestige of different makes of car, shops for clothes, and suburbs. Cars will all take us places but they also send out messages about their owner. Status may be enhanced by driving the latest model, and large and expensive cars. In modern society there are changing fashions, for clothes but also for other possessions. Veblen proposed that it is the rich who start fashions and others follow, so that there is a 'trickle down' of fashion, and status symbols keep changing. As soon as lower status groups have adopted a fashion the rich start a new one to distinguish themselves from their social inferiors.

Social status is not the only message symbolized by possessions. Another is group membership. For example football fans, punks and other youth groups proclaim their solidarity with the group by wearing the 'uniform' of that group. Such symbols express solidarity with other members of the group, they emphasize shared identity. Other symbols express uniqueness, deviation from the norms of groups, showing that someone is a scientific doctor, a high church clergy person, a left-wing politician, etc. It is hardly necessary to send signals announcing whether an individual is male or female but it is common to signal aspects of sexual orientation, e.g. being gay, celibate, promiscuous. For women at work it may be important to signal their degree of masculinity or femininity by their clothes and whether they get the job may depend on this. This whole process depends on there being shared meanings for objects; these shared meanings are not mainly created by special groups like the rich, however, but more by the media, advertising and the norms of different groups.

Buying, wearing and consuming things is a language the astute learn to speak. Much can be gleaned by going to a person's office or home. Their dress, accent, preferred lunch are often carefully chosen to communicate a message and an identity. Just as with products, the image and the reality may not be very close together. Never judge a book by its cover. But remember somebody has designed the cover in the hope that you will buy and even display it.

Consumer boycotts

Consumer boycotts are increasingly common in America and Europe. Some are media-oriented, where announcements and pleas are made with passion, drama and supposed legitimacy by individuals or organizations. Others are market-oriented where particular brand names are targeted by lobbyists and protectionists. Some pressure groups aim to 'educate', that is to proselytize, rather than to boycott. It has been suggested that boycott strategies can be judged thus:

Table 3: Boycott strategies

Boycott orientation	Target	
	Non-surrogate	*Surrogate*
Media-oriented boycott	Adverse effects on target firm's image lead to desired change in target firm's behaviour	Adverse effects on target firm's image lead to pressure applied by target firm on offending party, leading to desired change in behaviour of offending party
Marketplace-oriented boycott	Adverse effects on target firm's image and sales lead to desired change in target firm's behaviour	Adverse effects on target firm's image and sales lead to pressure applied by target firm on offending party, leading to desired change in behaviour of offending party

It seems that, to be successful, media-orchestrated boycotts follow certain simple rules:

- announcements and pleas should be made by well-known organizations and individuals.
- announcements should identify a few well-known organizations as the target;
- complaints and objections against organizations should appear legitimate and relatively uncomplicated;
- if possible passion and drama should accompany all announcements.

Factors that seem to predict the success of market place-oriented boycotts include:

- boycotted products/services should be easy for consumers to identify;
- boycotts should target just a few brand names, ideally one primary target;
- boycotts should be planned at a time when there are few, if any, competing boycotts;
- it is crucial that there are acceptable and readily available targets for the boycotted products and services;
- ideally, boycott targets need to be selected so as to ensure that consumer violations of the boycotts are publicly visible.

The lobbyists and protectionists are becoming increasingly sophisticated. Indeed there are now boycott consultants who advise nascent pressure groups how to proceed. Some, curiously and paradoxically, recommend approved, politically correct products. The purpose of this reverse discrimination is to encourage consumers to buy products and services provided by organizations that are somehow favoured (for ethical, political or other reasons). To this extent one might even see the boycott as an extremely clever bit of marketing!

What these consumer affairs activists have in common is that they purport to speak on behalf of others. Most behalfers claim to represent the consumer – which is patently absurd precisely because consumers have highly varied, indeed conflicting, needs. Have they ever been elected? Worse, there is no way they can know consumers' needs, wants or wishes. Newspapers through sales, companies through market research, even politicians through their surgeries get some idea of the feelings, beliefs and behaviours of the public, but behalfers rarely have access to the diversity of public opinion.

Most are against things anti this or that and in favour of more lifestyle control or legislation. It would be hypocritical to attempt to ban or restrict behalfers but no one should take them seriously.

Corporate culture

Hermann Goering, Marshal of the Luftwaffe, once said that every time he heard the word 'culture', he reached for his revolver. Some managers might feel the same.

For some time now 'culture' has been a buzz word in management circles. It can be used in two senses. It can refer to ethnic culture – that awfully sensitive issue with a heady mix of colour, language, and religious differences. There is a whole industry dedicated to keeping this issue alive and in the forefront of people's minds. Just as the past is another country where people do things differently, so cultural differences reflect different ways of seeing, thinking and behaving. The second sort of 'culture' is corporate, and it is this that is now the flavour of the month. Managers have found an excuse or explanation for their woes in this amorphous and vague concept but also, often naïvely, a source of hope for a quick fix.

The academics (often from different and mutually despising disciplines) ask, of course, academic questions about the aetiology, meaning, correlates, indeed even the existence of corporate culture. Popularist writers or speakers have more catchy phrases and models to describe culture. Thus, some say it's 'the way we do things around here' whereas others rely more on concepts like values or beliefs for defining culture.

Most ordinary people confront corporate culture directly, and somewhat confusingly, only when they change jobs. It is striking how people become socialized into distinct patterns of dress, language, time-keeping and so on in different organizations. Consultants often rely on very subtle cues to understand an organization's culture: the logo; job titles; the company's building, particularly the reception area; the attire of the managing director!

Being faced with a new and different corporate culture can present employees with tremendous problems, as some multinationals know to their cost. Large corporations often try to impose a unified, homogenized corporate culture across ethnic or national culture boundaries. Others adopt the approach that 'when in Rome do as the Romans do' – even though they might draw a line at the nepotism, corruption and inefficiency that they perceive in some cultures. The reaction to these differences often causes culture shock and managers deal with this syndrome in different ways. Whether it is corporate culture or ethnic culture shock, the results and reactions are much the same.

Discovering cultural differences (whether they are ethnic, gender, religious or linguistically based) is frequently an unpleasant experience. Organizations most often find out about corporate culture during restructuring or, most traumatically, during mergers and acquisitions. They discover that what they thought to be normal behaviour is not necessarily so and that people do things rather differently. In short, they suffer corporate culture shock. The reactions it induces vary considerably but people tend to fall into one of the various groups detailed below:

- *Chauvinistic imperialists:* 'Ours is the best way and others should learn our ways; differences are fairly minimal anyway and due solely to their ignorance.' This approach argues that 'we' have the secret to how to do things and corporate culture, and the sooner others learn our ways and our language the better.

- *Ashamed post colonialists:* 'Theirs is the best, most natural way and ours is the worst, most exploitative way. Others have the solution. We are, or were, arrogant and wrong.' This rather self-effacing approach seems to be more and more common especially among those who have lived and worked in an economically declining country or company. They believe the Japanese, the electronic industry, consultants, or someone else knows the real secrets of ideal corporate behaviour and working patterns.

- *Ignoramuses:* 'Cultural differences don't really exist and are emphasized by people who have ulterior (political) motives.' Here ignorance is bliss. They simply don't want to know about alternative ways of working or value differences.

- *Relativists:* 'Every culture does things differently and has its share of the truth. Nearly every aspect of culture varies and they are essentially incomparable.' Relativists feel rather overwhelmed by the whole business of culture and can find no way of making judgements about culture. They certainly don't believe there is one best way; they try to see the best in a variety of different styles and, as a result, are quite happy to stay as they are.

- *Vacillators and marginals:* 'All cultures are valid in some respect and the trick is to find which has the best answer to the problem. Cultures tend to be completely right or wrong on a specific topic and it is difficult to predict which is which and when.' With this approach, the group chops and changes its beliefs and behaviours, and is exceedingly capricious. Every so often there is an attempt to change the corporate culture.

- *Mediators:* 'The most sensible approach is to choose the most sensitive, veridical, and appropriate aspects of cultural tradition and attempt to live them out.' This is a sensitive mix rather than a homogenization. Mediators believe one can and should choose between working styles and behaviours.

- *Hybrid creators:* 'We should try to create a new hybrid culture that best meets our needs and that it is adaptive and healthy.' Creating a culture may be easier said than done.

Whatever one's reaction to corporate culture, it remains an issue that will not go away. Human resource experts talk about it the whole time; line managers attempt to change it; CEOs attempt to measure it even if none of them is quite sure what it is.

Working abroad often means confronting the heady mix of both ethnic (national) and corporate culture. All kinds of reactions occur: surprise, anxiety, bewilderment, even disgust. After some time people begin to slot into the above categories and then cope with the difficulties of being different. If only Goering's revolver could deal with these issues more effectively.

Creativity cannot be taught

It is both optimistic and naïve to assume that everything can be taught. With sufficient time, money and effort, it is certainly true that every skill can be partly learned or improved. The tone-deaf can be taught to sing; the computer phobic can be taught to be computer literate; the monoglot can become a polyglot but the cost-benefit analysis is often depressing. The effort is not worth the reward, the gain not worth the pain. In short, the amount of progress or progressive change is sometimes not worth the effort involved.

Are any of the creativity training courses on the market effective? Can one teach creativity? Is it essentially something one either has or not (like colour vision)?

The obsession with change means many managers believe that being innovative before one's competitors is the only way to ensure that businesses survive, let alone prosper. The *Zeitgeist* says we not only have to *adapt* to change but must *anticipate* or even *create* change ourselves. To have the reputation of an 'ideas' person is now more important than being an 'action' person.

Hundreds of consultants and trainers offer creativity training courses. Ironically, few are new, innovative or 'different'. Courses like this go back 50 years. Before the war, General Electric offered creative engineering courses. All courses seem to have certain key components such as stressing flexibility, uncertainty avoidance or tolerance for ambiguity; suspending judgement/assessment, teaching divergent, intuitive versus convergent and analytic thinking, and breaking down problems into more manageable component parts. All the techniques like brainstorming and mind mapping are 30 years old, but simply repackaged in the metaphor of the day, the most popular of which is currently the split brain analogy with the logical right and creative left side. The gullible and ill-formed actually believe this charmingly old-fashioned concept to be physiologically based. It is no more than a late nineteenth century re-emergence of phrenology, dismissed by those who know anything about cerebral laterality.

In reality, the only creative things about creativity courses are the new catchphrases and the new focus on marketing. Hence, we find techniques called synectics, morphological analysis and neurolinguistic programming. The problem is just like that of naming a new medicine: it has to sound right. Currently, 'bio-', 'neuro-' and 'eco-' are good prefixes and 'programme', 'software' and 'connection' quite good suffixes. Thus bio-connectionism or eco software would be a good term for any old techniques that might or might not have anything to do with creativity.

We do, however, know some facts about creativity (from years of careful, patient, deliberated research). We know, for instance, that brainstorming and meditational techniques do not work in the sense that they generate more or better creative responses. We know that people feel more confident about their ability to be creative after a course but that by any objective criteria most courses fail. We know that teaching theories of creativity is as effective, if not more so, as merely teaching techniques. We know that people are more creative in the company of those they like than those they dislike or merely respect. And we know that it is the particular combination of individuals (personality types) and situations (tasks) that leads to creative success. In the jargon of statistics, there is always an interaction effect, never a main effect.

Curiously, the way trainers like to demonstrate the effectiveness of their courses is through measuring what is called ideation. Before the course begins, ask people to write down all the things they can do with a brick or a paperclip and total this up. Do the same after the course, and the difference is a measure of success. This very crude measure takes no account of the quality or usefulness of the decisions and there is precious little evidence that quantity is related to quality. Most people come back from courses semi-deluded that they are creative, and therefore rate the course highly. 'Happy sheets' are no substitute for a demonstration of actual creativity long after a course has ended.

As scientists tell us, an experiment needs a control group. To evaluate a creativity course, those who experienced the course would have to be compared with a control group consisting of individuals who did not experience the course, or those who went on an opposite type of course (teaching advanced logic, for example) and those who went on an unrelated course (leadership training). If the scores of those who went on the creativity course are better after the course than those of the control group(s), this provides some evidence that creativity training works. However, it is very difficult to find anyone who has done this using real control groups.

When it comes to genuine creativity, organizations only 'talk a good game'. Put a creative person in an innovation-resistant organization and the latter always wins. The question is whether and how organizations are really interested in innovation. And what sort of innovation – products yes, even services, but alas, rarely management techniques.

Kirton, at the University of Hertfordshire, has distinguished between adapters (who seek solutions to problems in tried and understood ways) and innovators (who try radically different, even impractical solutions, rejecting past customs and the rules). The problem is that adapters are never really seriously creative and that organizations never select or maintain innovators. Because they are often difficult characters (abrasive, irreverent), they are seen as problems for management and are often ditched before they have had an opportunity to manifest their creativity.

The questions for organizations are thus:

- If someone or some group believes they have a good creative idea, to whom do they communicate it?
- What process or forum is set up to assess, implement and audit these ideas?
- Are people rewarded, ignored or punished through being genuinely innovative?
- Is the organization willing to take risks and fail or is it eager to watch others experiment and be first to adopt clearly successfully innovative ideas?
- Is the organization really interested in selecting creative people and putting up with their disruptive and anti-social behaviour?

Creativity can go too far. Tell people to attempt creativity at every turn and you end up with people applying endless divergent thinking, left brain, ambiguity-tolerant, mumbo-jumbo techniques. Creative thinking is a means to an end, but worshipping it means it soon becomes the end in itself.

There is no question that you can teach people techniques supposedly associated with creativity but this does not mean that those people will necessarily be more creative. It is more cost-effective to select and reward the creative types . . . if, of course, the organization really does want to be creative (see *teaching thinking*).

Cross-functional teams

Which is most productive – homogeneous groups of like-minded, similarly-trained, joint experts on a topic, or heterogeneous groups from different backgrounds and quite different disciplines?

The best argument for forming and using cross-functional teams comes from the use of business games. In one study a business school had marketing, accounts, production and HR specialists compete in separate groups in a lengthy simulated game with a measurable outcome.

The marketing group focused on sales and promotion. They achieved impressive market share but bankrupted themselves in doing so. The accountants, ever watchful of the bottom line, minimized investments in production and promotions. They maintained capital but had no new products and slowly faded away. The production specialists were, of course, interested mainly in the manufacturing process and new product development. They ended with excellent products, at the right price but no money left for promotion, so no customers.

To everyone's surprise and chagrin the HR team won. They tinkered around with the organizational structure, spent a little money on training and got the organogram (chart) right. Having avoided bankrupting themselves they won by default.

The moral of the story: we need people with different perspectives and priorities. Homogeneous teams with similar perspectives tend to be egocentric. Cross-functional teams may be less comfortable but much more effective.

Culture shock

Nearly every traveller must have experienced culture shock at some time or another. Equally, many managers have experienced corporate culture shock as they have either changed company or the company has changed around them.

It seems that the phenomenon has six facets: there is strain caused by the effort of making necessary psychological adaptations – speaking another language, coping with the currency, driving on the other side of the road etc. Secondly, there is often a sense of loss and feelings of deprivation with regard to friends, status and possessions. If you are in a place where nobody knows, loves, respects and confides in you, you may feel anonymous and deprived of your status and role in society, as well as bereft of familiar and useful objects. Thirdly, there is often a feeling of rejection – your rejection of the natives and their rejection of you. People who have experienced corporate culture shock after a merger and acquisition know all about rejection!

A fourth symptom of culture shock is confusion. Travellers can become unsure about their roles, their values, feelings and sometimes about who they are. When people live by a different moral and social code from their own, even for a comparatively short period of time, they can be very confused. Once one becomes more aware of cultural differences, typical reactions of surprise, anxiety, even disgust and indignation appear. The way foreigners treat animals, eat food, worship their god, guru or CEO, or perform their ablutions often causes amazement and horror to naïve travellers. Finally, culture shock often involves feelings of impotence from not being able to cope with the new environment.

There are two extreme reactions to culture shock: those who act as if they had 'never left home' and nothing has changed, and those who immediately 'go native' and embrace the new with enthusiasm. The former chauvinists create 'little Englands' in foreign fields, refusing to compromise their diet or dress and do things in their traditional manner.

Most travellers, however, experience less dramatic, but equally uncomfortable reactions to culture shock. These may include excessive concern over drinking water, food and bedding; fits of anger over delays and other minor frustrations; excessive fear of being cheated, robbed or injured; great concern over minor pains and eruptions of the skin; and a longing to be back at the idealized home 'where you can get a good cup of tea and talk to sensible people'.

As any seasoned traveller will know, one often begins to get used to, and even learn to like, the new culture. First, there is the honeymoon stage, which is characterized by enchantment, fascination, enthusiasm and admiration for the new culture, as well as cordial, but superficial relationships. In this stage, people are generally intrigued and euphoric. The second phase heralds crisis and degeneration. It is now that the traveller feels loss, isolation, loneliness and inadequacy and tends to become depressed and withdrawn. This usually happens after two to six months of living in the new culture.

The third phase is the most problematic and involves reintegration. At this point, people tend to reject the host culture, becoming opinionated and negative, partly as a means of showing their self-assertion and growing self-esteem. The fourth stage of autonomy finds the traveller assured, relaxed, warm and empathetic because he or she is socially and linguistically capable of negotiating most new and different social situations in the culture. Finally, the independent phase is achieved, characterized by trust, humour and the acceptance and enjoyment of social, psychological and cultural differences.

Curiously, people appear to go through the same series of reactions when returning home after a long spell abroad. However, it would be a mistake to assume that everyone will pass through each of these stages, or in this particular order.

Then there is the shock of being visited. Anyone who lives in a popular tourist town soon becomes aware that it is not only the tourist but also the native who experiences culture shock. The amount and type of shock that tourists can impart to local people is an indication of a number of things, such as the relative proportion of tourists to natives, the duration of their stay, the comparative wealth and development of the two groups, and the racial and ethnic prejudices of both. This experience may be like having a new change-oriented boss in the organization or being audited by consultants.

Of course, not everybody will experience culture shock. Older, better-educated, confident and skilful adults (particularly those who speak the language) tend to adapt best. Yet there is considerable evidence that some sojourners, be they foreign students, voluntary workers, businessmen, diplomats or even military personnel become so confused and depressed that they have to be sent home at great expense. That is why many organizations, including the Foreign Office, the British Council and many multinationals, attempt to lessen culture shock by using a number of training techniques.

Information and advice in the form of lectures, pamphlets and so on are very popular but not always very useful. The 'facts' that are given are often too general to have any clear, specific application in particular circumstances. Instructions tend to emphasize the exotic and ignore the mundane (how to hail a taxi, for example). This technique also gives the impression that the culture can be easily understood, and even if facts are retained, they do not necessarily lead to accommodating behaviour.

A second technique is 'isomorphic training'. This is based on the theory that a major cause of cross-cultural communication problems is that most people tend to offer different explanations for each other's behaviour. First, various episodes are described which ended in embarrassment, misunderstanding or hostility between people from two different cultures. The trainee is then presented with four or five alternative explanations of what went wrong, all of which correspond to different attributions of the observed behaviour. Only one is correct from the perspective of the culture being learned. This is an interesting and useful technique, but depends for much of its success on the relevance of the various episodes chosen.

Perhaps the most successful method is 'skills training'. Socially inadequate or inept individuals have not mastered the social conventions of their own society. Either they are unaware of the rules and processes of everyday behaviour or, if aware of the rules, they are unable or unwilling to abide by them. They are therefore like strangers in their own land. People newly arrived in an alien culture will be in a similar position and may benefit from simple skills training.

This involves analysing everyday encounters such as buying and selling, negotiations, refusal of requests. Successful culture models are shown engaging in these acts. Practice with videotape feedback follows. This may all sound very clinical but can be great fun and very informative.

Many travellers, unless working for an enlightened business and with considerable company resources behind them, do not have the time or money for training courses that prevent or minimize culture shock. They have to leap in at the deep end and hope that they can swim but there are some simple things they can do that may well lessen the shock and improve communications.

Before departure, it is important to learn as much as possible about the society you are visiting. Areas of great importance include:

- *Language:* Not only vocabulary, but polite usage; when to use higher and lower forms; and particularly how to say 'yes' and 'no' clearly.
- *Non-verbal cues:* Gestures, body contact and eye gaze patterns differ significantly from one country to another, and carry very important meanings. Cues of this sort for greeting, parting and eating are most important, and are relatively easy to learn.
- *Social rules:* Every society develops rules that regulate behaviour. Some of the most important rules concern gifts, buying

and selling, eating and drinking, time keeping, and bribery and nepotism.

- *Social relationships:* Family relationships, classes and castes, and working relationships often differ from culture to culture. The different social roles of the two sexes is perhaps the most dramatic difference between societies and travellers should pay particular attention to this.
- *Motivation:* Being assertive, extrovert and achievement-orientated may be desirable in America and Western Europe but this is not necessarily the case elsewhere. How to present oneself, maintain face and so on, is well worth knowing.

Once you have arrived, there are a few simple steps that you can take to help reduce perplexity and understand the natives:

- *Choose locals for friends:* Avoid mixing with compatriots or other foreigners. Get to know the natives who can introduce you to the subtleties and nuances of the culture.
- *Practical social activities:* Don't be put off more complex social encounters, but ask for information on appropriate etiquette. People are usually happy to help and teach genuinely interested and courteous foreigners.
- *Avoid 'good/bad' or 'us/them' comparisons:* Try to establish how and why people perceive and explain the same act differently, have different expectations etc. Social behaviour has resulted from different historical and economic conditions and may be looked at from various perspectives.
- *Attempt mediation:* Rather than reject your cultural tradition or theirs, attempt to select, combine and synthesize the appropriate features of different social systems, whether in dress, food or behaviour.

Travel does broaden the mind (and frequently the behind) but it requires some effort. Preparation, it is said, prevents a pretty poor performance and travelling in different social environments is no exception. This preparation may require social, as well as geographic maps.

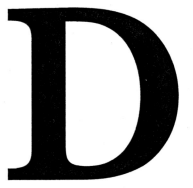

Definitions

As in many other forms of life, in business the reality and image are often far apart. What you see is not what you get. 'Business speak' is a subtle language – it can be decoded and translated – but for the uninitiated it remains perplexing. This is why jokesters and comics periodically list the real meaning of the words. These are funny but often true. It's where a manager for an organization refuses to see the truth of these cynical definitions that one may have the start of a problem.

This ever lengthening and unattributable or unattributed list may be general or specific. Thus the following 10 definitions are from business reports and how to read them:

It is in progress	So wrapped up in red tape that the situation is almost hopeless
A conference	Place where conversation is substituted for the dreariness of labour and the loneliness of thought
Expediate	To confound, confusion with commotion
Co-ordinate	Someone who has a desk between two expeditors
We will look into it	By the time we get around to doing anything about this, we assume you will have forgotten too
To activate	To make carbons and add more names to memos
To negotiate	To seek a meeting of minds without knocking together of heads
Reorientation	Getting used to work again after the holidays
Note and initial	Let's spread the responsibility for this
Clarification	To fill in the background with so many details that the foreground goes underground

The following are translations from marketing speak, one of the most impenetrable jargons.

Advanced design – The advertising agency doesn't understand it.
A – Parts not interchangeable with previous design.
All solid-state – Heavy as hell!

Breakthrough – We finally understood a way to sell it.
Broadcast quality – Gives a picture and produces noise.
Built to precision tolerances – We finally got it to fit together.

Customer service across the country – You can return it from most
    airports.

Designed simplicity – Manufacturer's cost cut to the bone.
Direct sales only – Factory had a big argument with distributor.
Distinctive – A different shape and colour than the others.

Exclusive – Imported product.

Field-tested – Manufacturer lacks test equipment.
Foolproof operation – No provision for adjustment.
Futuristic – No other reason why it looks the way it does.

Hand crafted – Assembly machines operated without gloves on.
High accuracy – Unit on which all parts fit.
High reliability – We made it work long enough to ship it.

It's here at last! – Rush job: nobody knew it was coming.

Latest aerospace technology – One of our technicians was laid off by
    Boeing.

Maintenance-free – Impossible to fix.
Meets all standards – Ours, not yours.
Microprocessor controlled – Does things we can't explain.
Mill-spec components – We got a good deal at a government
    auction.

New – Different colour from previous design.
New generation – Old design failed, maybe this one will work.

Performance proven – Will operate through the warranty period.

Redesigned – Previous faults corrected, we hope . . .

Revolutionary – It's different from our competitors.

Satisfaction guaranteed – Manufacturer's, upon cashing your cheque.

Unmatched – Almost as good as the competition.
Unprecedented performance – Nothing we ever had before worked *this* way.

Years of development – We finally got one that works.

Desks

There used to be a time when there was a positive association between one's power and status in an organization and the size of one's desk. All cartoons still show dictatorial, merchant-baron captains of industry seated behind half an acre of polished oak, glaring at a clearly intimidated employee.

In these desks there were drawers, trays, files and various other 'clever little niches' to store papers and other documents. Information was power. But now desks are out and tables are in. Indeed personal space of all sorts is on the way out. The 'lap-top' can be placed anywhere and store everything. The smaller the computer, the more impressive.

Further, the shape and size of the 'designer' office and desk/table reflect a rather different image. Desks are frequently oval; occasionally circular, rarely oblong, never square. Often their surface is bare, although the room should contain a computer terminal, one telephone, a couple of good pieces of art (never a portrait or certificates of degrees), a few comfortable chairs and a couch. Colours should preferably be pale so as to heighten the effect of openness. The crucial image, it seems, is one of space, lack of clutter, indeed a minimal emptiness. Because office space in 'super cities' (London, New York, Tokyo) is so expensive, to emphasize it by conspicuous emptiness is a powerful statement.

The briefcase – a sort of mobile desk– is an ideal icon of corporate culture. It certainly comes in many forms. First, there is the shabby, shapeless, donnish, somewhat battered leather bag. Then there are those fairly large square cases – the more hideous made of plastic (or some substitute) and designed not to be flexible but to have useful compartments for felt-tipped pens. Thirdly, there is the 'expensive material' designer case that follows no shape rule except that it is made of crocodile, calf or some other unfortunate animal and carries a gold monogram.

Now, however, status is distinguished not so much by shape or material but by size. Capable of carrying only the *Financial Times*, the new wafer-thin briefcase is remarkable for not looking like a brief-case at all. The less one can carry in the case, the better. This is due to the way in which we now use, store, and gain access to information. Top people are briefed by their underlings who, each in turn, has had to condense information about sale, production units, share movements etc from vast computerized printouts into pretty (prefer-ably coloured) computer graphics such as pie-charts, histograms and so on – a sort of visual image for the hard of thinking. The higher one is in the organization, the more interpretation and selection of data is required and the more it is boiled down.

Around the conference table, then, the decision maker may call for information about a particular issue. This information has, no doubt, been carried to the meeting by the lieutenant in a briefcase slightly bigger than the person's above him. This briefing has already occurred at various levels, each time with an underling providing more and more material and printouts, which the person above selects, edits and summarizes, and so reduces in size. Thus, as with the porters of David Livingstone and Edmund Hillary, the more one carries, the lowlier one is.

Consider the workstation and what it may tell us about its occu-pant. Any psychologist worth his or her salt could easily devise a book-length, chat-show type theory of its importance. A manager's or even support staff's typical desk state could be used to diagnose the following:

• *Personality.* The arrangement of papers and objects gives easy clues as to the nature of the individual. The obsessive individ-ual is compulsively neat and orderly (but should remember that a tidy desk is the sign of a diseased mind). The impulsive and creative individual is hopelessly disordered. Many managers personalize their workspace with photographs, *objets d'art*, awards and similar items, as well as necessary tools of their trade. The desk is an impressive management tool of considerable possibilities; the padded leather-backed chair shows gravitas; the brightly coloured Swedish design indicates the occupant has arty-farty tendencies; the battered functional standard supply shows the alienated manager.

- *Seniority and security.* In the old world, size of desk was a clear indication of seniority. Then other factors were introduced: better quality of wood, leather and design. Thus, nasty little metallic desks for juniors, polished oak for the CEO. But now, in the minimalist 1990s, the desk has been replaced by the meeting table – or even the coffee table. Some really serious managers have forsaken the desk for comfortable chairs and/or a couch. Desks are for paper-pushers, even computer johnnies – no longer for serious decision makers. But it is only the very secure, senior manager who is confident enough to give up the security blanket of the genital-protecting desk.

- *Workstyle.* Is a cluttered desk a sign of genius? Certainly the implements on the desk can give an indication of the working preferences of the desk's tenant. What does the in/out tray suggest? Or the time-zone clock? Does the position of the phone indicate its usage? Is the desk's position in the room an indication of whether it is used as an interview barrier or protector? Apart from the self-presentational features of desk-management, it can give an insight into the habits of the holder. The centrality of PCs, phones and calculators usually indicates centrality of locus. An in/out tray may possibly show a need to prioritize systematically, as well as a regular desire for closure. Time-zone clocks, of course, indicate the regularity of overseas calls made. Fluffy toys on the desk, as elsewhere, indicate a feeble mind.

Go into an empty office and try reading the signals. Predict the personality, status consciousness and work style of the desk holder. If you are correct, by matching your predictions with actualities measured by various ratings, you may feel eager to take up the exact science of desk psychology!

Diversity in business

People have one thing in common: they are all different. But how different? We were once taught to celebrate our common humanity; we are now taught at work to enjoy our differences. A latest fad in the American corporate world is diversity training. A country that once celebrated the melting pot concept, where assorted immigrants became good Americans, now encourages native-born Americans to become cultural foreigners.

Borrowed from the highly political correct world of 'environment speak' where bio-diversity seems necessary for survival, the management gurus believe that differences are now an asset within an organization. Having spent time and money on recruitment and selection to ensure a clear, distinct, homogeneous corporate culture, the human resource people are now trumpeting diversity of heterogeneity.

Whence this diversity talk? And what are the dangers of diversity training? In the late 1980s, American strategic planners and futurologists predicted that the predominance of white males in the workforce would be on the decline. More women and more ethnic minorities were assuming junior and senior work roles, so the pundits believed that companies needed to prepare for this change. They needed to prepare and plan for a different mix, although it was not clear how, or indeed why.

Migration to Britain has led to the setting up of various commissions like the Equal Opportunity Commission and the Commission for Racial Equality. The primary aim of these and other bodies is to ensure that legislation on these issues is followed. Although there are equal opportunity and discrimination laws, some organizations attempt to put in place 'affirmative-action' rules. Affirmative action is now a very hot topic with one extreme claiming it is just a smokescreen for anti-establishment discrimination and other extremes believing it is the only way to install real justice at work. Hence, companies choose to have affirmative-action guidelines, homilies and hype rather than rules. The following of laws, rules, procedures and guidelines is one strategy. The other is sensitization, indoctrination and seminaring.

For many, the favoured way of dealing with the diversity issues is not legalistic but training. Hence there are, at least in North Africa, a plethora of courses that attempt to raise sensitivity and reduce prejudice. They fit well with the prevailing culture of victimhood and stress how some feel misunderstood, undervalued and stereotyped at work.

To a large extent these programmes are a mix between the sensitivity training of the 1970s and lectures on racial and sexual discrimination. Some institutions make these courses compulsory, convinced that those who need them most are least likely to attend of their own volition. Their aim is to reduce out-group hostility and suspicion, make people more tolerant and accepting and ultimately to encourage multinational/ethnic teams. But do they work?

Like many good intentions they often fail abysmally. The following are the most common reasons. First, they choose the wrong presenter/trainer. Many believe a minority person – a black woman, a recent immigrant, a handicapped person – is the most appropriate person because they can tell the story of their own triumph over victimhood most clearly. But this ignores the perceptions and underlying values of the trainees. It is all very well to say that minorities/women or members of some other group are misunderstood while ostentatiously not understanding the values, fears and myths of the trainees. Insiders and those from the same group often make better, more trusted, trainers. They know best where the group is 'coming from'. Further, it is probably better that they do not advertise themselves as paragons of virtue, 'whiter-than-white'. Admitting shortcomings increases rather than decreases credibility.

Second, targeting certain groups, especially middle-class white males, is hypocritical. To preach non-prejudice by targeting one group is to practise the very opposite of what one preaches. This white Anglo-Saxon Protestant (WASP) knocking is the very example of what is supposed to be wrong with the current system.

Third, it is best not to pretend the programme or training is 'value free', 'value fair' or any of the other similar euphemisms. It is much better explicitly to state the values that are underlying the whole diversity training world. But once again we find a paradox. A sort of fuzzy, post-modernist relativism underlies most courses. This suggests that there is no right or wrong or best way of behaving and that different approaches are to be welcomed. Differences are good; no one is right; but Anglocentic, masculine behaviour is intolerable, unacceptable and wicked. Despite the rhetoric to the contrary, diversity programmes have clear messages about right and wrong. All they serve to do is silence, not convert, those of different opinion and to drive them underground into like-minded cells that now have a common enemy.

Fourth, the idea of making programmes guilt-driven is dangerous. To attempt to unearth racists and homophobes is a delicate matter. Focusing on past historic examples is unwise for two reasons: it encourages an emphasis on the past and it turns out to be a game where those who can find the best examples win. One cannot change the past nor is one often responsible for it. It is much better to agree on the present principles that should be put into practice to obviate agreed injustices. The way in which young Germans deal with their own recent and painful history teaches how this can be achieved.

Fifth, diversity, discrimination and oppression training is based on the 'attitude adjustment' idea. It makes for more heat than light, and rarely new skills. It is much better to teach attitude change through teaching skills. Diversity issues – meaning understanding and communicating with work colleagues – are far better addressed on real training courses to do with leadership, appraisal or team building. If courses focus exclusively on cross-cultural issues they nearly always fall flat. Taught as an integral part of business skills they often succeed.

Sixth, the most ridiculous strategy is 'language attitude change'. The ridiculous insistence on politically correct terms shifts attention to etymology and word games. The casualties of this lexicon-therapy are both humour and clarity. Language is the means not the end. That is not to say that language and naming problems might not be important to people at work but they are not the single or even major cause, nor are they the consequence, of occupational injustice.

Finally, the present is often ignored in these programmes. They move from the wild speculations of fantastic futurologists to a curiously simplistic rewriting of the history of the past. The present is too difficult to deal with. How people deal with each other in the organization *now* must be the focus of all training courses.

You change attitudes by changing behaviour. Let people from different backgrounds work together, interdependently, on a test that is ultimately successful. Let them mix under easy, structured circumstances and they will grow to appreciate each other. Let them be sensitively tipped off by one of their 'own kind' that certain behaviours go over the top and are neither appreciated nor understood. And, above all, don't make humour a minefield of emotional hype.

Ultimately most diversity training is diversionary. It is a stratagem for diverting attention away from what is really important in the organization.

Doubletalk

Although the word 'academic' is almost always used pejoratively by the business world, a few university practices have been borrowed. The two most favoured are the sabbatical and the concept of emeritus.

For the academic, the sabbatical was a sort of moratorium where one took stock, refreshed oneself intellectually and perhaps travelled – a kind of mid-life Grand Tour. It was time to write books and to read in an environment free from such distractions as e-mails, faxes and students. Every five to seven years, the dons would arrange the long-anticipated break; but in some universities, this privilege has been reduced, curtailed and even stopped.

For the middle manager the idea is most attractive. Although it is not clear what a manager does on his/her sabbatical except have an extended holiday, in some sectors the idea has really caught on.

Old academics don't die, or even retire. They become emeritus. That is, they can hang on to their title, and the supposed accumulated wisdom of experience that is therein contained. They potter about their old institutions, as much part of the furniture as the peeling paint and scuffed carpets. The term 'emeritus' has now crept into business, particularly in America. Still usually applied only to jobs with a proven skill base (wine taster, engineer) it allows the retired to behave as if they never have.

Drafting reports

Does the speed with which a document is produced have anything to do with its quality? Most people do more than one draft. They may read over the word processed output, but make few substantial changes. The typos need to be corrected, the infelicitous phrases adjusted, the odd sentence inserted or deleted and an afterthought attached. But this may take as little as a tenth of the time taken in the first, swiftly composed, sometimes even stream-of-consciousness 'draft'.

That is, however, very unusual for the average business person; and therefore much despised by them. It seems to be implicitly assumed that redrafting is a slow and necessary business in the painful journey to perfection. A very senior manager once did a record 26 redrafts of a 30-minute speech. Some people show colleagues various drafts, encouraging criticism and attempting to incorporate their suggestions. If a camel is a horse designed by a committee, then this redrafting technique leads to the most anodyne and compromising of texts. In attempting to please everyone, no one is pleased.

Why should redrafting lead to improvement? Certainly this is very dependent upon both the quality of the first draft and the method of redrafting. Start off with very poor quality and there is a good chance it will get better. Equally, however, it could get worse. Changing one's mind is not always a recipe for improvement. Handel composed 'The Messiah' in three weeks. And there are many other famous examples of much lauded and applauded work (prose, poetry, fine art and music) being 'dashed off'. No amount of polishing will make a poor piece of furniture great. If the first draft is not good, little can be done. Start again completely afresh. If the first draft is good, don't fiddle with it.

Dressing down

A consultant was telephoned recently a few days before a meeting with the HR department of a blue-chip company and warned not to be too surprised when he arrived at the meeting. It seemed that the first Friday in the month is 'dress casual day'. He was told that employees are encouraged to discard pin-stripes for jeans, and smart jackets for jerseys on this day.

It came as a bit of a shock to see the assembled bunch in a newly renovated, high-tech, designer-planned boardroom. Some of the men looked as if they were going on a fishing trip, others as if they were about to mow the lawn. The women were much smarter – their clothes were brighter and more loose-fitting, but hardly casual. Most had the look of someone setting out to shop on Rodeo Drive. It certainly seemed as if it took more money and imagination to look casual than it did to look smart.

The idea of dressing down or casual for one day a week or month is, of course, an American fad. The idea, no doubt, was that formal clothes somehow induced, reflected or encouraged formal communication. So, in order to facilitate more informed, co-operative behaviour, the 'dress casual day' would not only be a bit of harmless fun, a semi-PR coup, but also a very cheap way to increase morale.

However, the whole idea has backfired on various companies and the policy has been withdrawn. The reason was that, far from increasing co-operativeness and an easy-going atmosphere, it did the precise opposite. The day became a mark of one's fashion conscious-ness, one's artistic flair and good taste. Women, being more percep-tive and aware of sartorial styles, soon took to outsmarting each other and men (particularly senior executives) were forced into buying ever more expensive casual wear with soft pastel coloured cashmere jumpers. Cost and bitchiness escalated, and soon the company resorted to the old ways.

The old school debate about school uniforms was usually enlight-ened by the paradoxical point that, despite their cost, uniforms bene-fited the poor children most. They rendered everyone equal, so that there were few opportunities of showing wealth.

So perhaps we should ape the Japanese rather than the Americans. They, it seems, appear to favour the smart boiler suit from the CEO to the cleaner. There's no nonsense about dress competition there.

Economic success

One of the most depressing features about returning to Europe from the Pacific Rim is reading the appointments pages. It is not specifically the relative number of jobs, although that is striking (often the appointments section in the Hong Kong and Thailand dailies exceeds the very respectable size of the newspaper itself a few times over, compared with our rather modest page or two a few times a week). The noticeable distinction between the two lies clearly in the fact that their jobs are almost exclusively *wealth creating* jobs in the financial, manufacturing and service sectors. European jobs, on the other hand, are frequently about wealth distribution. European broadsheets have page after page of jobs with fancy but essentially meaningless titles like living standards facilitation executive, equal opportunities liaison officer or playgroup maintenance co-ordinator, whose job it seems to be to calculate the distribution of public funds while themselves being supported by them.

Precisely what factors led Hong Kong, an ex British colony on a barren rock in the South China Sea, to be so successful has exercised many minds. A recent legislator there identified six factors: political stability, a free market economy, the rule of law, serious attempts to control corruption, personal freedom and the growth of the economy of a powerful neighbour (China).

Although it may be possible to produce different lists, the above is pretty comprehensive. Could one use the same inventory of necessary, but probably not sufficient, criteria to predict or evaluate the success of different economies in the world? Put crudely, one could develop a 'score out of six', so that Italy, for example, would presumably fail on political stability and control of corruption and North Korea would fail on all except the China factor. Germany would score highest but not top because they don't have a huge and growing neighbouring market unless one mentions Russia.

And Britain – we are relatively politically stable, we have more of a mixed market system than a totally free one, the British and European courts certainly attempt to uphold the rule of law, we have personal freedom, Germany is a powerful economic neighbour, but what about corruption?

Electronic mail

Many organizations have enthusiastically adopted e-mail in order to maintain competitiveness and contain rising costs, but does it work? Its supporters argue that it accelerates and regularizes information flow: it's fast, cheap and, unlike the telephone, asynchronous, which means that parties do not have to be available simultaneously. It also offers a wider spread of contacts. It seems generally agreed that it may be less friendly but more businesslike and therefore useful for task-orientated communication.

Studies in the late 1980s reported that the introduction of e-mail reduced the use of telephone calls by 80%, saved 36 minutes per day in communication and millions of pounds in associated costs. Most importantly, the number of meetings was reduced, because on e-mail, everyone can 'talk' and 'listen' at their own convenience. However, recent British research suggests people spent more than 45 minutes per day on e-mail activities. They sent and received on average about 15 e-mails per day, and read their e-mails as many as 10 times per day!

An American study found that e-mail was typically used within organizations for four purposes: scheduling (such as announcing the time and place of an upcoming meeting), task assignment, reporting accomplishment, and general awareness. E-mail is democratic once it is introduced company-wide. One can easily, comfortably and regularly communicate with important people higher up in the pecking order, to whom one is unlikely ever to talk. Users report that they like the rapid speed of message delivery; access to a wider spread of contacts, the savings coming from fewer non-work-related discussions, and the fact that the sender and receiver do not have to be present at the same time.

But the system clearly has drawbacks. There are three sorts of concerns or disadvantages with e-mail. First, there are work-related problems. *Information overload:* because it is cheap and easy, too much trivial, irrelevant and redundant information is sent via e-mail.

Many people are tempted to communicate before they reflect, and injudicious messages can be the result. There is the issue of *security of information:* there is a small, but real chance that mail can be intercepted. Of more concern is the ease with which mail can be forwarded to a third party. Second, some concerns are system related. *Users require training:* certainly much more than telephone or fax users. The storage of outdated messages is commonplace but expensive and pointless. Finally, there is the social impact and this has three factors: social isolation (face-to-face contact is reduced); misinterpretation of messages (this often leads to angry, uninhibited, less empathetic messages being sent, seemingly anonymously) and the filtering out of social cues means less effective communication.

Some people like e-mail and feel in control of it, while others feel bewildered by it. Those who feel in control of their mail and successfully use e-mail in their work tend not to try to read all their mail messages, remove themselves from voluntary distribution lists, keep their inboxes small, and keep a small number of mail folders.

Those who describe themselves as out of control and feel that they are always missing possible important information tend to read mail at irregular intervals, or constantly; and try to read all their mail but often do not succeed. They tend to keep hundreds of messages in their boxes yet do not get to the bottom of an inbox. They seem to want to save a large percentage of their mail and maintain many mail folders on diverse topics yet have difficulty finding messages.

Some people want a system that manages their mail before they see it: a sort of cyber-secretary. Others are adamant about reading all their incoming mail first but want subsequent help to store and later retrieve messages. The first group can be classified as *prioritisers.* They are interested in limiting the time they spend with e-mail and in maximizing efficiency. They want help in selecting important messages to be read immediately, deleting finished ones, and organizing the rest for later reading. They are willing to risk missing an important message for the sake of increased efficiency in managing their mail. These people are not necessarily more successful at managing their time than others but they are more likely to describe time management as a central function in their work.

The second group is called *archivers.* These people want to ensure that they read every message and are willing to spend extra time with their mail so as to avoid missing a potentially important message. They want help in categorizing and storing messages and want better tools to aid in the later search and retrieval of messages.

Archivers are not necessarily just hoarders, afraid to discard anything. Instead, they regard the gathering, digestion and distribution of information as critical in their work. These users are not necessarily very well organized. Some display very efficient strategies for the storage and retrieval of messages. Others are very disorganized and spend a considerable amount of time searching for stored messages.

The psychological impact of e-mail lies in the effort required to complete normally straightforward conversation. Whether or not people send a message depends on the degree to which its relevance and urgency exceeds the effort required to compose the message and complete the transaction.

However, the main problem lies in the ability of people to write clear, comprehensible English. The irony is that the non-literary, monoglotic techies who are attracted to e-mail cannot write any better than they can speak. They might feel more comfortable communicating with the world electronically but there is little evidence that the quality of the communication increases.

Entertrainment

Most HR departments are encouraged or, indeed, forced to measure the efficacy of training. Perhaps the most common, simple, but least valid method is through post-course 'happy sheets'. These are evaluation forms of varying length and response format that request that trainees rate the course, the trainer, the venue etc.

One of the major consequences of this assessment method has been the emergence of the entertrainer. Somewhere between a comedian and a story-teller the entertrainers become the soap-box orators of the educational world. With quick quips, fancy slides, electronic gizmos, funny videos and a host of tall tales, the entertainers realize one way of getting maximum marks on the happy sheets.

The fact that few skills are learned and only odd snippets are recalled doesn't worry the entertrainer. They know that participants enjoy the cabaret style 'training' and rate it highly, and hence that they are likely to be re-employed or retained if the happy sheets are the only measurement criterion. This doesn't mean training can't be fun or that funny stories are a no-no. But it does mean that happy sheets will not suffice as a sole criterion of training success.

Eponymous fame

People or products whose name becomes adopted as a verb or a noun achieve a particular form of fame. A Scot, John McAdam, for example, lent his name to a form of road surface (macadam, the related verb being to 'macadamize') and an Australian, John Macadam, gave his name to a kind of nut (the macadamia nut).

Certain brands live forever: one Hoovers the carpet and Sellotapes a parcel. Americans, it is said, believe in the inalienable right of all nouns to become verbs. Thus 'auto-condimentation' of food is putting the salt and pepper on by yourself. The ideal situation for inventors and those after fame is when proper nouns, i.e. their surnames, become adopted into the language.

Occasionally people lend their names to principles and laws that enshrine succinctly an idea or a kernel of truth. The world of management is surprisingly rich in such eponymous laws. What most have in common, though, is their scepticism about the folly of the human condition. Furthermore, they frequently inspire numerous corollaries. Consider the following five:

- *Parkinson's law.* This states quite simply that work expands to fill the time available for its completion. The law was based on the observation that managers seek (and succeed) in multiplying subordinates, not rivals, and that they tend to make work for one another. Management preference, it seems, leads to payroll obesity rather than anorexia. Some managers even believe that if they don't receive complaints about overwork, the Parkinson syndrome has struck. It is precisely because of the operation of the law that re-engineering, delayering, rightsizing and other synonymous activities meet with such resistance and are so necessary.

- *The Peter principle.* This observes that in a hierarchial organization every employee tends to rise to his level of incompetence. The idea is that in any reward-based system those who do well are pushed up until they get a job beyond their abilities and competencies, and thus, are no longer eligible for rewards. Performance in one job is confused with potential in another (the next one up). Thus it is often the case that technical experts (scientists, engineers) are promoted to managerial jobs that they hate and at which they are hopeless.

- *The Pareto principle.* This has been adapted from an economic observation about the distribution of wealth to become the

80-20 rule: 20% of the variables (vital few) influence 80% (trivial many) of the results. Analysing a cause–effect situation makes it possible to isolate key factors (positive or negative) for remedial action, and either the vital few or trivial many may hold the secret of improvement. Thus in one case managers can obtain results by dealing with the vital few causes of excessive absenteeism, while in a cost cutting exercise it is the excessive expenditure on the trivial many that requires action.

•   *The Zeigarnik effect.* This reflects the tendency of workers to resist interruption. In the words of a now famous quiz master 'I have started, so I'll finish'. It tends to explain why some employees work late, with no overtime, to complete a project on which they are involved. It also 'explains' why employees sometimes balk at stopping one task and starting another – even one with much higher priorities. The Zeigarnik effect is the addiction of the completer-finisher and the grave of the prioritizer.

•   *Machiavellian power principles.* It is to this sixteenth-century consultant to the crowned heads of Europe that we owe the idea 'better to be feared than loved'. It is better to be parsimonious than generous and better to be known for being (and to actually be) cunning than for ethical behaviour. Machiavellians strive for a desirable reputation believing that is sufficient. Duplicity and audacity are thought of not so much as desirable characteristics but as the necessities of being a manager.

There are other eponymous concepts in management. Everyone knows Murphy's rule(s): 'When anything can go wrong it will'; 'Nothing is as easy as it looks'; 'Everything takes longer than you expect'. But why is it that eponymous fame comes to management thinkers only when they codify human foibles and not when they celebrate human kindness, worker motivation and organizational efficiency? Possibly because management scientists are exclusively cynics.

Equity at work

Odd things sometimes happen during office moving. Recently a group of American life insurance underwriters of varying degrees of seniority (ranging from underwriter trainees, associate underwriters to underwriters) were temporarily assigned (over a two-week period) to the offices of one of their co-workers as their own offices were being refurbished. Some were assigned to the offices of higher-status persons, others were assigned to the offices of lower-status persons. Finally, there was a non-movement group of underwriters who continued working in their own offices throughout the period. Over this fortnight a measure of productivity was made, taking into account the number of hours they worked and the difficulty of the cases they reviewed. A curious result occurred.

Although all underwriters performed equally well before the office reassignments began, these office reassignments had a profound effect on productivity. Those assigned to higher-status offices dramatically improved their performance; those assigned to lower-status offices dramatically lowered their performance; employees whose work space rewards were unchanged had performance levels that remained much the same during the study. As soon as the underwriters returned to their own offices, their performance returned to its original level.

Why did this productivity change? One answer is that people respond to, and 'correct' inequities created not only by the money they receive but also by other rewards such as the status value of their offices. Therefore if people in a state of equity get more they work harder. Take things away and they produce less.

But what is equity? Consider the example of a group of friends who go out for a meal and agree to 'go Dutch'. They usually divide the bill (plus tip) by the number of people present and pay equally. Everybody pays the same despite the fact that they have eaten differently priced dishes. This means, of course, that those who choose modestly priced food and 'drink tap water' subsidize those who have more expensive tastes and drink alcohol. The anorexics, as it were, pay for the gluttons.

As a consequence people who dine together tend to choose dishes of similar cost. They either all do, or do not, have a starter, a drink or dessert so that no one person or group eats more than the others. If, however, somebody wants an expensive item and the others do not, it is frequently agreed that he or she pays for it separately. The principle of equality – people all pay equally irrespective of what they eat – is replaced by the principle of equity – where people pay differently depending on what they eat. There is one other option – the richest in the group pays proportionally more. This principle, taxation, is the least popular.

Nearly everyone faced with the choice argues for equity, certainly in the world of work, and particularly when it comes to pay. Nearly everybody favours equity over equality because they feel it is the fairest system. Climate surveys, which are snapshots of a company's health, frequently show that people are most unhappy with the pay system because appraisal is not directly linked to pay. Strikes, walk-outs and go-slows are often the result not of complaints about absolute pay but comparative pay. Let one person discover that he or she is paid less for work of equal or equivalent skill, responsibility or 'messiness' than a colleague and all hell is let loose.

Where people feel unfairly dealt with and inequitably rewarded – nearly always underbenefited in the sense that they feel they give more than they get – they nearly always attempt to rectify the position. There are two ways working people bring about a sense of pay equity: increase their rewards or decrease their efforts (or both).

The first is to get more reward (such as pay) for one's work in terms of pay or benefits sometimes called a package. This is neither easy nor even feasible in public or poorly performing companies or in a recession. There are, however, other things people can take. For instance, employees more often do shoplifting (politely called shrink-age) than 'customers', partly because it is easier! Certainly stealing goods is one way of increasing rewards if, of course, one's organiza-tion produces or has something worth stealing. On the other hand one can steal time by coming late, going early, or simply going absent frequently. Time is money and can be relatively easily stolen as national absentee (and especially local council) figures show. The easier way of increasing one's pay is to work fewer days for the same money.

As it is frequently difficult, dangerous, or even impossible for people to increase rewards it is much more common to find that they reduce their input . . . their enthusiasm for the job; the amount of effort they put into their work; their willingness to do (unpaid) over-time; their attitudes to customers. In the last event, of course, the worker convinced he or she is unfairly dealt with might leave the organization, but the most common reaction is the alienated, uncommitted, unhelpful worker – the sort we have all encountered, even in the customer service industries.

Sometimes a feeling of inequity comes after promotion because although promotion usually means an increase in salary, status and benefits it also means an increase in responsibility and workload and the two might not increase proportionally. I know many people in the academic world who refuse promotion because although they feel equitably dealt with at their level, increased responsibilities simply outweigh rewards. In some jobs people frequently eschew promotion until the equity balance is re-introduced. Most frequently the feeling of inequity and unfairness occurs when we compare ourselves to others doing almost the same job but in different organizations in different countries. People at work need to feel fairly, equitably rewarded. Their perception of fairness may differ from their employer's because the value attached to rewards (outputs) such as free meals, sports/fitness facilities, company car and outputs (hours of work, attention to detail, customer responses) may not be shared by employer and employee. But if they feel unfairly dealt with they will do something about it.

Not everybody in a state of inequity feels angry because they are undercompensated. Some, the theory goes, feel guilty because they are overcompensated. To overcome this imbalance the fortunate inequitably overcompensated can either not take their full benefits or they can work harder. Or, of course, the easiest option is to persuade yourself (and others) that you deserve it through a mix of effort, ability and uniqueness!

Expert scientists

For most of us, all the authority figures in whom we used to trust and believe have lost a lot of their credibility. The local GP and the parish priest are no longer the voices of authority. Politicians and law enforcers have suffered a dent to their pride and credibility.

Academics are no longer seen as, as objective, detached and well informed as they used to be. Business consultants have long, and in many people's eyes deservedly, been ridiculed and have to win their expertise spurs with each new client.

One group has seen its credibility (and hence self-respect) drop spectacularly. This is the scientists. It is 'scientists versus the people' on some television programmes and rather than listening in awed and respectful silence, Joe Public argues with, and even sometimes succeeds in humiliating, the boffins. Neither trusted nor respected, scientists are frequently stereotyped as callous, calculating or simply interpersonally inadequate.

Equally, 'personalities' seem to carry more weight than professionals. Film and sports stars, despite their lack of education or information on highly technical topics, are seen as more honest than professionals who are trained to know. So activist groups now command the high ground despite their sometimes obscure findings, implicit ideologies and dubious methods. A nuclear protester is believed more than a nuclear scientist; a consumer protectionist more than a company's occupational medical officer. Many in-house managers and even PR managers say: 'The trouble is, the public doesn't understand us.' But the obverse is true: they do understand the public and how to inform them (see public relations).

Explaining away lack of ability

Some cynics claim that 'dyslexia' is Greek for 'dim' and 'acalculia' is Latin for 'very dim'. Cynics and sceptics have become wary of neoclassical labels for poor intellectual performance because they suspect, with good reason, that they are mere excuses for lack of ability.

There is now a growth industry in finding new explanations for poor scholastic performance. These are directed at two major groups: the middle-class parents of young people who are failing to fulfil their (often totally unrealistic) expectations and those adults on developmental courses who want to rewrite their own biographies explaining away school failure, university drop-out or other career-limiting academic experiences.

The diagnosis both groups are ignoring is 'you are, alas, not very bright', or, less colloquially, 'your IQ is low; your general intelligence is (well) below average'. What they are seeking to hear is that they are bright, possibly very bright, but because of some 'quasi-medical' phenomenon (attention deficit) or being forced into adopting a rigid educational approach (learning style), they seem (but are not) less able.

The preferred, most established and acceptable explanation is dyslexia. This is, of course, a genuine disorder that can be seriously debilitating. But the number of people claiming 'mild dyslexia' as an explanation for lack of skill, poor preparation, or simply sloth is on the increase. Third year students in the social sciences, approximately three months before their finals, are apt to discover their mild dyslexia and claim the partial victimhood benefits that universities now grant, such as longer time for every exam.

The two most popular 'explanations' can be seen in the use of the deficit and style concept. One has attention or memory deficits that supposedly explain poor performance. A newspaper advertisement for a self-improvement course runs something like 'IQ of 145 but still can't remember names?' The idea, which appeals to many, is that a deficit is like a faulty part in an otherwise perfectly functional, even super-effective, machine. They would never admit that attention, storage, retrieval, as well as analysis of facts (data) is part of intelligence.

Attention deficit is the diagnosis favoured to explain the behaviour of dim, hyperactive delinquent youths fed on a rich diet of cartoon television and e-numbered junk food. Parents like to attribute their offspring's poor academic performance, uncooperative attitude and uncontrollability to attention deficit disorder (ADD).

Adults eager to pick up on the quasi-medical psychobabble for themselves, will quote a 'short-term memory deficit' to explain why they can't understand computers, play bridge or get promotion. Most would not be happy to hear that this disorder can be caused by years and years of heavy drinking, or may signal the onset of Alzheimer's disease.

More recently there has been a rise in the popularity of explaining poor performance in quasi-educational terms with the concept of style. This line of dubious reasoning suggests that everyone has different learning, thinking and working styles. Psychometric consultancies have devised questionnaires to help people find their preferred style. The style argument goes like this: the reason individuals did not do well at school is that the teaching style of the school (disciplined, didactic) did not fit their learning style (creative). So the school was to blame for failing to establish and accommodate the pupils' preferred styles.

Equally, the reason why you are a failure at work – a 'passed over and pissed off' POPO – is that the imposed working style of your organization (focuses on productivity) is not your preferred or natural style (focuses on process). So 'they' – your bosses – are at fault because they do not understand you, your needs and your strengths.

Finally, there are even those who attempt to use the murky, primitive world of astrology, graphology, crystals and other new-age mumbo-jumbo that use the concepts of 'fit' and 'misfit'. These systems will apply the same taxonomy to both individuals and organizations. So a Libran may be in a job better suited to an Aquarian personality and, hence, is having difficulties. Most blame the organization for poor selection or insensitivity to the needs of their different employees, rather than their own lack of flexibility.

In this age of victimhood, no one need be 'intellectually challenged'. Some have banished the concepts of stupidity, dullness, 'a sausage short of a fry-up' and other fairly straightforward explanations for poor intellectual performance. As in Lake Woebegone, everyone is above average if pseudo and popular social/educational 'science' is to be believed. Either through minor faulty wiring (deficit) or poor teaching/managing (style), or selection (fit) your inner genius has not yet been discovered.

Alas the fault, dear reader, lies not in our stars but in ourselves.

Fear of giving feedback

Be honest now: when was the last time your manager called you to his/her office and you spoke exclusively (for at least 30 minutes) and consistently about your performance? In other words, when did you last get honest, accurate and comprehensive feedback on how your boss perceives your performance?

About half of middle managers surveyed say 'never', despite the fact that many may have been with the company for well over a decade. Another third remember a boss, whom they admired many years ago, who gave them an honest appraisal – and remember this rare, highly beneficial event very well. A small minority of employees is fortunate in that they get regular quality appraisals mainly because they have a good performance management system that requires their managers do it.

The question is why this fundamental process is so rare and, when it is done at all, why it is so frequently done badly. It is particularly important because feedback is necessary to all learning. All change and learning programmes – from Weight Watchers to computer skills – give regular, specific feedback on performance. The role of the sports coach is as much to give feedback as it is to encourage and give advice. Indeed, the video camera has replaced the coach for just this reason, and this accounts for why it is so often used in training.

There are several major reasons why managers do not carry out serious appraisals. The first is pusillanimity – they are too scared to give negative or corrective feedback. The more authoritarian the organization, the easier it is (consider the army for instance) but the rise of assertive, demanding, litigious staff means that managers always feel uncomfortable about negative feedback and simply duck the issue. Fearful of the tears, anger and sulking that may follow a negative performance review, most managers simply evade the task. Indeed, it's pleasant giving positive feedback, but it's rare that all feedback is exclusively good.

The second reason is related to the first. It is that managers have not been trained in the skill of appraisal. Many are offered but resist courses, partly through fear of being shown up. The skills are relatively simple – managers need to structure the appraisal interviews and have an agenda; they should ask the member of staff who is being appraised to summarize at the end; they should move towards establishing agreed action points that form the basis of the next agenda, and so forth.

The pusillanimous manager's most common excuse for not going on a course is that they 'appraise people all the time'. Their argument is that rather than having a couple of specific hour-long meetings over the year, they give subordinates constant feedback on a day-to-day basis. What they fail to realise is that discussion about software, the strategic plan, and sales figures are not appraisals. There is an easy way to test this. Ask reluctant managers on the course if they believe they do regular, relevant appraisals. Then ask those whom they (supposedly) appraise. The difference is salutary and sobering.

The third reason is that the organization, despite much rhetoric to the contrary, clearly does not take the whole process seriously. It is usually not modelled from the top; there are no consequences of appraisal ratings; there are no punishments for managers who simply do not comply. Indeed, there is a collective cowardice in many organizations that talk about merit, promotion and people being our greatest asset, etc. The problem lies not so much in rewarding the good performer, as dealing with the poor performer.

A good appraisal system is one that is transparently fair and equitable, where there are checks and balances on ratings, and where these have clear consequences. What sanctions do HR directors apply to managers who don't play the game, either by ducking appraisal or attempting to 'fix the system'? Most of the time, none. Human resources directors are not usually selected for their courage, so the pusillanimity starts at the top and that, rather than good appraisals, is modelled.

Sir Michael Edwardes, who faced the problems of British Leyland head on, said about British businessmen: 'We are tough and brave in war. We are soft and compromising in management.' The problem of pusillanimity is not that it leads to an unhealthy tolerance of poor performance but rather its effect on the morale and maturation of the good performers. Paradoxically, it is frequently the high-achieving, ambitious and hard-working who are most eager for feedback – good or bad – because they know it is helpful, and if the organization ducks the task, they feel deprived and poorly managed.

Good managers, like good teachers and good coaches, conduct 'appraisals' anyway, whatever the policy in vogue. They know the importance of feedback. Bad managers – the pusillanimous, the unskilled, the devious – do not give appraisals, whatever the HR type.

If you are not prepared to give each person a direct report, a minimum of two one-hour appraisals annually, you should not be a manager.

File thickness

Some years ago, a study tried to identify the single factor that most accurately predicted how long patients were kept in a mental hospital. Various theories abounded and it seemed a good idea to test them. In the end, the single best predictor turned out to be the thickness of the patient's file. The bigger the file, containing all sorts of official reports and assorted bric-a-brac, the longer the patient remained locked up.

Is the opposite true of the best predictor of management success? A top civil servant personnel officer once claimed his section had attempted, using retrospective data, to find out the best predictors of high flyers. Again, old hands, idle speculators and aspirant gurus believed they knew the answer. Some thought it was an Oxbridge conspiracy with a self-fulfilling prophecy. Others, of a similar sociological persuasion, thought it might have something to do with the father's occupation or the school attended. The educationally minded were convinced it was a mix of A-level results and participation in games. Occasionally, an odd suggestion was thrown in, such as whether the person was religious, the age they first acquired a home computer, even the number of first names they had.

The best predictor turned out to be the thinness of the personnel file. The fewer the assorted bits of paper that ended up in the file, the better the individual was rated by the organization. So pause before going to personnel to sort out your problems – it may thicken your file and reduce your chance of success.

Filthy lucre

Why do people, especially women, go shopping when depressed? One could argue that fondling the credit card is healthier than popping Prozac, although the former may be as addictive as the latter. The answer, according to the Freudians, lies in potty training. In all languages, money and defecation/dirt are linked. Hence we become stinking rich. We acquire filthy lucre; the rich are rolling in it; gamblers get cleaned out, while trying to make their pile.

During that long-forgotten or repressed stage of potty training, we all did battle with our parents. It was over control and possession. For the first time, we had pretty powerful control over Mummy and Daddy by simply saying 'no'. But having made those curious floating objects, one believed one had the right to play with them. Children, the psychoanalysts tell us, are confused by the ambiguous reactions of parents who, on the other hand, treat the faeces as gifts and highly valued, and then behave as if they are dirty, untouchable and in need of immediate disposal. Horrified, cleanliness-obsessed parents would beg, cajole and threaten, and once the little donations were received and rapidly flushed away, one received lots of conditional rewards. And it is the latter we recall from the grimy and murky unconscious when feeling a bit down. If children are traumatized by toilet training, they tend to have extreme money-related behaviours. The miser hoards money symbolically, refusing to submit to parental demands, while the spendthrift recalls the post-poo approval and affection rather too much!

So armed with filthy lucre, our laxative of love, we reward the high street trader when down in the mouth and in search of parental approval.

Financial year

Why do some consultants always appear to ask their clients (remarkably surreptitiously) when is the end of their organization's financial year? Many claim to have noticed that, near the end of the financial year, spending departments seem eager to yield up their last penny. The underspending departments know it becomes more difficult to justify a similar budget in future, let alone an increase. This is presumably because of the fact that departments are in competition for scarce resources and that parsimony and prudence are not rewarded. Rather, they are punished. 'To him who hath his budget spent shall more be given.'

So, six to eight weeks before the end of the financial year, avaricious consultants contact all major clients and float the idea of a quick project. They know there seems to be a far greater chance of selling business at this time of the year.

The other good time is soon after the budget has been approved. With lots of money in the bank, managers feel they can splash out on that new technology, or consultancy they want or need. The U Curve is, of course, an extrapolation of aggregated data, and is far from smooth, but it makes sense. It does seem a pity that organizations can't find a way of rewarding good financial management. Imagine making next year's budget a multiplicative function of the money prudently saved in this so that saving is rewarded and not punished.

Focus groups

It seems that not only advertisers, but even politicians and business-men are currently unable to make any decisions without first commissioning a series of focus groups. Focus group work is big busi-ness for market researchers – easily the most profitable work many do, with 'mark-up' nicely proportioned to client wealth, not quality of work carried out.

What are focus groups? Why are they so popular? Do they work in the sense that they provide valuable data for decision makers? Or are they a passing fad, providing little new or useful information?

The focus group is far from new, dating as far back as the Second World War when people were asked to openly discuss their reactions to a radio programme after rating it. Since then, they have been used primarily to discover consumer attitudes and motivation and to represent the views of particular groups and communities.

A typical focus group consists of a moderator questioning and listening to a group of individuals discuss a particular topic or react to a particular product. It usually lasts for one to two hours and is ideally conducted in a 'comfortable setting'. This 'sensitive, qualita-tive' technique is akin to a think-tank situation. Sessions can take on a life of their own, often revealing myriad unexpected outcomes. The moderator's tasks are to encourage and challenge, as well as manage disruption, diversion and other problem dynamics. Focus groups should ideally allow the moderator sufficient time and an appropriate setting to probe for, and draw out, important attitudes, perceptions, prejudices and opinions. Participant responses may be recorded by an observer/notetaker or a tape recorder, the former being easier to use because of the difficulty of knowing what was going on when listening to the tape.

The group is typically composed of six to 10 individuals who have something in common. The ideal is to run and run these groups until no novel information arises. This is, of course, potentially time wasting and enormously expensive because it is never clear when some new worthwhile data arise. There also remains no consensus on how to 'play the group' – to make sure everyone has equal time to speak; to encourage or discourage disagreement; how to deal with dominant, distracting or dreary participants. In short, there are no clear guidelines of best practice, which is not good news for the person commissioning the focus group report.

The central idea of the focus group is to hear the language and ideas of ordinary people; to see how 'amateurs' represent and debate topical issues. For some researchers, the process is as important as the content – how people who do not know each other negotiate, discuss and attempt to persuade. The product of focus groups is usually a report, differing enormously in length, style and depth. These reports are characterized by having many quotes and by the essentially wry, perceptive interpretations of the observer on what, how and why ideas were generated.

Some researchers like to call back groups over time, meeting, say, weekly, for a couple of months (like a company board or committee). Most, however, are 'one-off' experiences. The question of how to recruit and motivate participants is also unclear, but crucially important. Who volunteers for a focus group and do they have different opinions from non-volunteers? Some groups turn into self-help groups; others political debating chambers; still others become simply social occasions, with free coffee and biscuits, and a present to take home. Perhaps most important of all is the role of the report-writer, if that is not the mediator. The long, jumbled, indeed often garbled, notes or recordings, need to be 'written up' into a report. This, of necessity, involves interpretation, highlighting and selecting core themes; major points of dissension; even implicit and badly articulated ideas. Precisely how this is done and how reliable is the interpretation is never clear.

Why the popularity of focus groups? They are popular both with academic researchers and market researchers, for similar reasons. First, there has been a change in the *Zeitgeist* from quantitative, large-scale, numbers-based, smart-statistics research to qualitative, small-scale, words-based processed procedures. This is associated with post-modernist, anti-empiricist thinking and an epistemological revolution in science that has spread to market research. Secondly, there has been disillusionment with the promises of the empirical approach. No matter how sexy the stats or how representative the sample, it seemed that the ability to predict how people actually behaved (voted, purchased and so on) never improved much beyond a particular level. Thus the pendulum has begun to swing the other way and the focus group epitomizes the ideal for the qualitative 1990s. It seems more intuitive and also has the promise of revealing more than the standard survey.

But do they work? Do you get your money's worth? Much depends on what the commissioning client is expecting. Critics of this method are very clear about their limitations:

- Surveys are reliable and adequately sampled and can be used to make statistical inferences about populations. One cannot make generalizations from these small, deliberately unrepresentative, samples. Results are desperately unreliable. Run two groups and you will get quite different results. Have different moderators and interpreters for the same group and you will also have two very different reports. In short, the results are not replicable. And that which is unreliable can, by definition, rarely be valid . . . that is, they don't measure what they say they are measuring.

- Public ideas are problematic, pluralistic, conflicting, diverse and contradictory. The focus group stresses (indeed, often rejoices) in this and yields results that are of no help to the decision maker. Rather than clarifying the situation, they tend to make it worse. In a sense, the reports rejoice in indecisiveness and plurality, rather than consensus.

- Even the most skilful moderator cannot overcome the fundamental problem of groups making decisions, because:

  - people have evaluation apprehension – some self-censor, being scared to look foolish, so will never say in a public forum (the very open focus group) what they really think;

  - social loafers will go along for the spectacle and the freebies but contribute little, letting the garrulous speak for them. In this sense, the focus group reports are biased towards the eloquent and opinionated who might or not speak for the group. In fact, some moderators go out of their way to choose the talkative as they yield more material;

  - it is difficult to think about a problem seriously when some know-all is continually talking. Some individuals allow little or no quiet time to think about the issue before other members of the group are asked for their opinions;

> –   there are powerful conformity pressures to take sides
>   and follow certain individuals or subgroups; in short, to
>   obey explicitly and implicitly upheld norms, giving a
>   misleading idea of the spread of ideas in the group.

A few years ago, brainstorming groups were all the rage. The research on these groups showed that despite what protagonists said, compared with the pooled ideas of people working alone, brainstorming groups nearly always produced fewer and lower quality innovative ideas. Focus groups, being in many ways similar, share the same limitations.

Focus groups are fine for journalists. You often get great quotes, watch people fight and provoke powerful emotions. One can pretend that as the mediator or interpreter, one has special trained insights, allowing one to speak for or interpret the otherwise tongue-tied or incoherent. This is a dangerous myth. If you want to know what people really think, or even, more importantly, how they are going to react, you need to interrogate a large representative sample in a situation of sufficient anonymity and confidentiality to understand real values, motives and behaviour intentions. One needs to question their attitudes, behavioural intentions and past behaviours. Focus groups, it seems, are for the short sighted. Hocus-pocus is defined in the dictionary as a pointless activity, or words often intended to obscure or deceive. It is not that focus groups set out to do this, but the net result is that many do just that!

Graphology

It is one of those nice but sad ironies that, as popular interest and especially commercial application of handwriting analysis, or graphology, is on the increase, scientific scrutiny of its claims remains limited and may be on the decrease. Like many of the other '-ologies' that claim to be useful in describing and predicting human behaviour, it has a long past, with many notable figures like Goethe speculating that somehow one may expect that a person's character is projected in the way he or she writes. The term graphology in fact was first used in 1871 by the French cleric Michon, who spent 30 years studying handwriting.

Since the beginning of this century there has been more and more interest in the topic, and it is difficult to go into any large bookstore without finding among the self-help, occult, or even psychology/social-science books some texts on how to analyse handwriting. These tomes tell you what factors to look at (i.e. size, slant, zone, pressure) and what traits (temperament, mental, social, work and moral) are revealed. In fact there are schools of graphology, each with a slightly different history, approach and 'theory'. However, what appears to be missing most from the area is not a method of analysis so much as a theory of how or why individual differences are manifest in handwriting. For instance, is one to assume that personality traits are the result of genetic biological differences that predispose all social behaviour, including handwriting, or is writing style, like other social behaviours, a product of complex primary, secondary and tertiary education?

Despite the lack of any sound, illuminating, or indeed falsifiable theoretical base, there has been a great deal of interest in graphology by hard-pressed managers and administrators anxious for a valid and non-falsifiable way of measuring the desirable and less desirable traits of employees. Dispassionate and disinterested research, however, has severely questioned the usefulness of graphological analysis.

There appears to be two different basic approaches to both the assessment of handwriting and personality – holistic and analytic. This leaves four basic types of analysis:

- *Holistic analysis of handwriting.* This is basically impressionistic. The graphologist, using his or her experience and insight, offers a general description of the kind of personality he/she believes the handwriting discloses.
- *Analytic analysis of handwriting.* This uses measurement of the constituents of the handwriting, such as slant or pressure. These specific, objective and tabulated measures are then converted into personality assessment on the basis of a formula or code.
- *Holistic analysis of personality.* This, too, is impressionistic and may be done after an interview, when a trained psychologist offers a personality description on the basis of his/her questions, observations and intuitions.
- *Analytic analysis of personality.* This involves the application of psychometrically assessed, reliable and valid personality tests (questionnaires, physiological responses to a person, and the various grade scores obtained).

As a result of this fourfold classification there are quite different approaches to the evaluation of the validity of graphological analysis in the prediction of personality. These are:

- Holistic matching, which is the impressionistic interpretation of writing matched with an impressionistic account of personality.
- Holistic correlation, which is the impressionistic interpretation of writing correlated with a quantitative assessment of personality.
- Analytic matching, which constitutes the measurement of the constituents of the handwriting matched with an impressionistic account of personality.
- Analytic correlation, which is the measurement of the constituents of the handwriting correlated with a quantitative assessment of personality.

However you do it the answer remains the same. There is no validity in graphical analysis. At least five dispassionate reviews show this.

Graphologists do not do better than chance or than ordinary lay people. Most obtain their clues from the contents of material rather than the way in which it is written.

Although it would not be surprising if it were found that sloppy handwriting characterized sloppy writers, stylized calligraphy indicated some artistic flair and bold, energetic people had bold, energetic handwriting, there is no reason to believe that traits such as honesty, insight, leadership, responsibility, warmth and promiscuity find any kind of expression in graphological features. Indeed, if a correspondence were to be empirically found between graphological features and such traits, accounting for it would be a major theoretical challenge.

There are not enough constraints in graphological analysis, and the very richness of handwriting can be its downfall. Unless the graphologist makes firm commitments to the nature of the correspondence between handwriting and personality, one can find *ad hoc* corroboration for any claim.

As graphologists practise their craft, it appears that from a graphological viewpoint, handwriting – rather than being a robust and stable form of expressive behaviour – is actually extremely sensitive to extraneous influences that have nothing to do with personality (e.g. whether the script is copied, or the paper lined).

It is noteworthy that most graphologists decline to predict the sex of the writer from handwriting, although even lay people can diagnose a writer's sex from handwriting correctly about 70% of the time. They explain this by insisting that handwriting only reveals psychological, rather than biological, gender. Although common sense would agree that some women are masculine and some men are effeminate, it would be somewhat perverse to argue against the assumption that most women must be feminine and most men masculine. Could the graphologists simply be reluctant to predict so readily verifiable – or falsifiable – a variable?

The growth of graphology may be due to the inability of empirical scientists to discover or invent a simple, single, robust, and predictive measure of personality. But one cannot allow graphologists to fill this void, given that from any objective and dispassionate evaluation of their wares graphology is quite simply invalid. It is dangerous and incompetent to even think about using a graphologist in any organization.

Group think

When groups develop a very cohesive, internally consistent set of roles and norms, they sometimes become concerned about not disrupting the group's decisions. Group morale, happiness and contentment are more salient than the task (decision making) that the group has been forced to undertake. 'Group think' is the term given to the pressure that highly cohesive groups exert on their members for uniform and acceptable decisions and it actually reduces their capacity to make effective decisions.

The concept of group think was proposed as an attempt to explain the ineffective decisions made by US government officials, which led to such fiascos as the Bay of Pigs invasion in Cuba, the successful Japanese attack on Pearl Harbour, and the Vietnam War. Analyses of these cases have revealed that, every time, the President's advisers actually discouraged the making of more effective decisions. Members of very cohesive groups may have more faith in their group's decisions than any different idea they may have personally. As a result, they may suspend their own critical feelings in favour of conforming to the group.

The warning signals of group think are:

Symptom	*Description*
Illusion of invulnerability	Ignoring obvious danger signals, being overly optimistic and taking extreme risks.
Collective rationalization	Discrediting or ignoring warning signals that run contrary to group thinking.
Unquestioned morality	Believing that the group's position is ethical and moral and that all others are inherently evil.
Excessive negative stereotyping	Viewing the opposite side as being too negative to warrant serious consideration.
Strong conformity pressure	Discouraging the expression of dissenting opinions under the threat of expulsion for disloyalty.
Self-censorship of dissenting ideas	Withholding dissenting ideas and counter-arguments, keeping them to oneself.
Illusion of unanimity	Sharing the false belief that everyone in the group agrees with its judgements.
Self-appointed mindguards	Protecting the group from negative, threatening information.

When group members become tremendously loyal to each other, they may ignore information from other sources if it challenges the group's decisions. The result of this process is that group's decisions may be completely uninformed, irrational or even immoral.

Some of the potential consequences of group think include:

- Few alternatives are considered when solving problems; preferred accepted solutions are implemented.

- Outside experts are seldom used; indeed, outsiders are distrusted.
- Re-examination of a rejected alternative is unlikely.
- Facts that do not support the group are ignored; or their accuracy challenged.
- Risks are ignored or glossed over; indeed, risk is seldom assessed.

Fortunately, managers can take steps to reduce the likelihood of group think. Most of these steps can also reduce the effects of group think once it occurs. Reducing group think, however is much more difficult than preventing it in the first place because groups engaging in group think seldom realize that they are doing so. To prevent or reduce the effects of group think, managers can:

- encourage each member of the group to evaluate ideas openly and critically;
- ask influential members to adopt an initial external (even critical) stance on solutions;
- discuss plans with disinterested outsiders to obtain reactions;
- use expert advisers to challenge group views;
- assign a devil's advocate role to one or more group members to challenge ideas;
- explore alternative scenarios for possible external reactions;
- use subgroups (select committees) to develop alternative solutions;
- meet to consider decisions prior to implementation.

Gurus ideas

It has been said that journalists first used the term 'guru' to describe management theorists because they could not spell the word 'charlatan'. Partly out of envy, but partly because they clearly deserve it, there are numerous pejorative descriptions of guru business consultants.

They have been described as simple organisms designed specifically to convert doublespeak into air miles. Supposedly, gurus know some of the worst mistakes that can be made in business and how to avoid them. But many suspect the business guru is often a greedy dogmatist who peddles inane, simple solutions to difficult and complex questions.

A guru can be a mentor, a spiritual guide, or a far-sighted philosopher. The business guru is a product of the late twentieth century: a story teller and master of parables via telecommunications; a shrewd and remorseless (re)packager and marketer of ideas and catch-phrases; a writer of popular books.

Gurus don't necessarily have to be original but they have to be subtly aware of the *Zeitgeist* in the management community. Essentially, they need to memorably encapsulate in a phrase or term what people of their time recognize (or at least believe) to be true. Armed with their concept, slogan or model, they need a great deal of self-promotion, clever packaging or marketing – and a lot of luck.

Occasionally, they are deeply insightful. The ideas may genuinely help companies understand and deal with their problems. Often they are flawed. But having flawed theories in the world of economics and politics never stopped people carrying out even the most hideous ideas. Remember that Pol Pot, Karl Marx and Leon Trotsky were gurus to politicians.

How good is your knowledge of gurus and ideas? Below are 'theories' proposed by different gurus. Can you put a name to an idea/concept?

A. The theories

1. Whatever managers do, they have essentially three major roles: interpersonal (figurehead, leader and liaison person); information (monitor, disseminator and spokesperson); and decisional (entrepreneur, disturbance handler, resource allocator and negotiator). The last group is the most important. Management skills are as important as management ideas and concepts.

2. The employee and employer have a formal, legal work contract but also a psychological contract, which is expectations about how they are treated and encouraged to develop abilities and skills. Assumptions on both sides help form corporate culture. They also develop career anchors, which are perceptions individuals hold about their organization, and which encourage them to remain in it or leave it.

3. The key to quality is reducing variation in production. Among this guru's statistically derived recommendations (there were 14 in all) are: improve constantly and forever every process of planning, production and service; eliminate quotas and numerical targets; encourage education and self-improvement in everyone.

4. Managers need to be creative by lateral thinking, which has five steps: escaping from fixed patterns of behaviour, challenging

assumptions, generating alternatives, jumping to new ideas, and seeking to find entry points so that one can move forwards.

5.   Leaders of successful groups need to monitor three factors equally all the time – the task being set, the team and its morale and functioning, and the individual including oneself.

6.   An organization's competitive advantage comes from good strategy. All managers should analyse and plan with five factors in mind: the existing rivalry between firms; the threat to new entrants to the market and substitute products and services; and the bargaining power of suppliers and buyers. He believes that one can understand, predict and measure the competitive advantage of nations.

7.   Company excellence can be guarded by the eight Ss – structure, strategy, systems, style of management, skills, corporate strengths, staff and shared values. Managers need to move away from the hierarchical pyramid structure to one that is horizontal, fast, cross-functional and co-operative.

8.   Strategic advice comes from planning and strategy, which should be based on an organization's capability to increase market share/profitability; exploiting any relative superiority; challenging accepted assumptions; and the development of innovations such as new markets or products.

9.   The idea of empowering employees was stressed in the new 'fast entrepreneurial' flatter, decentralized organizations. Co-operation above competition and the operation of business without the 'crutch' of the hierarchies are stressed.

10. The originator of management by objective. Corporate goals should be divided into objectives and clearly assigned to units and individuals. Every organization should regularly inspect and assess the product, process, technology and service. Management of all organizations is essentially the same process, akin to that of the conductor of an orchestra.

B. The gurus

A: Adair
B: De Bono
C: Denning
D: Drucker
E: Kanter
F: Mintzberg

G: Ohmar
H: Peters
I: Porter
J: Schein

C. Correct answers

A: 5
B: 4
C: 3
D: 10
E: 9
F: 1
G: 8
H: 7
I: 6
J: 2

If you got nine out of 10, you are probably a guru in your own rightt
– or have too much time to read all that nonsense. If you got 0, 1 or 2
you have clearly escaped the guru hype and may even be better for it.
Reading management books and magazines will not necessarily
make you a better manager, but if you think knowledge acquisition is
expensive, try ignorance.

Hairiness

Baroness Thatcher does not like beards. She may even be pogono-phobic (the technical term, doctor). Given the number of hair pieces worn by politicians, media stars and businessmen, it seems we are generally not too keen on baldness either.

But is an obsession with hairiness or hairlessness a common phenomenon? Various researchers have asked this problem. Ordinary people are usually given photos or pictures – to keep the underlying attractiveness of the face constant – in which the same people are rendered bald, bearded, spectacle-wearing or whatever, often in combination. These photographs are then rated, on various dimensions: attractiveness, honesty, trustworthiness.

Men with beards are rated more masculine, extroverted, coura-geous and independent, but also less attractive, older and dirtier. Baldness is associated with greater intelligence and sometimes sexiness (thanks to the too-much-testosterone-leads-to-baldness theory) but also with lower attractiveness, less life success and with overestimation of age. Spectacles may help various competency-related traits like intelligence, industry and honesty but wearers are seen as more timid, fearful and independent than non-wearers. Glasses and beards have opposite effects on ratings of mental competency. Specs make one look mentally competent and alert, but lacking in social forcefulness, while beards make one look virile but dim.

Research therefore confirms the fearful suspicions of those sans their crowning glory and afflicted by myopia. Unless you want to be seen as donnish, get contact lenses. If you don't want to be thought of as a raping and pillaging Viking, get rid of the beard and if you don't want to be seen as a failure, get a toupee.

Haloes

Visitors to mental hospitals are frequently surprised by the patients. It is not that they are indistinguishable from the psychiatrists or even that they are dangerously erratic. They are, to a person, nearly always ugly. Indeed it has been demonstrated that physical attractiveness, or more commonly its opposite, is one of the best predictors of incarceration in 'the bin' and how long one stays there.

Similarly, it is not unusual for managers to hire their personal assistants on the basis of their legs rather than their word-processing skills. Or to choose the articulate Oxbridge graduate for a task quite unsuited to the skills obtained in those fine universities.

These selection mistakes are all based on a well-known, but equally well-abused 'cognitive or logical error' called the halo effect. It is the tendency to give consistently good ratings to people the rater likes, finds attractive, or shares beliefs with. The opposite, sometimes called the *horns effect* is to see only the bad in people. It appears that liking (or disliking) someone for even trivial reasons (hair-colour, accent, spectacle frames) does exercise a pervasive influence over all ratings of their ability, motivation and potential sentence. It has, in fact, been demonstrated that the length of a sentence given by a judge is as related to the crime as it is to the attractiveness of the criminal. More attractive: shorter time in the nick.

What is the moral of the story? The fact that halo-ing helps and horns hurt one's image and reputation. Hairiness is associated with horns (the low brow) and hairlessness (high brow) with halo. After all, the main job of image and PR consultants is to create and then polish a positive halo (see rating staff).

Headhunters

Many headhunters report a strong, positive, perhaps paradoxical correlation between seniority of targets and ease of approach. The closer you get to the top of the FTSE-100, the more clued-in and helpful the secretary and the more charming and polite the contact. Headhunter codes are understood; calls promptly returned; home numbers freely given. A director of a major bank may even appear to answer his own phone (surely a sign of our delayered times).

Isn't this Darwinian selection at work? You can't be headhunted for a senior position if you don't return 'personal' calls from people you've never heard of, or if you won't speak to callers unless your secretary/PA has grilled them first. And only the less successful will ask their PAs to enquire 'He hasn't heard of you – what's it about?'

Moral: If you want opportunity to knock, it's best not to have a soundproof door.

High flyers

Becoming a high flyer in management essentially takes three things – ability, motivation and reputation. All three are required, in varying amounts, depending on the particular field. Clearly one needs ability to get on, although the precise nature of this ability may differ from job to job, sector to sector and time to time. For some it is ability with numbers, while for others it is ability with words. Some high flyers need to be able to think logically, others laterally. Intelligent, clever people are usually good at most things. They have general intelligence. One certainly needs that to get on in business. Not perhaps a high amount, but enough.

One certainly does not have to be super-intelligent. In fact, psychological assessors are often surprised to note that the IQ results of CEOs are surprisingly 'average', whereas those of some directors are much higher. The very bright often get caught in analysis paralysis or obsessional research and don't make timely decisions. Hence all the talk of EQ not IQ – emotional intelligence, which really is no more than interpersonal skill and insight.

Next motivation. Intelligence is not enough. High flyers need to want to succeed; to be motivated by the job whatever it may be (money, prestige, power etc.). High flyers need to be driven. Some are pushed from memories of poverty, weakness or powerlessness, others are pulled by the high flyer lifestyle of those they admire or emulate. The path is rocky and the journey long, hence endurance and fortitude are required. No amount of wealth or flashy sports cars can make a short man tall. History cannot be rewritten, although it can be compensated for. Business is full of people whose motivation for power, wealth and popularity comes from deep-seated, even repressed factors in their past. These factors may shape personality, which is closely related to motivation. People whose needs are satisfied early are not driven . . . and rarely end up as highflyers.

The third factor, reputation, unlike ability, can be acquired. Shrewd people realize the importance of cultivating and maintaining a good reputation. A reputation of fairness, hard work and competence is always desirable, but often a reputation for certain less desirable qualities does no harm and may in fact be beneficial. The PR business is based on creating, enhancing and changing reputations. In a sense it is personal advertising.

Each of the above three factors is not enough on its own. Nor is it good enough to merely have two out of three. To be clever and motivated, but without any (positive) reputation, may mean that you are not noticed. To be able and with a good and helpful reputation, but without too much motivation, means you may be too reluctant to make the move that leads to success. And to be motivated and of good repute yet without ability surely means you are the victim of the Peter principle. One can go a long way with two-thirds of what one needs to really make it, and of course, we haven't mentioned that old favourite mentioned most frequently by the less successful – luck. But as Vidal Sassoon noted: 'The only place where success comes before work is the dictionary.'

In business, as in politics, there is a fair amount of *schadenfreude*: rejoicing on seeing the mighty fall. The great danger for many high flyers is losing a sense of reality (and humility). It is all too easy, surrounded by sycophants, to overestimate one's ability or personal contribution to business success. Hubris, and all its faults, can easily follow the canonization in the popular press of being labelled a high flyer.

Human resources

Human resources, it is said, is an anagram of 'overhead'. Human resources are often claimed to be costly, bureaucratic, unresponsive time-wasters who don't add value. They often appear to be a bunch of drones whose apparent missions in life are to create paperwork, recruit secretaries who can't type and issue memos whose impertinence is only exceeded by their irrelevance. Many believe HR specialists spend their careers worshipping files, devising pointless programmes and generally accomplishing nothing of any fundamental importance.

All HR is essentially management of people but all managers are involved with managing people and the management of an organization's human resources is primarily a line or operating management responsibility. The degree, however, to which HR activities are divided between line or operating managers and the HR manager and his or her department varies from organization to organization.

In some organizations, a human resource specialist may handle all negotiations with unions while, in others, operating managers may see union negotiations as their responsibility with the HR manager taking an advisory role, or having no involvement at all. Line managers in some organizations are now starting to compete with HR specialists to assume responsibility for many traditional HR activities.

In this sense HR people become redundant because their jobs are now taken over by newly empowered and better-educated managers who are taught HR processes and procedures before or while in the job. According to some writers, if the HR specialists are to survive – indeed thrive – they need to obey certain crucial rules.

Human resources professionals must, like all others (marketing, manufacturing, finance), understand the importance of, be sensitive to, and actually help in achieving bottom-line targets. This may therefore involve downsizing, instituting 'pay for performance' schemes and attempting to demonstrate the cost efficiency of training. All HR departments are of course also responsible for:

- Cost containment – HR objectives and activities should genuinely focus on cost reduction via reduced headcount and improved expense control. Indeed HR departments should themselves model the 'lean and mean' department.
- Customer service – HR activities should aim to achieve improved customer service through recruitment and selection, employee training and development, rewards and motivation and the like. Again, the department should have an eye on its own internal and external customers and seek out their feedback regularly.
- Social responsibility – HR objectives should centre on legal compliance and achieving improvements in areas such as equal opportunity, occupational health and safety and development programmes, while bearing in mind that their organization is neither a charity nor uncritical of political correctness.
- Organizational effectiveness – HR should focus on organizational structure, employee motivation, employee innovation, adaptability to change, flexible reward systems, employee relations and so on.

Managed properly, the HR function should demonstrate to the rest of the organization that rather than being a waste of space, it is a significant contributor to company strategy. Yet to see or hear about an excellent HR department is an exception rather than a rule.

Impostor syndrome

It is said that behind every successful man there stands an astounded woman. What is less often said is that many talented, conspicuously hard-working and able people who have achieved success somehow believe they do not deserve it. In fact, they believe that they are impostors. Those who feel themselves to be impostors seem to have difficulty accepting and enjoying the success that they earn. Many handicap themselves by stumbling through life and setting unrealistic goals they know that they (or anyone else) can never achieve. Feeling an undeserving person can be dangerously self-fulfilling.

The feelings may develop because of particular early parental expectations, or because their teachers and peers never expected them to succeed. So when they did, they assumed it was chance and that equally by chance their success might go away. Or, just as frequently, they may have been led to expect moderate success in another field. Thus if a sporty type became a successful businessman, he/she may believe he/she is an impostor because success may not be due to business acumen and knowledge but the fact that people like and admire sporting fitness and prowess. As Oscar Wilde shrewdly noted: 'In this world, there are only two tragedies. One is not getting what we want, and the other is getting it.' Sometimes, depression follows success because people with the impostor-worries question 'where do I go from here?' Some believe that because they are impostors, they cannot continue to be successful . . . and they make sure they fail!

One of the greatest dangers of the impostor syndrome is that of self-handicapping. This is a piece of psychobabble that refers to the many self-defeating actions that successful people use to impede success or justify failure. Drink, drugs and damsels may be used to achieve the strategic goal: in excess each interferes with a person's ability to perform as well as they could were it not for the handicap. This tactic enables many a self-defined impostor to attempt to obscure the meaning of subsequent evaluations. The prototype of a career self-handicapper is the alcoholic who began his drinking after his/her career was marked by early success, a lucky break or an important act so spectacular that it seems impossible to equal, let alone surpass. Of course, chronic procrastination, depression and panic attacks will also do to justify failure in anticipation of performance evaluation.

In an empirical demonstration of self-handicapping strategies in action, two psychologists asked two groups of students to work on a problem-solving task. One group received problems that were soluble, but the other unknowingly worked on problems that had no solutions. Before proceeding to a second problem-solving session, each was given a choice of two drugs that were ostensibly of interest to the experimenter. One of these drugs was supposed to enhance performance; the other was described as impairing performance. The students who had previously worked on insoluble problems generally chose the drug that would improve their performance. The other group, whose experience probably led them to believe that they might not do well on the next task either, showed a strong preference for the interfering drug. By handicapping themselves with a drug, they provided themselves with a convenient excuse in case they did poorly on the second task. What they had done was to prepare a good explanation for their possible failure.

But don't panic! One can be taught, quite easily, to avoid the success impostor syndrome and the nagging feeling one is an impostor. A few quite specific issues need to be addressed. First, challenging the expectations of oneself and others derived from success. Next, one needs to redirect attention to the process of succeeding rather than the products of success. It is also important to learn to accept affection and admiration from others, without believing all are sycophants after the spoils of success. Successful people also need to avoid the tendency to withdraw from, or be passive in, developing or maintaining personal relationships. The scorn (or paranoia) that successful people develop for those who pursue them is a naturally occurring psychological response to being in a position where they never have a need to initiate social contacts.

'Success,' said American poet Emily Dickinson, 'is counted sweetest by those who ne'er succeeded.' Paradoxically, real success, just like failure, may be difficult to deal with.

In-house trainers

The whole training department needs to be made redundant. It is inefficient, counterproductive and bad (worst) practice to employ in-house, full-time trainers in an organization. The attitude toward, enthusiasm for, benefit of, and cost incurred by training is actually improved if the whole department is outsourced. This is not an argument against training, but rather the precise opposite. It is often in-house trainers who give training a bad name.

Big organizations often have training departments, or sections, usually under the umbrella of human resources. Some may even own training centres like medium-sized hotels, which are permanently staffed by cooks, gardeners, waiters and other necessary functions. Training departments, like lemmings, are highly vulnerable to the economic climate. Cut back, culled and pushed over the cliffs in bad times, they have learned to breed furiously in the good times. From plethora to paucity and back again is often the experience of trainers. They are easy to cut and seem unnecessary during the downturns, even though the importance of training is acknowledged from Cabinet to whelk stall.

All staff need to be properly trained to do their jobs. They need specialist technical and generalist managerial training. They need to attend refresher courses to practise and perfect these skills. They need training on ever-changing computer systems. They need to be trained in fundamental business skills like letter writing, understanding financial statements, and project management. But this is best done by carefully selected, audited and monitored outside specialists.

What are the arguments against in-house trainers? First, in order to get *cost-effective use* out of trainers they probably need to be 'in the class room' about 70% of the time. That is a lot of training time – perhaps too much for the organization; certainly too much for the trainer. Optimal utilization of the training department is very difficult to achieve. Long summer holidays and peaks in the business cycle mean little training. Fallow training periods waste money. Equally, in busy times the staff may not be able to cope. Trainers argue that they need time for preparation, updating and so on, which is done in off-times, but there is little evidence of them doing this.

Trainers *burn out easily*. Training is exhausting – as any good trainer will tell you. They need to be entertainers, monitors, enthusiasts and educationalists at the same time. They have to coerce the unwilling, amuse the sense-of-humour failures and render the charisma-bypass manager charming. They have to pass on skills and knowledge ... but also what Americans call 'attitude'. To do all this takes its toll. Used too often even the best trainer can become tired, flat and boring. The working life expectancy of full-time trainers is rather short.

Trainers are notoriously *difficult to manage*. This is partly due to the sort of people that drift into training. Am-dram enthusiasts, intellectual *manqués*, failed preachers . . . all are attracted to training. They can be egotistical and are rarely team players. Attracted by bizarre and long-discredited ideas, trainers can often be heard espousing scientific nonsense because they do not, perhaps cannot, keep up to date with the literature.

Most trainers are not interested in, and do not understand, *business issues*. Yet employee training must be integrated with the business plan. It has to be responsive to current organizational issues. Training must be flexible and dynamic, yet courses and syllabi tend to have a life of their own, often being repeated because of the peculiar enthusiasm of particular individuals rather than business necessity.

Finally, over time, many trainers become *organo-centric*. Whilst it may be a huge advantage that they have a full understanding and knowledge of their particular organization, they tend to know less and less about other organizations. Despite talk of benchmarking, best practice and so on, they take their eye off others and become obsessed by internal issues and politics. Outsiders, by contrast, bring a wealth of comparative advantage.

The implied solution is to buy trainers from the outside. The ideal scenario is to have a portfolio of tried-and-trusted trainers whose individual expertise and outside experience enrich the company. 'Hired when required; fired when tired' is the optimal solution. But outside trainers need to be very carefully selected and audited. There is a growing army of one-man-bands, recently made redundant or retired HR managers who reinvent themselves as trainers. Some are excellent; others are appalling. Nearly all are curate's eggs – the trick is to find what they do well, at what price, and whether they fit the company culture. Sadly their CV, company blurb, even lists of clients is frequently little guide to their ability or style.

Any organization that buys in training really needs to do its due diligence 'caveat emptor' stuff. Often this can be done only by trial and error, which is expensive. But the trainers themselves soon get a sense of peer competence and can be used to derive information.

Avaricious, egotistical trainers need careful management. Managing trainers, it is said, is like herding cats. Organizations do need to invest in a bright, tough training manager; not just a training administrator. The function of training managers is to select and audit as well as co-ordinate. They need to negotiate prices and to make demands on those trainers who begin to drift. The audit function is crucial; they need to measure the effectiveness of training and to let the trainers know they are doing so. And they need to 'let people go' if outside trainers have exceeded their sell-by date and to be ever vigilant in choosing their replacements. Hence they themselves need to be very well selected and managed.

A good training manager with an understanding of business issues can run the whole training section with minimal support staff. The training manager need not be a trainer but should understand training requirements, delivery and assessment. There are few other areas of the organization that can be as economically and strategically outsourced as the training department, so often the dumping ground of personnel departments. Downsizing and outsourcing are not appropriate for every function in a company, but the in-house training department perhaps deserves a long, hard look.

Interview questions

Media interviewers and politicians have to become ever more skilled when dealing with each other. The professional de-bunker has to expose the humbug and balderdash of the professional obfuscator.

An American television interviewer has developed a brilliant wheeze. He starts the interview thus: 'By the way Senator, on the way to this interview a friend bet me that you would not give me one straightforward, honest answer to any question that I asked you. I took up the bet saying the chances were you would at very least give one, perhaps more.'

After this preamble the interview begins. But the interviewer periodically refers back to the opening by saying: 'Senator, do you think I have won my bet yet or not?' Apparently this new trick is likely to unnerve even the most oleaginous and skilled political interviewee into occasionally doing the unacceptable – answering the question directly.

Intrinsic motivation

Some jobs and some tasks, like hobbies, are intrinsically satisfying. That is, by their very nature they are interesting and pleasant to do. They can be enjoyable for a wide variety of reasons and doing them is in and of itself rewarding. You don't need to be paid to do intrinsically satisfying work/activities. But what occurs if someone starts paying you for something you do out of sheer love?

Take the case of a writer scribbling at home on a new novel. Local children had for three days played extremely noisily in a small park near his study and like all noise of this sort it was highly stressful because it was simultaneously loud, uncontrollable and unpredictable. What should be done?

(A)   Ask (politely) that they quieten down or go away.
(B)   Call the police or the parents if you know them.
(C)   Threaten them with force if they do not comply.
(D)   Pay them to go away.
(E)   All of the above in that order.

Play is fun: it is intrinsically satisfying and can be extinguished by rewards. The writer went to the children and said, somewhat insincerely, that he had very much enjoyed them being there, the sound of their laughter and the thrill of their games. In fact, he was so delighted with them that he was prepared to pay them to continue. He promised to pay them each £1.00 per day if they carried on as before. The youngsters were naturally surprised but delighted. For two days the writer, seemingly grateful, dispersed the cash. But on the third day he explained that because of a 'cash flow' problem he could only give them 50p each. The next day he claimed to be 'cash-light' and only handed out 10p.

True to prediction the children would have none of this, complained and refused to continue. They all left promising never to return to play in the park. Totally successful in his endeavour, the writer retired to his study luxuriating in the silence.

This story illustrates a problem for the manager. If a person is happy doing a task, for whatever reason, but it is also 'managed' through explicit rewards (usually money), the individual will tend to focus on these rewards, which then inevitably have to be escalated to maintain satisfaction. That is not to say that intrinsically motivating work requires no reward. Compliments, positive constructive feedback is always motivating. It is not that intrinsically motivated people do not need to be managed properly but they do not need their focus distracted by a series of extrinsic rewards used to motivate people to do dreary work.

Intrinsic motivation in part explains why some people continue in poorly paid employment. They do not need motivating in the usual way – through an astute mixture of carrot and stick – because they are intrinsically motivated. But, like all of us, they still respond to praise for the product or service that they supply. Everyone needs regular feedback, support, and compliments where these are due but giving other extrinsic rewards may shift the focus away from the joy in the activity itself to getting those rewards. For those limited few who enjoy doing what they do, working (like virtue) is its own reward.

Job-ad speak

By now, most people understand 'estate-agent speak'. This easy-to-pick-up language of superlatives and euphemisms can be mastered without difficulty for two reasons: a limited vocabulary and a single linguistic principle – lying.

Thus 'in need of minor renovation' means dilapidated to the point of structural precariousness; 'deceptively spacious' means exceptionally small and cramped, 'an industrial vista reminiscent of Lowry' means that it overlooks the gas works; 'traditional facilities' means old-fashioned, probably obsolete; and 'period fittings' may mean expensive, bad-taste reproductions. 'Cottagey feel' means you can't swing a cat in it.

Menu-speak follows the same principle and relies on about 30 adjectives and adverbs. They refer to 'exotic' origins ('Pacific salmon', 'Hawaiian pineapple and ham'), 'freshness' (dawn-harvested peas), and 'combinations' ('married to a tropical fruit coulis', 'chaperoned by baby carrots', 'consummated by mashed potato').

Job adverts have now employed the same doublespeak and the new applicant would do well to learn the real meaning of words. Thus 'challenging' usually means very stressful or impossible. Self-motivated may mean that the person will receive little guidance and probably no appraisal. A job that requires a 'highly competent self-starter' means that someone is needed take the initiative. 'Excellent calibre abilities and skills' means that someone is required to find out what the job is all about. And a 'good team player' means someone who won't upset the applecart, or the entrenched old hands. 'Computer literate' may mean that someone is required to sort out the IT while everyone else goes about their work.

Job advertisements written in advanced recruiter-speak, need careful 'unpicking' and translation. The following were found in one week of newspaper advertisements:

Ambitious with potential	you haven't put it all together yet
Attractive salary	as little as we can get away with
Bottom-line focus	nothing else matters
Career minded	grovelling will help
Challenging	impossible
Communication skills	wizard at e-mailing everyone in sight
Developmental role	we're not paying as much as we should
Direct and communicative personal style	rude
Enthusiastic	naïve
Exciting opportunity	probably not
Experience of implementing culture change	we want to see blood on your hands
Friendly environment	cramped offices
Hands-on management style	interfering by another name
Initially on a contract basis	this is all a bit of an experiment
Innovative approach	the ideas will be yours, the glory ours
Key position	you'll take the flak
Liaise at all levels	piggy in the middle
Motivation skills	enough charm to persuade people to forget their problems
Opportunity to develop new skills	you'll be thrown in at the deep end
Self-motivated	you're on your own
Tact and understanding	the politics are a nightmare
Undergoing radical structural change	fighting for survival
Unique opportunity has arisen	previous incumbent fired
Work under pressure	you will have inadequate sources to achieve the impossible

Job hobbyist

Some people are lucky enough not to have to work for the money. They may have a rich spouse, a private income, a very generous pension, but they choose voluntarily to spend 9 to 5 at work. Job hobbyists do not always choose jobs that seem intrinsically satisfying. They can be found doing mundane jobs, even moderately dangerous jobs. This is because their reason for taking on the job may be due to historical serendipity or environmental propinquity. They may have helped out as a temp and then stayed on. They may have chosen a job because it is close to certain schools or shops. Some choose jobs in companies that are associated with prestige, power or particular values. Job hobbyists are thus often found helping in charities although, strictly speaking, these are volunteers rather than job hobbyists.

What motivates the job hobbyist? Some are strongly motivated by the social side of work. They might like the contact of fellow staff members or meeting the public. Some like the time structure that a job imposes on the working day. Others enjoy using their skills and abilities in constructing a product or service.

But what is the job hobbyist like to manage? Is it easier or more difficult to manage the hobbyist or the extrinsically motivated, job-dependent employee? As money is not a crucial issue they are less likely to become demanding for higher salaries. Equally, they seem less interested in promotion or acquiring any of the material perks of the job – but do not assume that they are not sensitive to certain features of the work, like job title. All jobs give one a sense of identity, which may be manifest clearly by such things as uniform and job description.

Job hobbyists, like everyone else, are highly sensitive to comparative data. They need to be paid equitably as money differentials are the most tangible way of comparing oneself with peers. If the hobbyist is given less than a peer on a comparable grade and with similar performance output, he/she can feel slighted. Never assume that just because job hobbyists are primarily extrinsically motivated they can be abused and neglected in terms of pay. Robbing the hobbyist Peter to pay the extrinsic Paul leads to disaster.

The job hobbyist is nearly always easy to motivate. In fact they are self-motivated and require little extra stroking or encouraging. It is not always apparent what motivates the hobbyist, but slight changes at work may radically disrupt them. It is not downsizing and restructuring that affects the hobbyist, as much as subtle changes in their duties and responsibilities. Thus, unless their manager really understands the motives of hobbyist staff, they may be very unpredictable.

Job satisfaction

Is job satisfaction genetically determined? For some, the very idea of posing this question is not only politically incorrect but terrifyingly Orwellian. For management scientists it is not only a legitimate question but an intriguing one. Two sorts of findings led researchers to ask it. The first was the perhaps surprising fact from longitudinal research that, despite changes in pay, occupational status and environmental factors over time, people seemed remarkably similar in their reported satisfaction. The happy remained so, as did the dissatisfied, whatever seemed to happen to them at work. The second finding concerned identical twins separated at birth and showed that genetic factors seemed to relate to educational achievements and occupational choice. Could it be that job satisfaction is, in part, inherited?

An American tested 34 twins (reared apart) who were on average just over 40 years old. The analysis showed that a strong genetic component (30% of the variance) could account for differences (or similarities) in intrinsic motivation – that is, how essentially satisfying one finds the nature of one's work – but not motivation for specific rewards. Environmentalists, of course, argue that all the remaining variation is due to such factors as the nature of the organization, supervision and reward packages. This does not necessarily follow, although few dispute there is some effect on satisfaction levels of the conditions at work. These findings are extremely contentious but, if correct, have important implications for management. First, it seems that the attitudes and dispositions that employees bring to jobs are rather more difficult to modify than hitherto acknowledged. Thus, job enrichment and other expensive satisfaction-increasing programmes may have only marginal effects and are unlikely to please the dissatisfied. Second, if an employee's satisfaction is fairly stable over time and from job to job, future satisfaction may be predicted from current job satisfaction. Finding out that a potential employee was highly dissatisfied with his/her previous job may well be a very bad omen about how he or she will react when working for you.

Job title inflation

There are probably more admirals than ships in the British navy today. In the unacceptable jargon of politically incorrect speech, most organizations appear to have many more chiefs than Indians.

We might well have monetary inflation under control in Britain, but we could have the start of job title inflation. Most of us have got used to the fact that nearly all Americans over the age of 23 have the title 'executive vice-president' embossed on their business card and the trend may be coming here.

These new-fangled job titles have elaborate suffixes, usually 'manager', 'director' or 'engineer' if British, and 'president' or 'officer' if American, and prefixes like 'senior executive' or 'corporate' are also common. Hence, one can mix and match any set of these to come up with a grand, but meaningless job title. As a result, employees are more concerned about their official titles than their responsibilities. Some ask in interviews 'What will I be called?' more often than 'What will I be doing?' Hence secretaries, whose jobs consist of typing, filing, faxing and coffee making, prefer to be called 'assistant service directors'.

Traditionally 'flat' organizations – those with relatively few levels or grades – such as the Church or universities, are being pressurized to invent new titles to keep their ambitious staff happy, while traditionally 'tall' organizations, such as the army or civil service, go on inventing new titles by rendering generalists into specialists however minor the task. There are, in fact, statistics that suggest that with, say, 15 levels of seniority and the normal span of control (1 to 8 people), one could manage the entire British working population.

Why does this happen? At first glance it seems to many managers that this is a relatively cheap way to reward productivity or service. It's cheap because many people, eager to satisfy their unquenchable self-esteem thirst, are happy to accept an improved job title in lieu of a sizeable salary increase. And it follows that the more problems people have with self-confidence and respect, the more they like to compensate with fancy titles. Hence the market for bogus degrees, especially of the Ph.D. variety, allowing one to call oneself 'doctor'.

In service industries, people tend to be driven by the carrot (reward) rather than the stick (punishment) because they are more sensitive to it. The inflationary force of the job title is particularly rife in this sector as a consequence. And because employees are so good at judging themselves and their packaging against others in equivalent companies, once one group starts it there is no stopping this egotistical multiplication of job levels. One major airline had 54 levels, including four ranks of tea-lady; a bank has well over 30 with nearly a dozen of them known by the handle of 'manager'; and there is a hotel chain with well over 40 different job titles. Some sectors inflate title grandiosity but don't increase the number of ranks. This, happens in the publishing world where, to compensate for relatively low pay (if good expenses), everyone is 'director'.

But, as with all inflation, there are great dangers to this practice. There is a limit to the number of grand titles that exist; the more they are used, the more worthless they become. The term 'professor' in this country is clearly going down that route. It takes time to build up the worth of a job title but not long to destroy it. Despite the imaginativeness of Americans, calling a 'personnel manager' the 'vice-president of human resources' does not help much. Outsiders have no idea what these grand-sounding titles are and, like Polish counts, they are two a penny.

The major problem of going down this route, however, is that, far from being a cheap ego trip for staff, it not only becomes very expensive financially but it raises expectations that cannot, and indeed should not, be fulfilled. Traditionally job titles prescribed what one did and did not do. Secretaries made tea and typed for managers, who may have keys to the executive washroom, an additional phone or a company car. The title comes with perks. Give employees a fancy new title and they question whether what they do is appropriate for it . . . a title is part of a package, so it can be very costly.

Some companies, in a spirit of crypto-egalitarianism, have chosen to withdraw in-house signs of rank and privilege – the managerial dining room, car park, privileged toilets – while at the same time doubling the number of people with the title 'manager', 'director', or some other such term in the organization. If everyone is a manager it reduces the worth and the meaning of that title.

Not long ago a British quango had employees with the somewhat demeaning title 'general worker'. Although this term seems more often used in a beehive or an ant colony, it endured for many years until a job title inflation required it to be changed into 'chemical facilitator' or 'technical steward' or the like.

There are other, better and cheaper ways of rewarding good performance and motivating one's staff than doubling, or even tripling the number of levels in an organization or giving everyone (and therefore no one) an impressive grand title. Some business gurus, in fact, suggest that the flatter your organization is, the fatter your profits will be. But while inflation may be under control in the economy, it is still rife in the currency of the job title.

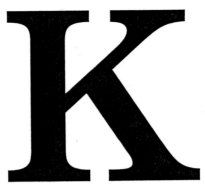

Keeping people waiting

Time is a scarce commodity – it can be saved, spent, traded, invested . . . and wasted. It is also a symbol of a manager's status in the organizational hierarchy. Thus he or she who is in a position to cause another to wait has power over them.

Research confirms anecdotal evidence: time spent by clients waiting to see executives varies in direct proportion to the executive's status in the organization. And the reason so many meetings fail to start on time is that the juniors have to wait on the (late) arrival of the dominant male (or female). But could it be that more important people are simply more busy?

Of course not all delays are caused by supply-and-demand economics. Some delays are purposive; they are a symbolic form of subordination. As our American cousins say – one can symbolically 'inferiorize' an interviewee terribly easily by pretending to be busy.

There must be an optimal delay after which the gesture backfires and is seen as bad business practice and bad manners. My guess for the British is about 20 minutes.

Knowledge of people

People have always been divided on whether management science is simply common sense or something more. It has been described as the art of systematic oversimplification, and a management scientist has been described as someone who would rather count than guess.

Others have seen management science as an expensive and pretentious waste of time. Furthermore, they argue that an MBA or any other form of management education is pointless unless one is in

123

possession of common sense. Many believe it is a thousand times better to have common sense plus an expensive business school education than to have the latter without the former. Others think that if a manager has common sense, then he or she has all the sense there is and that there is nothing more worth acquiring.

However, academics might argue that logic is one thing and common sense another. Indeed if common sense were as unerring as calculus, as some suggest, why are so many mistakes made so often by business leaders?

Can anybody be trained to become a good manager or do they need some sort of innate ability? For some, one pound of learning requires at least 10 pounds of application. Furthermore, education is only a ladder to gather ripe fruit from the tree of knowledge, not the fruit itself.

Cynics and biography readers are justifiably sceptical of a university management education. Too many really creative and successful entrepreneurs have done without going to university. Our best managers have no MBA. It seems quite possible that the socialization one receives at university results in poor management insight and skills.

Certainly the way that universities are run leaves a lot to be desired. Nepotism, inefficiency and corruption flourish yet in the groves of academe and provide a particularly poor role model for the budding manager.

Why not a little entrance quiz to determine potential management ability? Try the simple true-false quiz overleaf to determine your aptitude.

Many people believe simple management aphorisms. A considerable number of British managers believe that, for all workers, money is the most important motivating factor at work. They also believe, contrary to the evidence, that happy workers are productive workers, and that great leaders are born with the 'right type' of personality.

Education may not be the panacea for all management evils. It may not be at all helpful to people who lack some basic level of ability. It should, however, discourage people from holding simple, simplistic, naïve and even wrong views about how to get the best out of employees.

Do you have the ability to manage?

	True	False
1. Relatively few top executives are highly competitive, aggressive and show 'time urgency'.	T	F
2. In general, women managers show higher self-confidence than men and expect greater success in their careers.	T	F
3. Slow learners remember more of what they learn than fast learners.	T	F
4. To change people's behaviour towards new technology we must first change their attitudes.	T	F
5. The more highly motivated you are, the better you will be at solving complex problems.	T	F
6. The best way to ensure that high-quality work will persist after training is to reward behaviour every time, rather than intermittently, when it occurs during training.	T	F
7. An English-speaking person with German ancestors/relations finds it easier to learn German than an English-speaking person with French ancestors.	T	F
8. People who graduate in the upper third of the A-levels table tend to make more money in their careers than average students.	T	F
9. After you learn something, you forget more of it in the next few hours than in the next several days.	T	F
10. People who do poorly in academic work are usually superior in mechanical ability.	T	F
11. Most high-achieving managers tend to be high risk-takers.	T	F
12. When people are frustrated at work they frequently become aggressive.	T	F
13. Successful top managers have a greater need for money than for power.	T	F
14. Women are more intuitive than men.	T	F
15. Effective leaders are more concerned about people than the task.	T	F
16. Bureaucrats are inefficient and represent a bad way of running organizations.	T	F
17. Unpleasant environment conditions (crowding, loud noise, high or very low temperature) produce immediate reduction in performance on many tasks.	T	F
18. Direct face-to-face communication usually enhances co-operation between workers.	T	F
19. Women are more conforming and open to influence than men.	T	F
20. Because workers resent being told what to do, giving employees specific goals interferes with their performance.	T	F

Answers: 1 = T; 2–7 = F; 8–9 = T; 10–11 = F; 12 = T; 13–20 = F

How did you do?

Score 0–5	Oh dear, pretty naïve or even bigoted
Score 6–10	Too long at school of hard knocks, we fear
Score 11–15	Yes, experience has helped
Score 16–20	Clearly a veteran of the management school of life.

Leadership

Although long jettisoned by the academics, many managers still adhere to the great person approach to leadership. It was assumed that a finite set of individual traits – age, height, social status, fluency of speech, self-confidence, need for achievement, interpersonal skills, attractiveness, and so on – distinguished leaders from non-leaders and successful leaders from unsuccessful leaders. The sorts of traits more frequently investigated have been grouped under different headings: physical characteristics (height, energy), social background (education, social status), intellectual ability (intelligence quotient, verbal fluency), personality (self-confidence, stress tolerance), task orientation (achievement need) and social skills (personal competence, tact).

Over the years, a considerable amount of effort went into identifying traits associated with successful leaders.

Traits expected to characterize good leaders

Pleasant appearance	Self-confidence
Good grooming	Interpersonal sensitivity
Moderate weight	Tactfulness
Adaptability	Persuasiveness
Alertness	Fluency
Assertiveness	Creativity
Co-operativeness	Dependability
Ambition	Judgement
Aggressiveness	Achievement orientation
Enthusiasm	Extroversion
Stress tolerance	Integrity
Responsibility	Persistence
Intelligence	

Others have tried to put these in some order thus:

Importance	*Personality trait*
Great	Supervisory ability
	Occupational achievement
	Intelligence
	Self-actualization
	Self-assurance
	Decisiveness
Moderate	Lack of need for security
	Affinity for working class
	Initiative
	Lack of need for high financial reward
	Maturity
Little	Masculinity/femininity

Certainly, it is difficult to imagine anyone being a successful leader without such traits as vigour, persistence, originality, self-confidence, stress tolerance (hardiness), ability to influence, capacity to structure tasks, and willingness to take responsibility for the consequences of one's actions.

However, it has been recognized that, although statistically significant, many of the effects that were attributed to certain leader traits were quite small and of limited practical value. Moreover, although certain traits increase the likelihood that a leader will be effective, they do not guarantee effectiveness. The 'great manager' approach also ignores the roles of subordinates. The research in this tradition is inconsistent and non-replicable. The list of traits simply grows over time, leading to confusion, disputes and little insight into why leadership traits operate as they do. The 'great man' approach identifies people in leadership roles after they have been seen as successful. It is not certain therefore whether these traits make the leader or whether the leadership role shapes the traits. This approach may also be thought of as a fundamental attribution error: that is, explaining the behaviour (success or failure) almost exclusively in terms of the internal traits and motives of leaders, while ignoring the underlying organizational, social and economic factors that clearly play a large part. Managers remain trait theorists when it comes to explaining leadership, which means that this school of thought is still alive and well. Indeed, it can be observed today in those business managers who have replaced the term 'trait' with 'competency' and who believe a

particular combination or profile of competencies predicts leadership success. Yet at all levels, the trait approach is never more than
descriptive because very rarely do the trait theorists explain how,
when and why the traits they stimulate are necessary and sufficient
for the leadership process to be successful. They also do not stipulate
how much of a trait or ability one needs or, indeed, what occurs if
that ability is missing.

However, there is a refreshing move to look at what managers do.
In fact, it is possible to detect new themes in the literature.

Less emphasis needed on	*Greater emphasis needed on*
Planning	Vision/mission
Allocating responsibility	Infusing vision
Controlling and problem-solving	Motivating and inspiring
Creating routine and equilibrium	Creating change and innovation
Power retention	Empowerment of others
Creating compliance	Creating commitment
Emphasizing contractual obligations	Stimulating extra effort
Leader detachment and rationality	Leader interest in others and intuition
Reactive environmental approach	Proactive environmental approach

Left brain and right brain

Are you a trendy leftie or happily right-on? There are essentially two
sorts of people in the world: those who believe there are two sorts
and those who don't. Psychologists and management scientists have
long delighted in distinguishing people, types or categories, naming
different types of individuals and the way they go about their work
and play.

New developments in brain scanning and computer analysis led
various consultants to differentiate the way in which people process
information. In the wonderful world of brain mapping, real as well
as hopeful scientists have distinguished between left and right hemi-
spheres which control the left-hand side and right-hand side of the
body respectively. That is, their personal thinking style – not how
bright they are (capacity) but how they think and solve problems.
The metaphors they used were easily borrowed from the sexy cognitive neurosciences. So left-hemisphere processing styles are analytic,

reflective, logical, deliberative, single track, convergent and academic whereas right-hemisphere processing styles are impulsive, intuitive, global, liberative, multi-track and divergent. Lefties like language and unstructured images. Lefties like details, facts, logic, linear, reality-based, sequential and structured ideas: planned and organized types. Righties like the overview and the big picture, fantasy-orientated, holistic, analogical patterns: touchy feely types.

Before we get any more involved, test yourself. Read each of the following statements and give yourself a score out of 10 for each. Ten means 'totally true of me', 5-ish 'sort-of, sometimes', and 0 'never true of me'.

1. I like to keep my work activities scheduled and structured.
2. I prefer things to be generally stated and seldom worry about specific facts.
3. I believe I base work decisions on facts, not feelings.
4. I like using images in remembering and thinking.
5. I like things to be concrete and seldom make errors.
6. I have vivid dreams.
7. I can think of synonyms for words easily.
8. I prefer a playful approach to problem-solving.
9. I appreciate standard ways to solve problems and reach solutions.
10. I follow my intuition regardless of the facts.

Total up the odd numbers that give you a left-brain score (out of 50). Then total the even right-brain items. Subtract even from odd. If your score is greater than 20 you are very left brained; if it is between 5 and 20, you are moderately left brained; between −5 and 5 a bit of both; and between −5 and −20 moderately right brained; and if over −20 you are very right brained.

'Left-brain skills', it seems, limit one to being a manager, whereas 'right-brain skills' means one can be a leader. Poor old lefties like to administer (not innovate); they like to get involved with systems and structures (not people); they have a short-range, bottom-line obsessed view (not long-term, horizon-orientated), and they tend to imitate their bosses, happily accepting the status quo (they do not originate and challenge things as they are).

One argument goes that most businesses have enough analytic, rational, left-brained managers and need more holistic, intuitive, right-brained creatives. Lefties, it seems, are dull, obsessive and totally uncreative. Or is it that it is creatives who come up with all this? The trouble is, these desirable chappies don't fit in because:

- They are rather disorganised and find traditional time management strategies confining and unstimulating.
- They are non-conforming, breaking and even openly resenting, rules and regulations.
- They are chaotic, inconsistent and have trouble following through.
- They eschew logical calculations and data for those mysterious concepts called intuition and imagination.
- They are easily bored and seek novelty.
- They can be overly sensitive (perhaps neurotic), basing their arguments (such as they are) on personal values rather than data analysis.

Is it true that most businesses have selected out right-hemisphere holistics? Or is it that they either don't need them or don't like them?

Any accounts manager at an advertising or PR company will tell you the problems of managing right-brained, right-on creatives. Managing creatives is like herding cats. Many have minds of their own and are well known for being unreliable, unsocialized and (almost) unemployable. One of the great problems for organizations genuinely interested in using the services of right-brain creatives is selecting them.

Many talentless frauds and impostors hide behind the intuitive right-brain label. It is clearly easier to select and test lefties – you can or cannot do calculations, follow instructions etc. But creative solutions are not like that – except from a long-term, retrospective point of view. Charlatans know this and hence favour the creative position; even challenging established business practice of measurement and analysis.

The actual left–right brain description is, of course, a metaphor, not a physiological reality. In fact, real brain scientists are deeply disparaging about all this phoney anatomical talk. Further, many of the simple-minded left/right brain distinctions cloud and confuse many issues like preferences, skills, aptitudes and emotions. It may be a form of shorthand, but it is a barely legible form.

All businesses need original thinkers and visionaries. They also need people managers and charismatic, transformation leaders. What they don't need are vacuous airheads (who might be termed no-brainers) who threaten their business success with hare-brained schemes that are bound to fail. The trick is to know the difference.

M

Managing your boss

All good managers soon realize that they have to manage upwards as well as downwards. Ensuring your boss understands your needs and helps and supports you is just as important as directing or managing your subordinates. But to manage your boss you need to understand him/her. Imagine you had your boss's personality test profiles.

Psychological tests are meant to provide an insight into a person's preferences, predilections and potential. They are most often given to job applicants and middle managers to help in the process of selection, training and development. The test scores, at least valid ones, supposedly predict behaviour at work but also give clues about how best to manage a particular individual. Naturally, test scores are kept very confidential. Thus it is that few employees ever see their boss's profile.

A wise, if not good, employee should be able to read and respond to the boss's moods and foibles or weaknesses as well as knowing his or her implicit and explicit needs. Just imagine how useful it would be to have an accurate and sensitive personality profile on your boss or client. It certainly could provide a set of helpful hints as to how to charm and ingratiate yourself to them.

For instance, take *sociability*. The boss who scores low on this attribute is probably hard to get to know, perhaps a little shy, careful and ponderous. Those bosses who are very high on sociability are easy to be with and easy to get to know, but it is unlikely that they are interested in what you are saying. They prefer talking to listening.

Similarly, on a simple *likeability* or agreeableness dimension, bosses who score low like to argue with and challenge you. Combative, distrustful and moody, they are often the embodiment of the abominable 'no man'. On the other hand the manager or client who scores high on likeability is full of charm, agrees with everything you say but tends to progress things slowly, if at all. Conflict averse, those high on likeability prefer people to be supported rather than challenged.

The boss or client who is *intellectually short-changed* tends to resist new ideas and innovation. These types are not really interested in data and evidence and prefer simplistic, well-rehearsed answers. Bright bosses or clients accept the necessity of change and development. They are often interested in evidence and data and encourage its collection.

Similarly, the extent to which your boss is ambitious must dictate how he/she acts. The steady-as-you-go boss, lacking in ambition, avoids initiatives and is careful of being shown up. Security is traded off against ambition and they are neither ambitious for themselves nor for their staff. But the highly ambitious boss likes to 'run with the bull'. They may be opportunistic but it is pretty certain their eyes are on their superior and not you, their subordinate. Your best hope is to be seen to be helpful and influential in your boss's career.

Personal adjustment, or as politically correct American psychologists have now learned to call it, 'negative affectivity', is a very important facet of human behaviour and requires careful monitoring. Those a wee bit low on adjustment need reassurance and support. In fact it may well be that a bit of role-reversal occurs, in the sense that you become the parent and the boss becomes the child. But adjustment is another word for stability and the very instability of the low-adjustment boss presents problems. Coy, capricious, and irascible neurotic bosses and clients take very careful handling. Stable, adjusted bosses can take feedback calmly and can deal with crisis. They are often characterized by those wonderful British characteristics of phlegmatism and stoicism. Indifferent to pain and pleasure, bulls or bears, successes or failures, the adjusted, stable boss is a much-appreciated rock in the sea of business troubles.

Finally, *prudence*: beware the imprudent manager. They don't follow through, they don't pay their bills and they may be wildly incautious about financial arrangements. Their incompetence may easily lead to financial, if not moral, bankruptcy. The over-prudent manager may, on the other hand, be too tight-fisted and short-sighted to take any kind of business risk.

Of course, as the hapless employee or consultant knows, and as the psychometricians point out so clearly, one needs to read the trait scores in combination. Thus the ambitious, intelligent but unstable and imprudent manager may cause financial havoc in his/her wake whereas the intellectually short-changed, sociable and likeable manager may be charming and fun but is unlikely to get much done.

Certainly the intelligent, ambitious, and prudent employee soon becomes aware of the importance of managing up the organization. Managing your boss is not only politically wise but essential for a good working relationship.

Mapping values

Everything that exists, exists in some quantity and can, in principle, be measured. Measuring employee performance at work has always been controversial. Cynics argue that what is important can't be measured and, by inference, what is (usually) measured isn't really important.

All organizations measure and monitor people, products and processes. The engineering director, the finance director and the human resource director each have their figures to present to the board. They present the statistics gathered by each department supposedly monitoring the organization. Some keep detailed records of attendance whereas others would be hard put to give even the roughest idea of either the average or individual timekeeping or sickness levels of their staff. Certainly all (well almost!) measure the bottom-line variables: profit, sales, costs, budget over-spent etc.

What an organization chooses to measure depends on three things:

- First, what type of business it is in. Organizations count, measure and audit things that seem most relevant to them. Thus hotels measure room occupancy and airlines paid-for seats (load). Sales departments measure revenue, profit, sales-calls, repeat business as well as mileage, customer calls and even on occasion letters of compliment and complaint. Pubs and bars make a record electronically each time the server keys in an order and even academics are now measured by such things as student feedback forms, publications and exam success.
- The second factor that seems important is the nature of the professionals the organization employs and their particular expertise. 'Bean counters' and the 'grey men of the bottom line' (accountants and auditors) have been taught to count certain things in a certain way. Many become rigidly obsessed with the process and deservedly earn a negative reputation.

They seem exclusively interested in measuring only certain variables, happily – even disdainfully – rejecting others. The issue is usually about hard variables (revenue) versus soft (feedback forms).

- Thirdly, and most important, organizations measure what they really value. Take, for example, specifically the human resource function. If one is really interested in reducing absenteeism one measures attendance; and if one is truly interested in performance appraisal one measures performance and productivity. Ask yourself the following question: what HR data does your organization hold on you? What is in the dusty manila folder or computerized database on you? It may contain that initial application form with all those lies you wrote about why you wanted to join the organization. It may be an out-of-date CV or a few rather halfheartedly completed application forms. But it is unlikely to have accurate, useful, up-to-date numerical data on your performance, skills base, aspirations etc.

Despite eulogistic disclaimers about employees being 'the most valuable asset' and managers 'really caring' about staff, it is all too apparent that organizations rarely measure staff morale or productivity. Most fall into the trap of measuring whatever can be easily measured rather than what is important. Indeed many 'quant-jocks', as innumerate Americans call them, believe that what can't be measured really isn't very important, or worse, that what can't be easily measured doesn't really exist.

Those who resist measurement do so for ideological reasons or through incompetence. The ideological resisters know that data show up clearly individual and department differences in effort and ability. Those who favour equality (of reward) over equity like to believe that everyone is equal in terms of input and hence should be the same in terms of output. Data of practically every sort reveal this to be sentimental naïvety.

The incompetent resisters to measurement do so primarily because they don't know how to measure (not what to measure). Devising and putting into place robust, sensitive, accurate measures is not always easy (or cheap) and takes skill. Many have tried and failed and are, as a consequence, cynical about the value of measurement and they are often relatively skilled at shooting the messenger of measurement. They may have learned a little about the problem of sampling; issues of deceit, even some rudimentary statistics – just enough to confuse those eager to measure performance. But what they haven't learned is how to evaluate performance.

Many managers believe the 20/80 rule: 80% of sales are made by 20% of sales staff; 80% of good decisions are made by 20% of the managers; 80% of exemplary customer service is provided by 20% of the staff. The 20% need rewarding; more need selecting. But first they need to be identified by good measures. Productivity, morale, absenteeism can be measured accurately and reliably. It takes some effort, skill and resources but it can be done . . . if the organization really wants the data. Some prefer not to know; others don't really care.

Marketing speak

Marketeers are concerned with selling the comparative benefits of their products. In the world of competitive sport you come first, second or third and receive your medals made of metals of proportionate values (gold, silver and bronze). This is the world of honest decisions: good, better, best; heavy, heavier, heaviest; far, further, furthest.

But selling products requires of marketeers that they produce in everybody a 'feel-good factor' about their choice, or indeed lack of choice. Consider the world's favourite airline. First class does and will remain first class. No need to fudge at the top.

Nearly all airlines call first, first; as do railways, hotels and other service industries.

The problems, or challenges as we now have to call them, arise with second, or even third best. Thus business class is second class – not as good, not as luxurious, not as big. Some airlines favour calling their second class after some national hero, place or institution as long as it is positive, romantic . . . and vague.

. The real marketing problem lies in describing the poor blighters at the back of the bus; the 'little people who pay taxes' and have to endure hours of discomfort squashed into seats made for performing midgets. How best to describe the citizens of the third estate remains the issue. If God had wanted us to travel economy he would surely have made us narrower.

Measuring performance

Any performance-related management system must attempt to measure an individual's success at achieving objectives. Performance-related pay schemes must have ways of evaluating and qualifying individual performance. The principle of equity demands that the more people give (in terms of effort, ability) the more they receive (in terms of a wide variety of benefits). To ensure fair rewards, both inputs (blood, sweat and tears) and outputs (filthy lucre, promotions) have to be determined and equated.

However fair and common-sense performance management systems are, there is always much debate over the problems of finding definable success criteria that are specific, measurable, achievable, relevant and trackable (SMART). For some social scientists everything that exists exists in some quantity and can therefore in principle be measured. To many, however, particularly those not in the commercial world, this evaluation and measurement language is distinctly foreign. They argue that their job is different from others; it is so unique, complex and unusual that it cannot be measured at all. And therefore, alas, they believe it cannot be included in the evaluation system. One wonders, therefore, how individuals in these jobs where success is unmeasurable can be selected or promoted? Presumably that old prison criterion of time served has to suffice for reward or promotion.

Consider how success criteria might be determined for three quite different jobs: a salesperson; a waiter; or a lecturer. Measuring the success of a salesman is relatively simple and the different criteria that can be mentioned tend to focus on different facets of the job. Thus one could measure sales volume or revenue (related but not the same); one could measure the sheer number of sales calls, or the ratio of successful to unsuccessful calls; the costs in terms of advertising; the size of the client list; the number of repeat clients; letters of compliment or complaint. All provide objective, comparable criteria of success on the job.

Waiters may be measured by tips generated and by customer response on preset forms. Modern methods are electronic – many waiters and bar staff have a personal number that they put into the till before the total cost of the meal/drinks. From this anyone can measure at the end of the evening how many customers have been served as well as the total revenue generated. Aggregated over a few weeks it soon becomes apparent which waiters are busy, being attentive and seeking out customers as opposed to those with tunnel vision or a preference for hiding 'back-stage' in the kitchen or cellar.

Even the old academic could have his or her performance objectively measured. Many criteria could be applied: customer response in terms of students' evaluation; the amount of money generated by grants; postgraduate students; outside seminars; the sheer number of books written or papers published and/or the number of times they have been quoted or cited; the pass-rate of students or their future success.

Nearly every job can (and must) be evaluated in terms of multiple criteria. The reason is that all criteria have a particular source of bias, and the aim is to use many so that a pattern may be determined where all criteria point in the same direction. Some criteria are often wobbly – e.g. letters of praise or complaint. They certainly do not represent anything like the total number of people who are satisfied or dissatisfied with the service they receive. In fact some people have become professional complainers because they have learned the rewards (such as free air tickets) of being a whinger. Equally, few bother to write in having had exemplary service.

Essentially, success is measurable by five types of criteria: money, time, customer response, measures of quantity (such as percentage increase) or measures of quality (such as a particular level of decrease in defects). The better the mix of criteria, the more subtle, accurate, and bias-free the result.

The use of electronic means to determine job success grows apace. Telephones can be set to determine the number of rings before being picked up. Lorry drivers have long accepted the 'spy in the cab', which measures all aspects of their driving. Even the humble pedometer can be used on traffic wardens to measure how far they have walked on their beat.

Mission statements

The 'vision thing', as ex-President Bush memorably put it, appears to have reached its sell-by date. At the high point of this missionary zeal every department in every organization was encouraged or cajoled into writing and displaying its mission statement. Like traffic wardens, they were truly ubiquitous.

Consultants told bemused managers that these statements motivate employees. Staff needed to know what business they were in and what they were trying to achieve . . . as if they didn't know.

The task of writing these bland, wish-list statements often turned out to be an exercise that was something between a philosophy seminar about the meaning of words and a furious argument between self-interested individuals as to what is important. But what is most curious about this slightly outdated exercise is that radically different organizations, with very variable products or services, ended up with indistinguishable statements.

A good mission statement should not say what a firm must do but what it chooses to do. It should not be filled with meaningless, unmeasurable superlatives like 'optimum' or 'maximum' etc. It is no more than hypocritical hype to have a mission statement that does not change the behaviour of the organization measurably. A good mission statement should also define the business that an organization wants to be in, not necessarily the one that it is currently in! It should try to find a unifying concept that enlarges its view of itself and brings it into focus. Most statements address themselves only to managers (who write them) and shareholders (who notice them). Unless it is directed equally at employees, customers, suppliers and even the public it could backfire.

Although it is rather too American and not English, a mission statement needs to be moderately exciting and inspiring. The mission statement 'To get back the Holy Grail' worked pretty well in the Crusades, even if it was ultimately rather unsuccessful.

Money madness

Nearly everyone is in business to make money. But saying so – indeed, talking seriously and honestly about money at all – is pretty rare. Money matters are frequently discussed – the rate of tax, cost of living, property prices – but personal finance still remains a taboo topic. Celebrities and ordinary mortals seem happier to talk about the intimate ramifications of their sex lives and mental health than about their monetary status, salary or financial transactions. Secrets about money matters do not occur in all cultures. In the openly materialistic cultures of South East Asia, enquiries into others' and open discussion of one's own financial affairs seem quite acceptable. In our culture, money issues are often denied, overlooked, or ignored in courtship, argued about constantly in marriage, and the focus of many divorce proceedings. Contested wills between different claimants can turn mild-mannered, reasonable human beings into irrational bigots.

Many philosophers and playwrights have written about the irrational, immoral and downright bizarre things that people do with, and for, money. The media frequently focuses on compulsive savers and hoarders (who live in poverty but die with millions in the bank) or compulsive spenders who recklessly run through fortunes often obtained unexpectedly. The former are compelled to save money with the same urgency that the latter seem driven to lose it. Robbery, forgery, embezzlement, kidnapping, smuggling and product-faking are all quite often simply money motivated.

The dream to become rich is widespread. Many cultures have fairy tales, folklore and well-known stories about wealth. This dream of money has several themes. One is that money brings security; another that it brings freedom. Money can be used to show off one's success as well as to repay those who in the past slighted, rejected or humiliated one. One of the many themes in literature is that wealth renders the powerless powerful and the unloved lovable. Wealth is a great transforming agent that has the power to cure all. Hence the common desire for wealth and the extreme behaviours sometimes seen in pursuit of extreme wealth.

There are two rather different basic fairy tales associated with money. The one is that money and riches are just deserts for a good life. Further, this money should be enjoyed and spent wisely for the benefit of all. The other story is of the ruthless destroyer of others who sacrifices love and happiness for money, and eventually gets it but finds it is of no use. Hence, all such an individual can do is give it away with the same fanaticism with which he or she amassed it.

Money is a hot topic because it has powerful associations. It can stand for security. Emotional security is represented by financial security and the relationship is believed to be linear – more money, more security. Money is an emotional lifejacket, a security blanket, a method to stave off anxiety. Evidence for this is, as always, clinical reports and archival research in the biographies of rich people. Yet turning to money for security can alienate people because significant others are seen as a less powerful source of security. Building an emotional wall around oneself can lead to fear and paranoia about being hurt, rejected or deprived by others. A fear of financial loss becomes paramount because the security collector supposedly depends more and more on money for ego-satisfaction. Money bolsters feelings of safety and self esteem.

Money, of course, also represents *power*. Because money can buy goods, services and loyalty, it can be used to acquire importance, domination and control. Money can be used to buy-out or compromise enemies and clear the path for oneself. Money and the power it brings can be seen as a search to regress to infantile fantasies of omnipotence.

Money is *love*. For some, money is given as a substitute for emotion and affection. Money is used to buy loyalty and self-worth. Further, because of the reciprocity principle inherent in gift giving, many assume that reciprocated gifts are a token of love and caring.

For many people, money is *freedom*. This is the more acceptable, and more frequently admitted attribute attached to money. It buys time to pursue one's whims and interests, and frees one from the daily routine and restrictions of a paid job.

There are a number of pathologies surrounding money because of all the complicated emotions and associations it has. Five are well-known:

1. *Misers* who hoard money. They tend not to admit to being niggardly, have a terrible fear of losing funds, and tend to be distrustful, yet have trouble enjoying the benefits of their own money.

2. *The spendthrift* who tends to be compulsive and uncontrolled in his/her spending, particularly when depressed, feeling worthless and rejected. Spending is an instant, but short-lived gratification that frequently leads to guilt (and debt).

3. *The tycoon* who is totally absorbed with money making, which is seen as the best way to gain power, status and approval. These people argue that the more money they have, the better control they have over their worlds and the happier they are likely to be.

4. *Bargain hunters* who compulsively hunt bargains even if they do not really want them, because getting things for less makes people feel superior. They feel angry and depressed if they have to pay the asking price or cannot bring the price down significantly.

5. *Gamblers* feel exhilarated and optimistic when taking chances. They tend to find it difficult to stop, even when losing, because of the sense of power they achieve when winning.

Perhaps there is no way to be normal with money. As Vic Oliver observed: 'If a man runs after money, he's money-mad; if he keeps it, he's a capitalist; if he spends it, he's a playboy; if he doesn't try to get it, he lacks ambition; if he gets it without working, he's a parasite; and if he accumulates it after a lifetime of hard work, people call him a fool who never got anything out of life.' So how normal or sane are you about money? Consider the following 20 questions. Circle 'Y' for yes or 'N' for no.

Questions	Yes	No
1. Do you find yourself worrying about getting or spending money most of the time?	Y	N
2. Are you very inhibited about talking to others about your money (income, investments, savings)?	Y	N
3. Do you buy things you don't need because they are said to be bargains?	Y	N
4. Do you invest considerable effort in attempting to find out a way to spend less money and save more?	Y	N
5. Have you often been told that you are careful with money?	Y	N
6. Do you regularly exceed the spending limit on your credit cards?	Y	N
7. Does gambling give you an unforgettable burst of excitement?	Y	N
8. Would you happily walk a long distance to save an easily affordable fare?	Y	N
9. Are you constantly puzzled about where your money goes and why there seems to be none left at the end of the month?	Y	N
10. Do you sometimes use money (be honest, now!) to control or manipulate others?	Y	N
11. Do you refuse to take money seriously, believing that it is not that important?	Y	N
12. Do you resent having to pay the full price for any item when you shop?	Y	N
13. Do you regularly lavish presents on others?	Y	N
14. Do you spend a large proportion of your free time shopping?	Y	N
15. When you legitimately ask for money from others, are you overcome by guilt or anxiety?	Y	N
16. Are you increasingly anxious about whether you can pay your bills each month?	Y	N
17. Do you spend money on others but have problems spending it on yourself?	Y	N
18. Are you addicted to retail therapy – shopping when angry, depressed or upset?	Y	N
19. Are you reluctant to learn about practical money matters, like paying bills?	Y	N
20. Do you think about your finances all the time?	Y	N

Score five yes's or less and you're OK. You are unlikely to suffer from any major form of money madness. After all, 'it's only money'. Score between six and 12 and you're pretty normal but, depending on which questions you answered 'yes' to, you may have a hint of the miser or spendthrift about you. Score over 13 and you may be classed as obsessive.

Others must have remarked on this pathology. You may need help ... but for goodness' sake don't go to an 'independent financial adviser'.

Remember what Henry Ford said: 'There are two fools in this world. One is the millionaire who thinks that by hoarding money, he can somehow accumulate real power, and the other is the penniless reformer who thinks if he can only take the money from one class and give it to another, all the world's ills will be cured.'

Money as a motivator

One topic that never goes away is money and, more importantly, its ability to motivate the average worker. Hard-bitten middle managers, especially experienced supervisors, believe that money is the most powerful motivator. Paradoxically, it is nearly always those who do not have it in their power to motivate by monetary rewards who believe this to be the case. And by contrast, the people who have control over the purse strings may not regard money as a very relevant major job motivator.

Does money motivate people? Is money, the poor people's credit card, a constant and powerful motivator of work performance? What of economic motivation?

Until the Second World War, industrialists assumed that workers had to be made to work by the carrot and the stick (this may often have been true during the Industrial Revolution). A similar view has been taken by most economists, with their concept of 'economic man'. Psychologists cite support from surveys in which workers were asked which factors were most important in making a job good or bad – 'pay' commonly came sixth or seventh after 'security', 'co-workers', 'interesting work', 'welfare arrangements'. This has been confirmed in more recent surveys, which have found that job security, pensions and other benefits are valued more.

The basic psychology of incentives is that work behaviour can be influenced if it is linked to some desired reward. Speed of work is an example. There is little doubt that people work harder when paid by results than when paid by the time they put in. Look at the timekeeping of the self-employed. There is also evidence that money can act as an incentive for people to stay with their organization. Some talk of the 'golden handcuffs'.

Money is but one motivator at work. Job security, a pleasant environment and a considerate boss are all motivators as well. Consider the following: Would you prefer £1000 (tax free) or a week's extra holiday? £1000 or a new job title? £5000 or a job guarantee for life? £1000 or meaningful and intrinsically satisfying work? Put like that, as a choice between money alone and other motivators, the power of money declines.

If, indeed, money is a powerful motivator or satisfier at work, why has research consistently shown that there is no relationship between wealth and happiness? In fact there are four good reasons why this is so:

- Adaptation – although everybody feels 'happier' after a pay rise, windfall or pools win, one soon adapts to this and the effect very rapidly disappears.
- Comparison – people define themselves as rich/wealthy by comparing themselves to others. However, with increased wealth, people usually move in more 'upmarket' circles where there is always someone wealthier than themselves.
- Alternatives – as economists say, the declining marginal utility of money means that as one has more of the stuff, other things like freedom and true friendship seem much more valuable.
- Worry – an increased income is associated with a shifting of concern from money issues to the more uncontrollable elements of life (e.g. self-development) perhaps because money is associated with a sense of control over one's fate.

Money does act as a work motivator, but to a large extent in the short term, for some workers more than others, and at a cost often to the morale of the organization. Money is only one of many motivators of behaviour.

Monitoring workers

Over 20 years ago, many long-distance lorry drivers were faced with a new form of measurement; the tachograph. They called it the 'spy in the cab' because it monitored fairly accurately various aspects of the vehicle's performance. It can record not only miles travelled but such things as speed (range, average) and the engine being on or off. It caused a storm in those grey, trade union-strangled days, but became widely used. Managers could thus monitor closely and accurately the behaviour of their drivers. Many observers at the time felt the system seemed reasonable, but impersonal. After all, if the driver was doing what he said, there should be no problem. Only the skivers should be afraid of being caught. And, unlike the milometer, the tachograph is not too easy to fiddle.

The idea that workers' performance can be monitored mechanically or electronically is not new. Factory workers have 'clocked in' for a hundred years. But the idea has become more, rather than less, popular as performance management has spread. Also the development of technology has meant it is now much cheaper and easier to use gadgets to measure what (if not how) a person performs. Consider the following examples:

1.   *The pedometer.* How can one measure the performance of traffic wardens? One possibility is counting how many tickets they issue. This will certainly increase their attentiveness but also their somewhat Stalinist image. Why not use a cheap pedometer, calibrated to one's stride, to measure distance walked. No doubt traffic wardens and policemen have their rounds and these can be measured and compared to the distance they have walked on a daily basis.

2.   *The phone monitor.* Customer service businesses have found it possible to measure electronically how many times a phone rings before it is answered or the caller hangs up. This can be aggregated over the day or week and can measure both whether a person is near their phone and how eager they are to use it. One hotel expects no more than two rings before the phone is answered.

3.   *Corporate identity card.* This is not the 'flexible friend' type card, useful in wining and dining colleagues and filling the car with petrol. Rather, it is an all-purpose card that can be used as an identifier to enter and leave buildings, but also to list all activities. Activities such as photocopying, eating at the canteen or acquiring equipment can be monitored by these 'smart cards'. The information they provide can let the company know when a person leaves and enters buildings and the costs of all the items they use. It might not measure revenue generated but it can measure costs.

Is the electronically or mechanically monitored employee a prisoner of the Orwellian nightmare of Big Brother? Or is it a cheap, efficient and fair method of recording performance that one can reward appropriately? Some would argue that conscientious, hard-working employees would benefit as there would be objective, indisputable and specific evidence of their performance. Certainly, it would be most interesting to look at the work record of those who line up either pro- or anti- to determine if self-interest is their primary motive of the argument.

Multiple feedback

Managing performance involves, by definition, evaluation, rating and giving feedback. In competitive leisure activities, as in the world of work, judgements of worth, excellence or ability have to be made. Whether the activity is growing and showing roses, disciplining and exhibiting dogs, or blending and tasting wines, a judgement of quality and quantity is required. The question is 'who is best suited to make the most astute but impartial judgement?'

Few jobs or competitive hobbies have a clear, first-past-the-post, way of assessing success. The Darwinian rules of survival of the fittest may work but only over the long term. And because people need feedback on their performance, they have to be evaluated along a range of dimensions. From a very early age we are given tests of our ability, knowledge and skill that are rated by parents, teachers and peers. School exams, driving tests, and assessment centres all involve the rating of performance.

Performance can be rated in many ways. Sometimes it can be done by machines that can measure strength, fitness and similar attributes. Machines can also accurately score multiple choice answers on a test by reading pencil marks. However, the more subtle, important, and higher-level skills, abilities and products cannot be rated by multiple-choice objective tests. No chemistry analysis can discriminate a great wine; no simple selection test can infallibly choose the best CEO. Given that someone has to make a judgement, the question remains who should that be? An expert, one's superiors, one's colleagues, one's friends (reference writers)?

Who should be the judge of one's work performance? Traditionally it is a superior – usually a person to whom you report, possibly the boss. But it could equally be a peer. Even more radically it could be a subordinate or, for greater reliability, a whole group of them. Why not be evaluated by your customers – and don't say you don't have any! What about your shareholders? The idea of customers or shareholders judging senior managers sends a shudder up the back of most people, but it could be argued that these groups are making judgements of our performance all the time, even if not explicitly.

Different groups of raters have quite different perspectives and therefore different sources of bias. In the jargon of experimental science one needs multi-trait, multi-rater appraisal. That means evaluation of various traits (or behaviours, or skills) by people is most accurate. Consider the advantages to the average middle manager of being rated by his/her boss, peers, subordinates, customers, shareholders (if appropriate) and possibly a self-rating on various work-related behaviours.

For most companies self-evaluation is out because it leads to self-aggrandizement and delusional high scores. Some people give themselves unfair and unrealistic positive haloes whereas the depressed and morbidly self-critical do the very opposite and give themselves extremely low scores. Both are inaccurate and poor discriminators.

Most employees are rated by their boss. He/she supposedly knows their virtues and their faults, strengths and weaknesses, abilities and foibles. That may well be true if one has a sensitive, perceptive boss with not too large a span of control. For many people, the quality and quantity of interaction with their boss is so low that there is really no possibility of sensitive and accurate judgements being made.

What about your peers? Some studies have found they are amongst the most accurate and predictive of judges. Research on officers' training corps and other high-powered assessment centres found that the participants were better predictors of success than the judges themselves. Why? Simply because the peers had more opportunity to observe all the antics of their colleagues during the 'up-front', more public times and also the 'back-stage' activities.

Some companies are risking upward feedback – that is, feedback from subordinates. This may be inaccurate either because subordinates have an axe to grind (leading to very negative evaluation) or are sycophantic (leading to positive evaluation); none the less it is subordinates who experience and therefore know the consequences of a manager's behaviour. If all subordinates give similar ratings, this is surely a statement of reliability. Service jobs have external customers and it is not uncommon that they are asked to rate performance. Hotels, banks, airlines and restaurants are used to doing this. How seriously these ratings are taken varies in practice, but the principle is a good one.

Much is now made of 360-degree feedback or ratings from top, bottom and both sides. In theory this must be a good idea, as long as the raters are trained and the rating dimensions are relevant to the job. All examiners need to be trained and their criteria need to be relevant to the skill or performance evaluated. Given these conditions (often not fully considered) multiple raters help to remove the bias and subjectivity in the whole process. Feedback from many sources can be used for formal appraisal or self-development (see upward ratings).

Music while you work

One of the more enduring black-and-white images of the war, and its associated grim years of rationing, is of teams of young women faking pleasure by rhythmically moving to 'music while you work'.

The message was that even tedious, humdrum, mundane tasks performed to 'catchy tunes' made for higher productivity and better morale.

There have been recent press reports of a surgeon who likes to operate to music. Presumably, one can always choose appropriate music to fit the complaint – Handel's Water Music for those suffering from bladder problems; the 1812 Overture for excessive flatulence; Schubert's 'Unfinished' for plastic surgery; the New World Symphony for childbirth; and Fingal's Cave for stomach ulcers.

Until recently, there was piped music at Waterloo station, which presumably was intended to encourage commuters to approach the working day in a better mood. Some killjoy seems to have objected to this, so the masses now trudge along in sombre silence.

Since the turn of the century, industrial psychologists have been interested in the possible benefits of music at work. They found that feelings of euphoria during periods of musical stimulation have a physiological basis (changes in blood pressure), which could help with certain types of work. It seemed that young, inexperienced employees engaged in doing simple, repetitive, monotonous tasks increased their output when stimulated by music. But they also found that not all workers liked music. About one in ten complains, and the number increases sharply as they age. Further, quality of work can be adversely affected by the use of music in the work environment.

Early studies showed that the benefits of background music depended as much on the type of music as on the task performed. Simple rather than complex, instrumental rather than vocal, soft rather than loud was preferred and was beneficial overall. School children who claim not only to be able, but to be better at doing their homework with television in the background are simply deluding themselves. Builders, plumbers, and 'rude mechanicals' who insist on inane pop stations played loudly so as to annoy others are unlikely to be distracted from their physical labour. It may make the time pass more quickly, but it is not likely to improve communication.

Some shops in this country play 'background music' or 'Muzak'. Some follow the research advice that suggests that slow, soft, repetitive, low-information music provides optimally arousing conditions. Others like to play seasonal music: carols at Christmas and Caribbean music in the summer to focus the customers' attention on certain products. Others – often shops with products aimed at young people – play pop music loudly, both as an attractant into the shops as well as a stimulant to the attention-deficit customers inside. But does it increase sales?

Music can be used to soothe, but also to excite. It is often an effective mood indicator, as all movie-goers know. But what is its effect at work? Some people have radios, tape recorders and CD players in their offices and workspaces. Many listen to the car radio and the odd Walkman can still be seen on the odd walking man. Essentially, for most, non-routine office work, music, or indeed any background information, be it music, speech or pictures, is a distraction. And because distractions distract, they have a poor effect on performance. Music can certainly help relieve boredom in tedious tasks like driving, but listening to a complex play on the radio while negotiating traffic may increase the likelihood of accidents rather than lessen them. The human information processor simply becomes overloaded.

Generally, extroverts like and need distraction more than introverts. Stimulus-hungry, they can be quite comfortable working in noisy environments. In fact, they may create noise if it is too quiet. Introverts, on the other hand, because they are usually cognitively over-aroused, actively seek 'peace and quiet' to work in. Being chronically under-aroused, an extrovert's whole life is dedicated to finding stimulus fixes. Their impulsivity, sociability and excitability are all a function of their need for stimulus; whereas introverts who are over-aroused seek the precise opposite. Music is just another stimulus. Extroverts concentrate longer on mundane, mechanized tasks with music and their performance in complex, concentration-demanding tasks is less inhibited by music than that of introverts.

So, if you run an assembly plant employing extroverts, you should seriously consider the idea of introducing a good sound system. But if you have introverted workers, ban radios and keep the noise levels down. Perhaps that is why the latter group is so opposed to open-plan offices.

National differences

To all intents and purposes the business world is dominated by four sub-civilizations: the Saxon, Teutonic, Gallic and Nipponic. Partly because of the formal education and informal socialization that every culture affords, they have rather different and diverse ways of reaching decisions. Cultural diversity is a bit of a 'flavour of the month' in management circles, yet there is no doubt that national (and corporate) culture does have a powerful impact on business. Culture affects feelings and relationships, how we accord status, manage time and relate to nature. It also affects how we marshal evidence, present arguments and make decisions.

The Saxon style fosters and encourages debate and discourse. Pluralism and compromise are overriding values and there is often the belief, particularly in America, that the individual should be built up, not put down. Accepting that there are different perspectives and convictions, the general approach is that these should be debated and openly confronted so that not only a compromise but a synthesis be produced – a sum greater than the parts. The price of ecumenism is anodyne blandness.

This is quite different in Teutonic and Gallic traditions. First, less conflict is likely to arise because groups are often more homogeneous, being selected and socialized for being 'sound on the salient issues'. Teutons and Gauls love to debate but not with antagonists, which would be considered a hopeless waste of time or an act of condescension. There is less tension-relieving humour and back-slapping – the tone is stiff, formal, caustic.

The Japanese from the Nipponic tradition don't debate, partly through lack of experience and partly because their first rule is not to upset pre-established social relations. They show respect to authority

151

and collectivist solidarity. Questions are for clarification, and debate is a social rather than an intellectual act.

The British have a penchant for documentation; the Americans for statistics. Both believe that data (reality) unite and theory divides. The British are distrustful of theories, '-isms' and '-ologies': these are considered to be 'sweeping generalizations'. Reports, graphs and tables are seen as necessary backup to support decisions.

The Germans like theories that are deductive in both senses of the word: that the theory may be deduced from other more fundamental principles and that it is fecund for practical applications. It is not that they eschew data – quite the contrary – but they like to know the philosophical or economic model or theory that drives both data collection and decision making. The Gauls are impressed by the elegance of theories and approaches. The aesthetic nature of the argument is appreciated. The use of *bons mots*, double entendres, alliterations and allusions to obscure cultural artefacts are celebrated, if not shunned. For the Teutons it is rigour before elegance, but for the Gauls it is the other way round. Sometimes the sound of words is more important than their meaning.

The Nipponese might fear inconsistency, ambiguity and contradiction but seem able to live with it. Arguments are less categorical and it is perfectly acceptable to see things as tentative, not fully formed. Ideas and theories are very cautiously elaborated with various kinds of excuses and apologies for their incompleteness.

In decision-making groups, the Anglo-Saxons pretend they are all equal but different; the Teutonic leaders have to pretend that they have nothing much to learn; the Gauls that they are all irrelevant to each other and the Nipponese that they all agree. Given a proposition the Saxons question 'How can you document or measure this?' the Teutons want to know 'How can this be deducted from first principles?' the Gauls, of course, wonder 'Can this be expressed in French?' while the Nipponese approach is to ask 'Who is the proposer's boss?'

It is no surprise, therefore, that courses on international management styles are so popular.

Need for power

The power-crazed, power-hungry, power-mad manager is a familiar demon in our press. The late Robert Maxwell and James Goldsmith were often portrayed thus. But is the need for power such a bad thing in managers?

What really motivates the successful businessman: money, power, prestige, the possibility of a knighthood, or all of the above? Is the desire to influence others a necessary part of being successful? Certainly a successful manager's need for power ought to be greater than his or her need to be liked; affiliative managers who need to be liked tend to be erratic and weak. Their disregard for procedure leaves employees feeling directionless, vulnerable and ultimately irresponsible. Of course, it goes without saying that the need for power (to influence others) must be disciplined and controlled and directed towards the organization as a whole and not the manager's personal ego. A manager motivated by personal power is not a good institutional builder because when he or she leaves, the clarity and team spirit generated quickly deflates. A strong desire to influence others, combined with little need to be liked and a good grasp of self-control is the ideal combination.

Power is something of a taboo subject in this country. A desire for power is often confused with dictatorial authoritarianism. Words like influence, charisma and personality are sometimes used as synonyms for the exercise of power. But power is somewhat different. Powerful managers have impact; they help their subordinates feel confident and responsible and foster a sense of team spirit and loyalty.

Management is a game of influence. Managers with a power motive empower their subordinates; the authoritarian leader does the opposite. There is nothing inherently contradictory in a manager with a high need for power who works democratically and spends a great deal of the time 'coaching' his subordinates.

What are the characteristics of the healthy power-motive manager – healthy in the sense that the manager directs power at institutional development, not personal aggrandizement?

1.   They tend to like working in organizations and feel personal responsibility in building them up.
2.   They like the discipline of work because it satisfies their need for getting things done in an orderly way.
3.   They are quite willing to sacrifice some of their own self-interest for the welfare of the organization.
4.   They have a keen sense of justice and are strong upholders of the principles of equity.
5.   They tend not to be egotistical, are less defensive and are willing to accept, even seek out, advice from experts.
6.   They are not scared of making mistakes – they fear not learning from them.

Power in organizations is not always easy to discuss or research. Those who have power deny that they do; many people seek it but pretend not to, and those who have achieved it are secretive about their methods. Power is not a fixed structural characteristic, nor the property of any one individual or group. Power is produced in some relationships and not others. People have quite different power bases depending on their particular resources (money, information, allies) and how much they are valued by others.

Where does power come from? What bestows power on an individual, group or organization? Early researchers were interested in categorizing the bases and sources of power. Eight types have been distinguished, based on two factors.

Position power (formal position)

Legitimate: based on the belief that the individual has the recognized authority to control others by virtue of his or her organizational position (i.e. a high-ranking corporate official).

Reward: ability to control valued organizational rewards and resources (e.g. pay, information).

Coercive: control over punishments (e.g. suspensions, formal reprimands).

Information: the extent to which a manager provides a subordinate with information to do the job.

Personal power (individual qualities)

Expert: based on the accepted belief that the individual has a valued skill or ability (e.g. expert medical skills).

Reference: based on liking of the power-holder by subordinates (e.g. the superior is friends with the subordinate). Allegiance to the relationship.

Persuasive: ability to use facts and logic to represent a case persuasively.

Charisma: attitude of enthusiasm and optimism that is contagious.

The underlying assumption is that most managers will prefer to use tactics that are socially acceptable and feasible in terms of the agent's position and personal power in relation to the target; which are not costly in terms of time, effort, loss of resources, or alienation of the target; and which are likely to be effective for a particular objective – given the anticipated level of resistance of the target. Some tactics are easier to use in a particular direction because the agent's authority and position power are greater in that direction or because their use is consistent with role expectations.

Essentially, the greater A's dependency is on B, the greater power the latter has over the former. Dependency is inversely proportional to alternative sources of supply – if everyone is educated, education gives you no special advantage or power. Power over others, or their dependency on you, is a function of three aspects of control:

- Importance: the thing(s) one controls must be seen as important. Thus, because people and organizations do not like uncertainty, individuals who reduce it have power. Therefore, during industrial unrest, the HR negotiators have increased power.
- Scarcity: any resource that is plentiful is cheap. Knowledge is power and this explains why certain groups refuse to share or pass on their knowledge.
- Non-substitutability: the source of power is unique and cannot be replaced by something else.

Although power involves the formal capacity of the control of 'others' in the organization, influence may be defined as an attempt to persuade another to behave as desired. Influence may be regarded as a form of control, if it is successful.

Different strategies require different resources and have different consequences. First, there is push and pull: these involve the threat of force, the withdrawal of resources and other coercive measures. Blocking support, using sanctions such as loss of promotion and perks, and assertiveness such as setting deadlines and enforcing rules, all come under push strategies. These strategies are more acceptable in some corporate cultures than others. Second, persuasion: this is the use of argument, evidence and facts to bargain and reason with others. Whereas most managers like to believe this is the most preferred strategy, there is no evidence that it is. Third, preventive strategies: these are really non-decision-making strategies aimed at keeping people out of the decision-making process. Finally, there are preparatory strategies: these are coalition-building strategies that aim to secure the help and support of others.

The desire to have and wield power in organizations is not bad, unnatural or pathological. Senior managers have positional and personal power that they can use for the ultimate benefit of the organization. It is when megalomaniacal, menopausal managers in search of power as an aphrodisiac use their positional power to further their own ends, against the interests of the company, that power – absolute or relative – corrupts.

Negotiating the Pacific Rim

The cry is clear: 'Go east, young(ish) man! The Pacific Rim is where it's at.' Growing, sophisticated markets; cheap labour; strong currency. The bars of downtown hotels in the capitals of the Asian tigers still overflow with European and New World businessmen seeking their fame and fortune even following the recent stockmarket crash.

How successful are the British? Despite the fact that half of the countries on the Rim were once British colonies, the eager salesman, as negotiator, often fails to 'close the sale'. Why do so many return empty handed with the opposition having clinched the deal?

One reason is the way we negotiate. We tend to make classic mistakes. The first is probably the most common. Negotiation and selling of any kind means entering into a relationship. The negotiation process is not over when the meeting ends. It continues at dinner, during sightseeing trips and even during shopping expeditions.

The Asian is not alone in wanting to get to know, even to understand, his opposite number. The British, however, too easily drop their guard, change their tune and reveal their hypocrisy when out of the formal environment. The gin and tonic can be the lethal discloser on one's real thoughts. Indeed, in some parts of the Pacific Rim, the real decision making is done outside the formal, meeting-based negotiation setting.

Second, many British negotiators have been conditioned from birth to believe in the concepts of fair play and supporting the underdog, and cannot grasp the elusive idea of the win–win. Many Asians have been socialized into a rather different view. Business is war; the negotiation, although disguised, is a battle. 'You let up, you lose' is the catchphrase of many in the Pacific Rim, and the quest for the idealist win–win situation may be fruitless because 'they don't want you to win'.

There is another, possibly particularly British characteristic that backfires. Battering Britain: its industry, politics and economy, is thought by some negotiators to be helpful in establishing a good relationship. To British ears, the self-effacing, self-critical approach may be charming. To many Asians, it seems both curiously disloyal and unpatriotic. Further, they may read into it a state of desperation and helplessness and demand lower prices because they perceive the negotiator to be on his or her knees.

Colonial guilt, felt by some, is often not dealt with by a new generation of business people abroad. The past is not forgotten, but does not bear close scrutiny. Seeking forgiveness for past imperial insensitivity may sound patronizing, if not insincere. That air of condescension that seems to characterize certain ex-colonial Britons, is popular with no one. Let lying dogs sleep – unless historical ties are referred to, they may not warrant a mention.

Another legacy of guilt attributed to the British in the Far East is their alleged ignorance of Asian culture and etiquette. 'The inscrutable complexity of Asian culture' message is deeply counterproductive. We are no more or less culturally insensitive than them but believing we are may cause self-fulfilling prophecies and also lead them to exploit us. Astute Asians exploit any signs of cultural pusillanimity.

It would be wrong to assume that the Asian 'opposite number' will conform to his/her cultural stereotype. All the cultural sensitizing courses and books in the world will be useless if your Asian negotiator has been educated out of his supposed cultural framework. The higher one goes, the more one meets the Harvard, LBS and Insead trained manager. They, like you, are individuals and need to be recognized and treated as such. A feeling of mutual affection is not necessary, but sensitivities must be respected. Astute observation of their dress, manner and speech will usually provide the required cues.

The cardinal sin of the monoglot Briton involves language. Whatever you do, do not assume that if your contact chooses not to speak English, or speaks it badly, that they do not understand it. We all comprehend much more than we can speak. Asians have been raised on the World Service, American TV and films and can pick up and fully comprehend the *sotto voce* asides foolishly muttered by monolingual Britons. Everyone appreciates it if you attempt to speak their mother tongue – after all, most have struggled to learn ours.

The new Asian manager and negotiator is tough, shrewd and insightful. He or she may well have had a Western education and possesses a good understanding of British ways and foibles. Doing business in Asia is no more easy or difficult than in Eastern Europe but it may require something of a rethink.

Nepotism

Does the appointment, from outside and at the same time, of a husband and wife to an organization constitute sleaze at work, or simply a fairly negotiated package deal? In the university world it is very widespread but because females keep their maiden names it is difficult to detect. Some organizations frown upon the process, believing that nearly always one of the pair is a freeloader often appointed to a position or role less for ability, effort or motivation, but more because of a relationship by blood or marriage. A sort of 'job for the relatives' idea that we used to dismiss as unacceptable nepotism.

Others have come up with a rather grandiose theory based on the biological idea of assortive mating. This argues that in general tall people marry tall people; the bright seek out the bright; the sociable each other – so that couples are frequently similar to one another.

A wonderful study done years ago showed that people with the name of Schneider (or Taylor) – that is people who took their name from their job and were required to be nimble of finger but not large of stature – were in fact shorter than those called Schmidt (Smith) who being blacksmiths needed to be big and strong. Hence, appointing two spouses of near equal merit is hardly corrupt but a double bonus for the organization.

If this story were true, though, wouldn't one find lonely-hearts columns involved in mate selection mentioning such things as consciousness, computer literacy and managerial competence? Ever seen: 'Male with strategic perspective, decisional flair and organizational ability seeks prioritizing female to implement proactive visioning'?

Newsletter begging

Having degrees from various universities means many people are the unwilling recipients of many increasingly glossy newsletters and magazines. This is a relatively recent phenomenon. For years, all of them appeared to have forgotten one; then someone must have pointed out that old boys and girls made up an invaluable and unique mailing list.

Cashing in on the nostalgia of our halcyon days of study, these magazines purport to keep one informed about the alma mater, one's old classmates and the triumphant strides of the institution at present. The Oxford magazine is most glossy; the LSE equivalent more interesting.

Rather cleverly, these publications encourage one to fill in lengthy biographical forms. One recently asked how many times in the last year one had travelled first class by air and to indicate present salary bracket. The answer to these questions, no doubt, is fed to potential advertisers in the magazine but also to university officials concerned with fund raising.

Where will all this end? Will one's Sunday School class run one to ground? It took nearly 20 years to escape the omnipresent tentacles of the *Reader's Digest*. Will the old school and the alma mater follow one to the grave? Clearly, like giving money to beggars, the last thing one should do is to encourage these people. If one does give a donation, perhaps it should be anonymous.

Norms: knowing what is average

All children have had the experience – proudly telling their parents that they have achieved 87% in the arithmetic exam, only to be questioned about the class average and having to admit they came last in the class.

Clothing manufacturers have to keep very exact and up-to-date figures on the size of the population. Every so often, we get interesting data that suggest that we, as a nation, are getting bigger. The average shoe size, bra size, and dress size is increasing and woe betide the manufacturer who ignores the population norms and over-produces in the wrong size.

The establishment of good norms is especially important in the selection business. Most people know that IQ has a near-perfect bell curve with the average score of 100, two thirds of the population being between 85 and 115, and the top 2% scoring over 130 IQ points.

What about other abilities or scores on personality tests? Many people who have completed those bogus but amusing magazine quizzes on 'Are you a demon or a dodo under the duvet?' have turned anxiously to the page that indicated to what extent they are above or below average. These test constructors are, of course, in the amusement business and simply make up the norms. They have not gone through the important but essential business of doing a representative population survey and empirically establishing what percentage of people do think and feel about particular issues.

Many widely used psychological tests have norms – quite often extensive norms on large and representative population groups – but not British norms. The Americans, who are enthusiastic developers and marketers of tests, have their own norms, but are they relevant to an equivalent British population? Is the middle-aged, middle-brow, middle manager from Birmingham really the same animal as his/her demographic counterpart in Birmingham, Alabama?

If stereotypes are to be believed, Americans are more extroverted, enthusiastic, optimistic and more open with their emotions than we phlegmatic Brits. There have, over the years, been many speculations about these two peoples having a common language and heritage but somewhat divided in popular culture.

There remain amazing observations about the habits and beliefs the two nations do not share. David Frost and Michael Skae pointed out that most Americans are puzzled by various British behaviours. Why, ask many Americans, do the British still find men in drag funny? Why do Britons apologize if you tread on *their* toes? Why do they watch sheep-dog trials on television? Why don't preordered interval drinks get stolen in the theatre? The British, on the other hand, ask why cash or personal cheques seem so often to be shunned in America; why few New York cab drivers speak English; why rubbish bins and post boxes look so alike; and why the nation that worships fast cars obeys a 55 mph speed limit. The trouble is that tests tap into local national beliefs and behaviours. What is normal for Americans is not always normal for the British or, indeed, any other nation.

John Cleese said that what he liked about Americans was their enthusiasm, and what he disliked was their naïvety. Equally, he admired British scepticism, but abhorred British cynicism. The British cultivate world-weariness and earn praise from making the best of a bad job; they have mixed emotions about work. Americans are taught that it is appropriate to express fiscal fitness and simple solutions to old problems. Whereas the former distrust professionalism and technology, the latter are taught to embrace it.

No wonder that personality tests looking at attitudes, beliefs and values in the two cultures do not tap into the same motives and traits. What may be naïve pestering for the British is healthy enthusiasm for Americans. Hence American norms, which show British managers to be depressive, anti-innovative and prone to paranoia. British tests, on the other hand, show the average American manager to be megalomaniacal and prone to delusions of grandeur.

One of the issues is that the British express their emotions less openly than the Americans and so do not show much of a range. Comparing a Briton with an American tells you very little, but comparing members of the British population with each other tells you a lot. Some American studies suggest that up to 70% of the US population are extroverts, but a UK study suggest that only 49% of Britons are extroverts. The UK data also suggest that Britons are much more comfortable with facts than with ideas (UK 80:20; US 70:30). The British are also less comfortable with tough-minded logic and prefer value-based (i.e. 'softer') thinking (UK 40:60; US 53:47). The British are similar to the Americans in preference for older decision making and planning (60% of both populations) compared with a preference for a more easy-going attitude to life (40% of both populations). Scores on one measure suggest that the British are less of almost everything than the Americans (including being less dominant, achievement oriented and flexible). However, they do score higher on self-control (the 'stiff upper lip') and good impression ('keeping up appearances').

The idea of establishing norms is not simply an academic exercise. It is also about that most American of pastimes: litigation. There have been a number of British court cases this decade where rejected job applicants have attempted to sue employers on the decisions they made using psychometric tests. This is important in the workplace, as older UK legislation about employment discrimination begins to bite and new laws such as the Disability Discrimination Act are introduced. Employers who do not phase out US-based assessments may find themselves having to explain to an industrial tribunal why the US population of 20 years ago is a valid comparison group.

Providing good, up-to-date national norms is essential. It does not provide any evidence for test validity, but it does settle arguments about what and who is average. Knowing what the majority of employees, as well as customers think and feel, and especially how they behave, is essential for managers as well as marketeers. Not having such data leads to guesswork and speculation, and that most common of follies: the belief, on the part of managers, that all internal and external customers are like them.

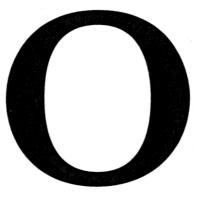

Opportunism

Opportunism and opportunity may be etymologically related but in the minds of many they are opposites. To be an opportunist, at least in this country, is thought of as extremely undesirable, but to have and seize an opportunity is thought of as good fortune. Is it that we disapprove of people who are fortunate through insight and luck, and approve of those who, with ability, effort and planning, work steadily and conscientiously towards a goal? Is it simple jealousy or the politics of envy that makes us despise the opportunist?

Opportunism (noun): allowing of due or undue weight to circumstances of the moment in determining policy; preference of what can be done to what should be done, practical politics, adaptation to circumstances; putting expediency before principle or place before power, political time-serving.

Opportunity (noun): opportuneness; favourable juncture, good chance, opening.

Opportunists then, may seem to compromise a moral or ethical position whereas those spotting an opportunity do not fall foul of these problems. Funny that the British, famous for their ability at, and liking of, compromise, are also those who are accused of investment short termism. Perhaps it is the recognition of the trait of opportunism that makes the British self-loathingly hypocritical of it.

Opposing innovations

Machiavelli, that no-nonsense, straight-talking management guru of his day, understood organizations' deep-seated hostility to innovation. He wrote: 'It must be remembered that there is nothing more difficult to plan, more doubtful of success, nor more dangerous to manage than the creation of a new system. For the initiator has the enmity of all who would profit by the preservation of the old institutions, and merely lukewarm defenders in those who should gain by the new ones.'

As all those attempting organizational innovations know, they are usually met with either antipathy or euphoria and nearly always the former. For those interested in executive level innovation, it is clear that the number of innovative proposals for serious change is inversely proportional to the innovator's rank. It is those middle-to-senior managers with 15 years and two ranks to go who are most opposed to change. They have invested in the system and are highly vulnerable to downsizing/rightsizing.

So the innovation opposer has recently become more skilled in opposing the innovative. They are masters of the 'killer' phrase, the sarcastic one-off jibe and also the sustained campaign against those enthusiastic for renewal, re-engineering or re-anything that shakes the boat. They strive for the status of abominable 'no' man.

In government executives are called administrators; in business they are called managers; in unions they are called leaders. Traditionally administrators favour the status quo; managers direct and control change. Administrators believe they are neutral implementers of the present policy but they do publicly advocate that things go most smoothly when the status quo is maintained and change is slow, cautious and evolutionary.

American politicians, despite public display about being decisive, innovative and change orientated, have been remembered more for their advice on how not to change. President Truman said 'If you can't convince them, confuse them', whereas others believed: 'When in charge ponder; when in trouble delegate; and when in doubt, mumble.'

Decidaphobia is the close companion of statusquophilia. The greatest asset for sufferers of decidaphobia is the committee. Committees only decide when most people are absent. In fact, the possibility of avoiding decisions or acts of change rises in proportion to the square of the number of members on the committee. The point of total ineffectiveness in any committee is usually reached when the membership exceeds 20 (especially if they are prima donnas).

Committee members know that trivial issues are handled promptly – even decisively – whereas important matters are postponed and rarely solved. Further, as all members of the ritualised 'Monday Morning Prayers' know, the meeting itself (its rules, norms,

roles) becomes much more important than the agenda and the problems it was intended to solve.

Through disagreement, committees generate heat and hot air,
not light. If a genuinely new, original idea is presented it nearly
always affronts the consensual agreement – indeed it wouldn't be a
new idea if it didn't. It has the effect of uniting the group against it.
Hence, paradoxically, committees most frequently agree when they
are most likely to be asked to change.

A member of that change-avoiding committee meeting usually
observes and then learns to use the vocabulary of the pussy-footer. 'It
would not be prudent at present'; 'the idea is a bit premature';
'having tried that before'; and 'research has shown'. The rules for
trying to suggest something new, on the other hand, prescribe that
one begins 'you'll correct me if I am wrong'; 'I'm only thinking
aloud'; 'it's a crazy notion that crossed my mind but . . .'

Delay, as Parkinson observed, is the deadliest form of denial. So
the change avoider never responds to letters, assuming the sender
will write again (and then visit in person) if the matter is of sufficient
importance.

A prominent American statistician observed the two best and
most common principles of administrative delay. The first leads to
the urge to centralize; the second to group think and both lead to
nothing being done:

- *The whole picture principle.* It is axiomatic that division managers
  are so wrapped up in their own endeavours . . . that they cannot
  possibly see the whole picture of anything, including their own
  divisions. It naturally follows that big programmes . . . should be
  guided not by managers but by trained administrators who can
  grasp the whole picture.
- *The combined thinking principle.* It is axiomatic that two heads are
  better than one, and a dozen is a nice even number. Given that
  administrative practices require that directors have councils,
  consultants and committees . . . if anything goes wrong, the
  responsibility can be graciously divided and erroneous decisions supported by the full minutes of the committee. Small
  wonder, then, that the management mantra of the 1990s is
  that 'the only constant is the need for change'. Even smaller
  wonder that staff at all levels constantly appeal for a 'period of
  stability' following the last round of manoeuvres.

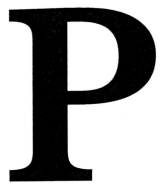

Pay

There is still regular press criticism of the large salaries earned by the American CEOs of poorly performing companies and directors of newly privatized British companies The beneficiaries themselves provide justifications, rationalizations and well-researched comparative data to support the case for their 'generous' packages but students of relative deprivation, the politics of envy and a muddled belief in equity, appear outraged at both the percentage increase in salary over time and the gap between the highest and lowest paid.

The British seem highly ambivalent in their attitudes to high achievers. Many approve of the Australian love of cutting down the tall poppy (*à la* Alan Bond), perhaps to ensure bland mediocrity. Many agree with the sentiment that it is important for society to support and encourage people who are very successful. Not as many believe that people at the top deserve their high position or believe their rewards are commensurate with their achievements.

It is, however, widely held that people who are successful get too full of their own importance. Indeed, the stories about top people falling from grace and being knocked off their pedestals is the very stuff of much journalism. It is not success *per se* that offends, however; it is the accompanying arrogance and self-satisfaction. Hubris, as my history master pointed out, is nearly always followed by Nemesis.

Well-paid executives, then, should be cautious in agreeing to appear on radio programmes or in pages of glossy magazines showing off their wealth. It may be tempting and flattering but rather than being a publicity coup it might well lead to a *coup d'état* followed by a *coup de grace*.

Performance-related pay (PRP)

Some companies have always had performance-related pay. Nearly all sales forces rely heavily on it. Others have had it for a decade or more, particularly large American companies. Recently many British companies have volunteered for it, while many public sector organizations are encouraged, then forced, screaming and resisting the whole way, to take it on board.

Does PRP work? Of course it depends on what one means by 'work'. Its aim is to boost both productivity and morale by introducing the concept of equity (rather than equality) at work, such that performance is directly related to pay, and it is unusual for any two people to receive the same pay. There are different types of PRP systems depending on who is included (to what level); how performance will be measured (objective counts, subjective ratings or a combination) and which incentives will be used (money, shares and so on).

For some organizations this experiment with PRP has not been a success. Sold as a panacea for multiple ills, it has backfired to leave a previously dissatisfied staff more embittered and alienated. There are various reasons for the failure of PRP systems. First, there is frequently a poor perceived connection between pay and performance. Many employees have inflated ideas about their performance levels, which translate into unrealistic expectations about rewards. When thwarted, employees complain, and it is they who want the system thrown out.

Often the percentage of performance-based pay is too low, relative to base pay. That is, if a cautious organization starts off with too little money in the pot, it may be impossible to discriminate between good and poor performance, so threatening the credibility of the whole system. But the most common problem lies in the fact that, for many jobs, the lack of objective, relevant, countable results requires heavy, often exclusive use of performance rating. These are very susceptible to systematic bias – factors such as leniency or the 'halo' effect – which render them neither reliable nor valid.

Another major cause is resistance from managers and unions. The former, on whom the system depends, may resist changes because they are forced to be explicit, to confront poor performance and to reward the behaviourally more successful. Unions always resist equity-based systems rather than equality-based systems because the latter render the notion of collective bargaining redundant.

Further, many PRP plans have failed because the performance measure(s) that are rewarded were not related to the aggregated performance objectives of the organization as a whole – that is to those aspects of the performance that were most important to the organization. Also, the organization must ensure that workers are capable of improving their performance. If higher pay is to drive higher performance, workers must believe in (and be capable of) performance improvements.

Performance-related pay plans can work very well indeed provided various steps are taken. First, use a bonus system in which merit (PRP) pay is not tied to a percentage of base salary but is an allocation from the corporate coffers. Next, make the band wide while keeping the amount involved the same: say 0–20% for lower paid employees and 0–40% for higher levels. Take performance appraisal seriously by making management raters accountable for their appraisals; give them trainers and train them how to rate behaviour accurately and fairly at work.

Make sure that information systems and job designs are compatible with the performance measurement system. More important, if the organization takes teamwork seriously then include group and section performance in the evaluation. It is possible and preferable to base part of an individual's merit pay on team evaluation. Finally, consider special awards separately from an annual merit allocation with which to recognize major individual accomplishments.

Any PRP system must support the strategy and values of the organization. If they emphasize entrepreneurial activity and independent effort they are all the more crucial. Closed, secretive, bureaucratic cultures do not take to PRP and undermine it. Openness and trust must be apparent if employees are to accept the standards and believe in the equity of rewards. Clearly, rewards valued by the worker must be linked to the outcomes valued and provided by the employers. For those who consistently rehearse the problems without the benefits of PRP, perhaps one can shout 'there is no alternative' as was the custom of Margaret Thatcher. There *is* no alternative – or at least none that is demonstrably more successful at improving performance and morale.

Place dropping

Businessmen and women, who nowadays are peripatetic itinerants, have started to indulge a newer form of the art of name dropping: place dropping. Like name dropping, this is also a form of showing off but naturally involves saying where one has been, on business or holiday, rather than whom one has met.

Modern place dropping depends on two factors. The first is the *exclusivity* of the place dropped. Exclusiveness may be obtained in many ways, but the most usual is by wealth. Most of the best places to drop are far away and hence expensive to get to. Some do not have any form of regular transport so one has to organize this oneself at great expense and difficulty. Occasionally a place may be out-of-bounds, privately owned or exceptionally remote, and hence, very exclusive. Exclusivity is not enough, however.

The second critical factor is *authenticity*. One's experience of the place in question must be authentic in that one does things as a native and not as a tourist. It is essential to refrain from the pseudo-events, contrived experiences and artificial products of tourist activity. The essence of authenticity, then, is that one meets, interacts with, behaves as, and hence obtains, a deep insight into the natives. When in Rome do as the Romans do, go where the Romans go, eat what and where the Romans eat and, most important, learn to pronounce things in the native way. This is a very cheap and effective means of emphasizing authenticity in one's place-dropping routine. That is why the highest compliment that can be paid to a foreigner is to be stopped in the street and asked the way by a local.

Go somewhere exclusive (Branson's private island; Cuba; Tashkent; Pitcairn; Angkarwat) and do something authentic (deep sea fishing; examining the effect of Stalinism on manufacturing; making yak butter). You won't get any points for sunbathing in Majorca.

Power ordering

Recently a successful businessman with 'old' money was having a post-opera meal in a trendy brasserie. He studied the varied and comprehensive menu for a few moments, slapped it down on the table and called the waiter over. He said that what he really wanted was a mushroom, broccoli and spinach quiche. This item was not on the menu and he was indulging in the practice of 'power ordering'.

Real power ordering is not having a starter as a main course, or recombining various separate options. It is simply informing the kitchen of what one fancies, presuming they have the skill, ingredients and inclination to provide it. Power ordering takes only two things: assertiveness and money.

Presumably, one could have even power ordered a non-black coloured Model T Ford from Henry, had one had the nerve. What power ordering reflects is the fragmentation of markets. This is the mass producer's nightmare (you don't power order in Burger King). As some people become more fastidious and organizations more customer sensitive, some are building in the flexibility necessary to deal with power orderers. Watch how first-class air passengers get what they want, as opposed to what they are offered. Set menus have been replaced by an *à la carte* selection. Now it seems all we require is a lively imagination to get what we fancy. The organization that is able to provide it will be the winner.

Procrastination

Few business meetings start on time. The corporate culture dictates not only how late a start is acceptable but how the organization deals with latecomers. Most institutions in this country simply wait 10–15 minutes for the latecomers whatever the excuse. In effect this punishes the on-time performers and rewards the laggards. More upbeat, macho organizations, or simply those for whom time-consciousness is part of their product or service, devise ways to deal with and eradicate this problem.

Some organizations lock the door at the assigned start time, as they do in the theatre. Others fine latecomers (say 50p per minute) and give the resultant 'pot' to on-time performers to spend, perhaps on a drink at the end of the day, a light lunch or a celebratory cake. Another technique is to humiliate the latecomer. Dame Edna Everidge is famous for this in her shows. Some chairmen and women draw attention to the latecomer skulking in hopefully unobtrusively. One group tries an odder, one-off strategy. They agree with the on-timers that when some specific person says a particular line (e.g. 'the executive committee decided' or 'according to the strategic plan') everybody laughs out loud. The puzzled latecomers are usually somewhat bewildered and know they have missed something. You can't use this strategy too often but it can have considerable impact.

It is possible to conceive times when procrastination is quite acceptable: prioritizing tasks or waiting until crucial information becomes available. Procrastination can be functional since it may maximize the likelihood of success at certain tasks. Psychologists, of course, are more interested in dysfunctional procrastinators, which they have divided into two types. First, there are the decisional procrastinators, who delay thinking about conflicting alternatives and they avoid stressful confrontations. They tend to claim forgetfulness, absent mindedness or simply being too busy. Decisional procrastinators apparently try to create situations whereby they never have to commit themselves to a choice, requiring others to make decisions for them, so that others can, if necessary, be blamed for failure.

Behavioural procrastinators delay doing things to protect their vulnerable self-esteem from failure. Thus by avoiding doing something, the procrastinator's perceived (or actual) inability at the task is never tested: they can maintain the illusion of, and possible reputation for, talent. All the research confirms that people who have low self-esteem or low self-confidence expend less effort, give up more easily and construct self-serving rather than accurate accounts of why the task is never finished.

So decisional procrastinators are interpersonally dependent, tend to be submissive and rely on others whereas behavioural procrastinators simply have low esteem. Maybe it doesn't take psychological research to demonstrate that chronic procrastination of any type is self-defeating and desperately handicapping. Perhaps some don't realize how much it says about one's underlying pathology.

For those of us who believe in time management, meeting deadlines, or on-time performance, procrastination is not just a curious and amazing habit: it is a dysfunctional aberration that ensures procrastinators and others dependent upon them waste time, miss opportunities and, worse than that, do not lead authentic lives.

Some see procrastination as irrational, others as immoral, and still others as pathological. All sorts of theories have been offered to account for chronic and acute procrastination. Of course, parents have been blamed: the procrastinating adult is supposedly a victim who was plagued by over-ambitious and demanding parents. In later life, imposed deadlines lead these people to re-experience early frustrations, so they dawdle and stall rather than attempting to meet imposed demands. Others simply argue that in some settings, procrastination has been learned because, paradoxically, it has been rewarded rather than punished. Some researchers have noticed that procrastinators tend to be perfectionistic rather than neurotic individuals, and assume that this may be the cause. Moralists point out that conscientiousness is associated with timely performance, not the evil of procrastination, and so they feel happy about condemning the latter.

Answer each question honestly noting whether it is true (T) or false (F) for you. To what extent are you a procrastinator?

1. I often say 'I'll do that tomorrow'.	T	F
2. I do routine maintenance on things as often as I should.	T	F
3. I waste time on trivial matters, avoiding big decisions.	T	F
4. When planning a party, I make all my arrangements in advance.	T	F
5. I frequently rush madly to meet deadlines.	T	F
6. I usually pay my bills on time.	T	F
7. I really need a time-management course.	T	F
8. I generally return calls promptly.	T	F
9. I think most people who know me expect me to be late.	T	F
10. When it's time to get up, I usually get straight out of bed.	T	F
11. Frankly, I am not good at meeting deadlines.	T	F
12. I usually accomplish all the things I plan to do each day.	T	F
13. A letter may sit for days before I post it.	T	F
14. I get most important things done with time to spare.	T	F
15. I always end up buying presents (birthdays, Christmas) at the last minute.	T	F
16. I am prompt and on time for most appointments.	T	F

Give yourself a score of 1 for each even item where you marked 'true' and for each odd item where you marked 'false'.

Score 0–5   No time-related problems, possibly impulsive.
Score 6–11   Fairly normal with a hint of sloth.
Score 12–16   A full-blown, incurable procrastinator.

Treatment may be at hand, however. There are, believe it or not, not only group workshops but also individual sessions for the procrastinator. Clinicians have found out five myths (cognitive distortions) used by serious procrastinators. In psychobabble, these are:

1.   Overestimation of the time left to perform a task.
2.   Underestimation of time necessary to perform a task.
3.   Overestimation of future motivational states. This is typified by statements such as 'I'll feel more like doing it later'.
4.   Misreliance on the necessity of emotional congruence to succeed in a task. Typical is a statement such as 'people should only study when they feel good about it'.
5.   Belief that working when not in the mood is unproductive or suboptimal. Such beliefs are typically expressed by phrases such as 'it doesn't do any good to work when you are not motivated'.

So procrastinators are 'cured' by being taught to think differently. They are also given homework exercises about meeting trivial and serious deadlines and they are given lots of positive rewards after success. The trouble with the therapy, of course, is not that it doesn't work but that too many serious cases put off attending (forever).

Public relations

A disgruntled colleague 'whistle-blows' on you and your organization. The press claim they 'have a right to know' about your management style. What do you do?

Most organizations have, at one time or another, been the unwilling focus of media attention following revelations of sleaze, corruption or incompetence. An increasingly litigious public, inquisitorial press and cock-up prowess, particularly in newly privatized companies, have provided rich data on what not to do. So how should one prepare for the eventuality of a PR disaster? Can one lay down some rules and regulations?

Consider the following, reasonably realistic scenario. As part of a major new product launch, your marketing department buys 5000 T-shirts, with your logo emblazoned on them, as giveaways. A few days into the launch, it is reported that a 10-year-old child wearing one of these T-shirts at a barbecue has been fairly badly burned. It emerges that the T-shirts were not only not flameproof – they were highly inflammable. There are many other topical examples that occur daily after transport crashes, chemical leaks and the malfunction of simple equipment. The local press gets hold of the story and the television news reporters want a statement – now! Indeed, there are also radio and television programmes entirely dedicated to investigating 'cover-ups'.

What should you do? The two most common responses are to blame the victim or maintain a tight silence. The former approach involves a company spokesperson saying that the company can hardly be held responsible for the problem as it was either the parents' or the victim's fault for being careless. This approach, however, is guaranteed to goad the parents and relatives into becoming more, rather than less, litigious. It will also paint a picture of the organization as being hard, unsympathetic and uncaring; the precise opposite of the 'we care about our customers' image that most like to portray.

The second approach is to preserve a determined silence: the 'no comments' option. The company lawyer, fearful of admitting any responsibility, may advise the PR department to stay quiet. This strategy may seriously backfire. Imagine what the investigative media do when faced with silent PR people and senior management.

They hunt for a talkative secretary or a garrulous security guard, flattered by media attention, and more than happy to comment. The media may simply interview staff leaving the plant or office, and finding the angry, alienated employee who slates the company's safety procedures is an easy task. The media like to unroll a crisis, to keep a 'human interest' story alive for as long as possible. These creeping crises are often more damaging than a 'one-off' disaster. Seeing a company duck and dive, refuse to admit responsibility and appear callous about its victims, leads to a true PR disaster.

Organizations must learn they can only control that which they manage. They need to be prepared for what follows. What the public want to know is what happened and why; whose fault it was; when the company first thought it might happen; what they did immediately it did happen, and what they are doing now. In other words, they want to know the full story of the incident. They also want to know that it won't happen again. Finally, they need to be convinced why they should trust the company again.

What all organizations, particularly those in manufacturing, need to do is essentially the following. First, when news of the crisis breaks, assume the worst-case scenario. This is not unduly pessimistic, but focuses the effect clearly. Second, be prepared to survive the media gaze. Choose articulate, intelligent people and keep them. Next, make sure you are communicating directly with your most important audience, whether customers, shareholders or staff. Centralize the flow of information, ensuring it all goes to, and leaves from, one specified point. Create a good crisis team and empower it to make the crucial decisions. It will always have to attempt to define the real problem and desired outcome throughout the crisis. The problem must be contained, even if it leads to short-term costs or loss of face. It is far too easy to escalate a relatively minor problem by dealing with it badly.

Lastly, and perhaps most important, resist the combative instinct. An exasperated research and development scientist, harassed by journalists, gives in to his emotions and shouts on camera. This is just not good. What the public wants to know is what is being done to prevent the crisis recurring. They are not a naïve, gullible, litigious mass, baying for the destruction of your company. They would prefer you to say you are doing your best, are truly sorry, and will endeavour to stop this kind of thing ever happening again. In short, you must demonstrate that you are a responsive and responsible company.

Punishing the punctual

Only little people arrive on time. Notice the schizophrenic way in which airlines deal with their customers. The sardine-canned economy passengers must be there two hours before international departures and may even be signalled to board, or at least be transferred to another lounge, 30 minutes before the engines are even turned on.
First-class passengers are discreetly whispered to in their peaceful private lounges. There is no rush to drain the champagne flute, or hasten the progress of the smoked salmon: they know they are special. They are only called when it really is time to board the aircraft and then, quite appropriately, first comes first. There is nothing morally wrong with treating people differently according to their ability to pay but it does seem silly to punish those economy passengers who are on time rather than those first-class passengers who are late. There is, of course, no real punishment in most instances, except added discomfort.

Each organization has its own way of setting acceptable time boundaries and methods of how to punish those who do not keep to them.

Yet there is real punishment for those who frequently arrive at meetings and talks on time. Not many business meetings start punctually. Most Western countries see time as a scarce resource, which must be rationed and controlled through schedules, appointments and through doing one thing at a time. Hence, spare time or time spent waiting is wasted and needs to be 'killed'. In some Eastern cultures, the maintenance of harmonious relationships is crucial and time needs to be flexible in order that one does the right thing with people to whom one has obligations.

National attitudes to time are related. An American psychologist called Levine compared various aspects of time management in seven countries. He found clear relationships between the accuracy of clerks in public places, the speed at which people walked down the street and the speed at which the post office staff sold stamps. The Americans and Japanese were fast; the Indonesians and Brazilians were slow. Further, in complete contrast to the Americans, in Brazil, a business person who usually arrived late for appointments was considered more likeable, happier and more successful than one who arrived on time. Hence the problems of relocating companies in other countries.

The reason why the punctual are punished is that some individuals simply have no concept of punctuality. They are time estimators, not contractors. If the meeting is scheduled to start at 15.00 hours, the contractor believes it means 15.00 hours, not 15.10. The estimator believes that 15.00 is a reasonable estimation of when things begin, but has the old colonial 'rubber time' approach, believing the meeting will really start at 15.15.

Dinner parties are different. If the invitation says '7.30 for 9.00', it means that drinks begin at 7.30 and food is served at 9.00. But in practice, few would ever dream of arriving at 7.30 lest they were thought of as gauche, crude or ignorant. Indeed, they would be punished if they followed these instructions. In fact '7.30' means 'about 8.10'.

Too many people, it seems, apply the rubber-time rules to business. How does your organization rate? Consider the following 12 statements and circle 'T' for true or 'F' for false.

1. All of our work is tightly scheduled.	T	F
2. Working fast is not really important.	T	F
3. People here get upset if you are late for work.	T	F
4. People here do things when they are ready, not on a schedule.	T	F
5. People here expect you to know how long it will take to do something.	T	F
6. People here feel that deadlines don't really matter.	T	F
7. Most people here are concerned about using their time well.	T	F
8. To be honest, the organization doesn't notice or measure what time you arrive for work.	T	F
9. People here plan their time carefully.	T	F
10. No one really cares if you are late returning from a meal break.	T	F
11. It is very important to be 'on time' for everything.	T	F
12. Most people in this organization don't think about how they use their time.	T	F

Give yourself a score of 1 for every 'true' you circled that was an even number and for every 'false' you circled that was an odd number. If you scored 10–12, you work in a serious time-conscious organization. Score 7–9 and you are about average for the UK. Score 4–6 and your organization is rather laid back, and score 0–3 and it will soon be laid out.

The corporate culture to a large extent dictates how time-conscious or obsessed the employees should be. The message of the 1990s is to work smart, not hard – but it's smart to optimize time use.

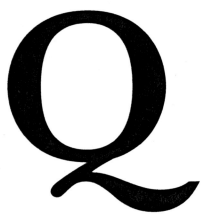

Quantum mechanics and administration

Recently there has been a modern myth going around that illustrates nicely the problem with administrators, bureaucrats, and other regulators . . . the way they multiply. It is reported that the heaviest element known to science was recently discovered by investigators at a major British research university. The element, initially named administratium, has no protons or electrons, and thus, has an atomic number of 0. However, it does have one neutron, 100 assistant neutrons, 50 vice neutrons and 200 assistant vice neutrons, which gives it an atomic mass of 350. These particles are held together by a force that involves the continuous exchange of meson-like particles called morons. They have to be passed regularly on different networks, cc-ed to others and grow regularly.

Since it has no electrons, administratium is inert. However, it can be detected chemically as it impedes every reaction with which it comes into contact. According to the discoverers, a minute amount of administratium causes one reaction to take over four days to complete when it would have normally occurred in less than a second. Every reaction becomes slow, inefficient, cumbersome.

Administratium has a normal half-life of approximately three years, at which time it does not decay, but instead undergoes a structural reorganization in which assistant neutrons, vice neutrons and assistant vice neutrons exchange places. Some studies have shown that the atomic mass actually increases after each reorganization. Administratium is indestructible . . . it grows consistently and like plants, more vigorously after being pruned.

Research at other laboratories indicates that administratium occurs naturally in the atmosphere. It tends to concentrate at certain points such as government departments, large companies, local councils, and universities. It can usually be found in the newest, best-appointed and best-maintained buildings.

Scientists point out that administratium is known to be toxic at any level of concentration and can easily destroy any productive reaction where it is allowed to accumulate. Attempts are being made to determine how administratium can be controlled to prevent irreversible damage, but results to date are not promising.

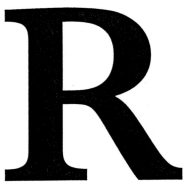

Rating staff

Customer satisfaction surveys and rating forms for people at work are now, like traffic wardens, ubiquitous. Hotels, airlines, restaurants, even churches provide one with cards and forms asking one to rate service, products and personnel. Not many people choose to tick the boxes and give institutions the feedback they require. Indeed, some give little incentives – a free drink, even a cheap calculator – to encourage us, the customers, to comply and improve the response rate.

Most managers also have to provide an explicit evaluation of the performance of their subordinates at least annually, by completing a, usually short, appraisal form. For some this is a bit like a school report with the most common phrases being satisfactory or adequate but, given the general loathing of unstructured report writing, most organizations devise appraisal forms where boxes are ticked to indicate the quality of performance against various criteria.

Rating others may be deeply counter-cultural to the British, although it is popular in America. We prefer to fudge with nice but meaningless phrases. Despite, or perhaps because of, the fact that we have all experienced the capriciousness of school or university grading, we resist inflicting it on others.

Many managers are hostile to, or resistant about, rating subordinates, precisely because they are supposed to be objective, impartial evaluations. They know, all too well, the errors and injustices that occur in the process.

Perhaps the most common error is called the *halo effect*. It can be illustrated by two examples. What most people are struck by when visiting a mental hospital is not that the inmates are dangerous or obviously 'mad' but that they do tend to be ugly. It is rare to find a physically attractive mental patient. The same is true of prisoners for similar reasons. When judges and psychiatrists decide on 'sentences' it seems they are influenced by the looks of the person. What is beautiful is good and vice versa. It is also not unknown for female secretaries and PAs to be selected more for their legs than their word-processing ability. All interviewees for selection know that appearance may be as important as, if not more, important than, ability in getting a job. Most attempt a positive halo by emphasizing their best qualities, whatever they are.

A second cause of error and lack of objectivity lies in being too lenient, or indeed, too harsh. The error is called *central tendency*. However long the rating form, and whatever its contents, some managers happily tick all the central boxes and avoid extremes. They do so because they do not want to overpraise an individual as this might cause an inappropriate and unfulfillable rise in expectations for promotion, or salary increase. They also avoid the low scores because they want to avoid controversy over the appraisal and having to deal with the anger, sulking and resentment of a poorly rated subordinate. The net result is that everybody comes out as average and the whole exercise is a waste of time.

A third problem is memory, also called *recency bias*. As managers rarely keep detailed notes, they do not always remember all the behaviours they have to rate. It has been said that when workers score any major success nobody remembers, but if they make one major mistake, nobody forgets. Certainly most people rate the recent past no matter how representative it is. Of course, another very common problem is personal bias and prejudice. This may be overt or covert, sophisticated or simple. We all have our preferences and prejudices based on past experience and it is often fairly difficult not to let these influence the ratings.

Thus, notwithstanding the quasi-scientific, and certainly numeric, feel of evaluation and appraisal forms, many managers complain that they are far from objective. They argue that there are so many sources of bias, like the few mentioned above. But this iconoclastic attitude doesn't take into account the fact that people can be taught to use the forms effectively. Coffee-tasters, dog-show judges, driving-licence testers are all open to the above errors when they rate beans, animals or driving behaviour, but they learn to overcome them.

When it comes to managing people, it is crucial that they are appraised and given accurate, specific and comprehensive feedback. Filling out forms encourages that and can be most helpful. Most managers would like their boss to provide them with detailed feedback but they all seem more hesitant about appraising their own staff often because they don't know how to conduct progress reviews with subordinates. So what do those who are sceptical and cynical about rating forms want in their place?

References

Despite what we all know about their shortcomings, the employment interview and the reference letter of recommendation remain the two most prevalent methods of evaluation used by prospective employers. Why do we retain the quaint and curious custom of requesting letters of reference and testimonials? Why do employers call for them? Are they at all useful or valid? How easy is it to spot classic lies and attempts to fudge or obfuscate?

Letters of recommendation are often called for in numbers roughly proportional to the status of the job. What employers are usually doing when they seek out references is to increase the size of the selection committee, adding to the number of people making judgements about the candidate, and spreading the blame, or at least diffusing responsibility. Furthermore, reference writers are supposed to know the candidate extremely well and be in a position to comment on his or her behaviour, skills, health, abilities and temperament on, as well as off, the job. In this sense they have a potentially important role as a source of privileged information about a candidate. This input may be significant given the difficulty of trying to get rid of people that one has mistakenly appointed and the need to find out about anything that a candidate is trying to hide.

Requests for references come in many forms. Some simply tell the referee that a person known to them (and presumably nominated by them) has applied for a certain position and would they be so kind as to state the extent to which they feel the candidate is suitable. Other requests require comment on a range of features of job-related behaviour of candidates, such as the extent to which they are punctual, socially adept, computer literate and prone to taking uncertified sick leave. More commonly, thanks to marketing mentality, some references invite the source to fill out rating scales going from 'outstanding' to 'poor' and using those wonderfully schoolmasterish phrases such as 'satisfactory' and 'average'.

There are three factors that render references of whichever sort pretty worthless. First, referees are frequently chosen or nominated by the candidates and so are likely to be biased. Second, an interviewer cannot be sure of the motives of the referee in completing the reference request. Third, there are unwritten, implicit, and hence ambiguous rules for writing references in code. The first problem lies in the nature of the source from whom the references are obtained. Some interview panels are completely non-specific, requesting letters from 'two people who know you well'. Others specify one's boss, immediate superior, former lecturer . . . but these often give the candidate extensive leeway to choose another alternative. For instance, if candidates suspect that the person directly above them will not write a good (possibly dishonest) reference, they may simply go up the ladder or along the organizational chart to find somebody who will.

The serious problem lies in the motives of the reference writer. The loss of an employee has consequences – some good and some bad – and it is difficult to see how these might influence the writer of a reference. What a temptation it is to put in a positive recommendation hoping that someone else will inherit your problems. This is a more common and more serious sin than writing a bad reference for a good employee who one may wish to retain. By definition, if they are good, employees will be clever enough to do well despite poor or even non-existent references.

Also, the fact that references are written in a sort of code of their own makes them difficult to crack. References are like Low Church funeral eulogies in that they may only contain praise. They can be dreadfully one-sided and it is, on occasions, quite difficult to recognize the dear departed or the refereed, however well one knew them. Some nationalities are worse than others; they write as if every student is an Einstein, every worker a Stakonovite, every leader a Churchill. These references are completely worthless because they fail completely to discriminate the able from the unable, the competent from the incompetent, the efficient from the inefficient.

The British, however, are uncomfortable with excess, particularly when it comes to praising others, preferring instead to understate. They also like a hint of criticism, believing that it is better to praise with faint damns. They also use wonderfully coded phrases that earn them the reputation for being perfidious. It is difficult to know whether this behaviour, namely writing in code, should be seen as pusillanimity in the face of having to give negative feedback, or just a method of encoding messages for native speakers only. It means, of course, that when British employers write references that are sent overseas they should be aware of not being understood. Many also love the double meaning found in phrases like 'he left us fired with enthusiasm' or 'you will be very lucky to get her to work for you'.

For those struggling in these politically correct and heterogeneously obsessive days, here are some pointers for writing a reference for the hard of hiring.

> These include such things as [being] *good at the big picture* (never starts anything) to its opposite: a *meticulous worker* (an obsessive who never finishes anything). There are many ways of saying the person is inflexible, changephobic or currently Peter principled to his appropriate level of incompetence such as *has a firmly based value system* (doesn't like powerful women), *does not believe in change for change's sake or is a solid middle manager* (hanging on for a redundancy payment). A *stable, long-term employee* possibly means insufficient drive and initiative even to look for another job. Other opposite but equally meaningless phrases include *is ready for a new challenge* (has tried and failed in a new position), or *we can no longer offer the necessary challenges*.

The British military writes officer fitness reports. The form used for Royal Navy and Marines fitness reports is the S206. The following are actual excerpts taken from people's 206 reports:

- *His men would follow him anywhere, but only out of curiosity.*
- *I would not breed from this Officer.*
- *This Officer is really not so much of a has-been, but more of a definitely won't-be.*
- *When she opens her mouth, it seems that this is only to change whichever foot was previously in there.*
- *He has carried out each and every one of his duties to his entire satisfaction.*
- *He would be out of his depth in a car park puddle.*
- *Technically sound, but socially impossible.*
- *This Officer reminds me very much of a gyroscope – always spinning around at a frantic pace, but not really going anywhere.*
- *This young lady has delusions of adequacy.*
- *When he joined my ship, this Officer was something of a granny; since then he has aged considerably.*
- *This Medical Officer has used my ship to carry his genitals from port to port, and my officers to carry him from bar to bar.*
- *Since my last report he has reached rock bottom, and has started to dig.*
- *She sets low personal standards and then consistently fails to achieve them.*
- *He has the wisdom of youth, and the energy of old age.*
- *This Officer should go far – and the sooner he starts, the better.*
- *In my opinion this pilot should not be authorized to fly below 250 feet.*
- *This man is depriving a village somewhere of an idiot.*
- *The only ship I would recommend this man for is citizenship.*
- *Works well when under constant supervision and cornered like a rat in a trap.*

Reinventing one's discipline

As patterns of employment change and the rules of supply and demand alter, so individuals have to acquire new skills. Or, at least, many are required to repackage and relabel themselves.

One anthropologist turned his attention from kinship patterns of primitive people to the peculiar rituals of the boardroom. He argued that anthropology was ideally suited to revealing the implicit bonds, power structures, and functions of ceremonies in the organization. He also noted that business schools have money, and the jobs available for academic anthropologists are now as rare as some of the tribes they investigate.

So we now have a small but growing breed of business anthropologists eager to share the prestige, pay and high-flying life of business school dons. Others have seen the advantage of joining the gravy train. Academics from many of the sturdy humanities disciplines have dusted themselves down, swallowed their anti-materialism and invented new disciplines, and therefore courses for the ever increasing band of smart young MBAs bent not so much on changing the world as changing the colour of the Barclay or Amex card.

Thus we have business ethicists who may have been theologians but embraced Mammon. Business historians are a new form of economic historian. And the less number-crunching orientated business schools may have business dramatic artists to teach presentation skills, as well as business sociologists who teach organizational behaviour (OB).

Psychologists have not been slow to find a new role, particularly in America. Thus business Freudians analyse organizations just as if they were patients – the neurotic organization, the paranoid organization and the schizoid organization. The business behaviourist is heir to the old-fashioned time-and-motion specialist with his stopwatch and clipboard. They are masters at inventing all sorts of new rewards, so important for the reinforcement-orientated behaviourists.

English dons may find a role teaching executives how to write in plain, clear English. All other 'foreign' language academics could offer short courses in business French, German and so on, or even contribute to the increasing fascination with international comparative business studies. The business schools are increasingly the main catalyst for changes in academe.

Selecting selectors

Human resource professionals often claim expertise in recruitment and selection. Hence they provide line managers with the only models they ever get on how to do it. Yet very few in the selection procedure attempt to ascertain the candidate's actual technical knowledge of his or her subject. They often look at qualifications, experience, even personality, but rarely test what applicants actually know. As job knowledge is assumed and rarely tested, it is not difficult for charlatans to slip through undetected.

For many years, HR professionals have fought against their widespread negative image. Bureaucratic timewasters, failed middle managers, and corporate social workers are the sort of labels they have been given. Most rightly reject these images, stressing the professional and technical nature of their work. They claim that HR has a theoretical and technical base that requires specialist training and examination. Indeed, there are Masters level degree courses at some 'new' universities that offer, one presumes, a rigorous analysis of the HR function. Lack of technical knowledge may even extend to recruitment and selection.

HR managers rarely make it to being the CEO of a major company. Coming from an administrative background, many HR specialists have a bureaucratic approach to work and find it difficult to make a contribution to the creation of future strategy. Unlike colleagues in operations or finance, they frequently lack management information, particularly financial data, which will guide senior managers' decision-making. Many do not know how to set up and exploit relevant databases. It is often difficult or impossible to detect the effect of the personnel department on an organization. Most other departments' effects are readily discernible, and their impact is immediate because they regularly collect data on their performance.

Lack of technical knowledge may even extend to selection. HR professionals are often not sufficiently computer literate or statistically trained to use sophisticated appraisal systems that generate information useful in actually tracking performance. Thus, because they do not know how to measure, monitor and improve their performance, many HR heads do not find themselves on the board, let alone in line for the top job.

Traditionally, assisting in the selection of personnel is a core HR function. This often includes job analysis and specification, recruitment and the selection procedure itself, conducted via the assessment centre and/or interview. Psychological tests of ability, preferences and personality have become particularly popular over the past decade, with as many as 60% of big companies using them. Many HR people like the apparent sophistication that many tests provide, with pretty computer printouts of individual profiles. It offers a privileged insight into the person, whereas, for others, it absolves them from making difficult decisions themselves. As a result, many HR managers have to be trained in the appropriate psychometric knowledge to use these tests.

It is surprising that so few knowledge-based questions are asked in interviews. There may be various reasons for this: the most probable is that the interviewers themselves do not know the answers. It is equally probable that they do not know which questions to ask because they are not specialists. There is also a peculiar form of embarrassment where certificated evidence of education is presumed to be sufficient and knowledge questions appear to doubt the 'evidence' of the paper qualifications.

So we all get to learn that it mainly presentation that gets you the job. The smart outfit, the easy charm, the apparent openness; all seem as important as the carefully doctored and embellished CV. It is very easy to bluff about actual knowledge, let alone experience.

There is no reason to assume that HR is any more or less guilty than any other specialization for not testing applicant knowledge. But just for fun, why not ask the next senior HR johnny applying for a job the following questions:

1.   Define: biodata; competency; demographics; ipsative; psychometrics; sten and z score; standard deviation.
2.   Distinguish between: context, concurrent and construct validity; massed versus distributed learning.

3.   What is: Cronbach's alpha; the fundamental attribution error; a polygraph test.
4.   How would you go about: doing a job analysis; calculating a selection ratio; evaluating a training course.

These are not particularly difficult questions and tap a modest but fundamental base of knowledge one may expect from anyone involved in selection. If there is nothing but flimflam for over 50% of the answers, probe more deeply into other areas of expertise. One might ask some traditional industrial relations questions about recent changes in the law, or even what they know about gurus like Denning or Peters. You may have a skilled impression manager who knows very little.

Selectors of HR specialists should test actual knowledge. This includes *functional expertise*: HR professionals should strive to be experts in fields such as learning, employee relations, compensation or benefits, in order to have something to 'sell' to their organizations, or alternatively, to sell to other employers. To give advice on a particular topic, you need to have a detailed knowledge of what that topic is. The tragedy is that many so-called professionals simply are not sufficiently knowledgeable about their chosen field. A *second factor* is people management, where one should look for the ability to set objectives, the ability to motivate staff, to deal with employee relations, to exhibit qualities and characteristics of leadership and to delegate adequately to subordinates.

Other factors include *personnel skills* and the desire for *constant improvement*. Self-evidently, these require *organizational knowledge*: clearly, to make progress within an organization, individuals need to know the structure of their business, the people, the functions, the strategic direction, the values etc. Knowing your context and the key decision makers is again a statement of the obvious but it is very often not understood.

Curiously, even internal candidates can be surprisingly ignorant about what business they are in and the key business indicators are worth watching. Of course, *business knowledge* is fundamental. All serious players in organizations need to know something about sources of competition, business performance measures, financial statements, and customers. Human resources, in particular, is still financially illiterate, all too often with little or no understanding of the concept of added value, profit, cost or, indeed, the world-wide context in which the UK operates.

In the jargon of competencies, the value-for-money HR director/manager needs knowledge of the business world, the skill to deliver traditional human resource services and the ability to manage the change process. There is a respectable body of knowledge and technical skill about the HR function and the successful professional needs to know it.

The moral is simple: use the selection interview to genuinely find out what candidates know. It ensures that one gets a real professional.

Selection fallacies

It is one of those curious ironies that those who know about recruitment often pretend they know the 'secrets of successful selection'. This pretence is similar to whistling in the dark to give the impression that one is not afraid. Selection decisions are fraught with difficulty.

There are those who do not doubt their ability always to appoint the best person. Maybe they lack self-insight; or real feedback; or have frankly made what turns out to be serious selection errors.

A number of truisms and fallacies surround the business of selection, which can be pretty dangerous. The most common and potentially disastrous is 'I can't describe what I am looking for but I know instantly when I have seen the right person.' Those who believe that their intuition, their hunches or their 'experience' is the best litmus test are seriously deluded. They infer too much from too little and forget that the job interview is a game; a charade of bluff and pretence, a hall of illusions – not a clinical surgery.

Those who feel they have instant, privileged or special insight often fall prey to psychopaths and other charming rascals found in used car lots. They forget that the people who appear best balanced, charming and experienced are often dissimulators. Secure, mature individuals have less need to sell themselves and may seem a little cool, even offhand. Further many 'ideal' people – clever, creative, judicious risk takers – do not present well to the conformist grey rulers of organizational employees. People frequently recruit in their own image if they merely use intuition, and this leads to organizational homogeneity.

Another fallacy is that of *committee reliability*. We form selection committees predominantly to diffuse responsibility when the decision goes wrong but the fallacy is that multiple selectors will minimize error. This can easily be nothing more than the blind leading the blind. The number of interviewers means nothing if they don't know individually and as a group what they are looking for or how to find it. Further, group interviews, or 'beauty contests' as they are called, nearly always favour compromise candidates – the average, the anodyne, the mediocre. The fallacy of multiple rating ends up with the lowest denominator.

The third fallacy is the *fallacy of human perfectibility*, of the development processes of the counselling cures. This fallacy assumes that giving people feedback and counselling can improve any problem they may have. Many ability and personality issues cannot be 'cured'. It is better to see oneself as a selector of the best rather than a reformer, repairer, counsellor or shaper of the second best.

The fourth fallacy is the misapplication of the idea that the past predicts the future: that *history is destiny*. If one can believe CVs, and they are at best a very selective view of history, all candidates are excellent: mature, talented, experienced and above average. The idea that success in a previous organization means success in another ignores the reality of the Peter principle. It could also be that past success has led to hubris and complacency. Success at work can extinguish underlying drive. Also, because of fundamental differences in corporate culture and success criteria, success in one organization might not transfer to another. As all gardeners know, the quality of the bloom is a function of the soil and the seed, not just the latter.

The fifth fallacy is to rely on the supposed impartiality of the *objective reference*. Inevitably, referees are inadequately qualified to give a good opinion as to a person's likely success in a new and different company and role. The referee eager to let go the second-rate can hardly be trusted to be a reliable witness. And, if the candidate actually nominates the referee, it is quite likely that the referee is far from objective.

There is no secret to successful selection. It begins inevitably with a careful job analysis to determine what abilities, traits or 'competencies' are required. Interviewers then need to be taught what questions to ask in what domains (early childhood experiences, current job, hobbies and aspirations), to look for consistencies and patterns, and to avoid classic errors like the 'halo' effect, but the fallacies persist.

Selection fallacies render all managers very vulnerable given the difficulty of sacking poor staff. Better to put effort and money into the quality circle rhetoric or eradicating all problems at source rather than quality control after the product has been made.

Selection versus training

All human resource managers need to have the courage (and budget) to teach the things they can train; the acceptance (and tolerance) to admit, accept and adapt to the things they cannot change; and the wisdom to know the difference.

Talk to some trainers and they will tell you that everything can be changed. They come from the can-do school of naïvety which assumes that with enough enthusiasm and enough multi-media training tools, everyone can be taught to be an Einstein, Stakanovite or a Branson. But is this true?

If the skills or gifts cannot be imparted by training, they can be selected for. Just as the former Eastern bloc had talent scouts always on the hunt for highly talented children to be shaped into Olympic athletes, so some organizations believe it is altogether more efficient to invest in careful recruitment and *selection*.

Others believe that the best selection and training device is the *Darwinian method of 'throwing them in at the deep end'*. This is not so much the gentle induction class, but rather the SAS survival course. The idea is simple: the department of hard knocks at the university of life is the best training ground.

A third system is the old-fashioned *apprentice model*, now revived in a lukewarm way by the mentor concept. Here, it is argued, the newcomer learns best at the side of the skilled worker (the master craftsman), gradually but surely picking up the skills of the master through initially trivial assignments.

The final system assumes that the above are too difficult, dangerous or ponderous and that chalk and talk, tooth and tongue training is the solution. But rather than start with training, it might be wise to use it only as a last resort.

Slogans

The wearing of T-shirts with slogans is commonplace, especially among the young. They are, in a sense, personal mission statements. As well as places ('I love New York') and institutions ('the University of the North Circular'), T-shirts often contain what Americans call 'motivation messages'. Occasionally on tropical holidays one may see middle-aged, rotund-of-girth managers indulging in the same habit. The 1980s school of triumphalism produced: 'you let up, you lose' and 'no pain, no gain'.

Why is there no entrepreneurial manufacturer printing T-shirts for managers? Are they short of copy? What about the following for starters: 'we deserve the Phillips curve'; 'if you think research is expensive, try ignorance'; 'a diamond is a piece of coal that stuck to the job'. Perhaps something for the fledgeling economist such as: 'maximize your marginal utility' or 'be bullish about bonds!'

The Americans sell posters and desks with 'motivational messages' that could be printed on T-shirts. How about the following: 'persistence prevails when all else fails'; 'if it is to be it's up to me'; 'never, never quit'. Or those crisper aphorisms – 'seize the day'; 'desire creates power' and 'I make it happen'.

Successful sales staff

In theory, selecting good sales staff should be easy. Unlike most other branches of management where it is fairly difficult to comprehensively and regularly measure performance, the sales function can, and does, provide frequent feedback on an individual's performance. Sales targets achieved, revenue, new versus repeat customers, costs, and a whole host of financial ratios can be calculated daily, as well as weekly, with any salesperson.

Given that the output or productivity is fairly easy to measure, one would think, by now, that those ubiquitous psychometric experts would have looked at ability, biographical or personality trait correlates of successful sales staff and have a list of answers. But this seems not to be the case.

Selecting and retaining good, effective salespeople costs insurance, pharmaceutical and retail organizations millions of pounds. The dropout rate is phenomenal. The really successful sales staff are worth their weight in gold. However, they are often mavericks with skeletons in the cupboard, and possibly even a dodgy CV.

Beware managers who say: 'I can't tell you what I am looking for, but I can recognize it when I see it'. They are either talking out of their derrière or inarticulate. But what should one be looking for? Essentially, these are the things that may be necessary and sufficient:

Coping with rejection (or ego strength)

Perhaps the most distinguishing characteristic of the successful salesperson who sticks at it and thrives at it is coping with rejection and how resilient one is in the face of criticism. Most sales companies report about 40% loss of sales staff one year after hiring and this attrition rate may go as high as 80% after the second year.

The problem is simple: you need salespeople to continue believing in themselves and their product in the face of overwhelming rejection. It is rejection of the product or service, not the former, but it is all too easy for salespeople to begin to believe that they themselves are being rejected.

Successful salespeople need the ability to handle (product and personal) rejection and accept criticism positively, taking it as helpful, not damning. They need, in the jargon, to be dispositional optimists believing their success is due to their effort and ability, and failure due to temporary, specific factors outside their control.

Ego strength is self-fulfilling. It leads to greater confidence, which permits one to be more immune to criticism. But one needs to start at a point where virtuous, rather than vicious, cycles begin.

The hunger (or ego drive)

This is not to be confused with ambition, energy, conscientiousness, nor even willingness to work hard. It is not even the aggressive drive so fondly spoken of by transatlantic sales people. Ego drive or internal motivation is the need to persuade and sell not only for the money but to persuade others in order to enhance the salesperson's own ego. Closing the sale must be a conquest for the psyche.

Ego drive does not go away. The harder the psychological challenge, the better. Not because of the monetary rewards, which should never be ignored, but the thrill of the chase and the joy of conquest. Stalk, hunt, bring down . . . the successful salesperson has a hunger for others to say 'yes'.

Closing a sale must boost self-esteem as much as the wallet. Of course, what one can do with large fees successfully earned as a salesperson can also satisfy an increase in self-esteem. But there must be intrinsic and extrinsic motivation.

Empathy and social skill

Of course, good salespeople need to be charming, socially skilled, and empathetic. They need to be able to accurately and objectively perceive another person's feelings without necessarily agreeing with them. A good salesperson can read the customer, picking up the verbal, vocal and visual cues the latter is always showing.

Empathy is the invaluable, indispensable ability to obtain subtle feedback. This enables the salesperson to adjust his or her own behaviour appropriately in order to deal effectively with other people.

Is it instinctive or can it be trained? The answer is both. Many courses attempt to teach 'the tricks of the trade'; the magical power of non-verbal communication or what to say in response to the customer. Good salespeople should have picked this up in childhood and early adolescence. In fact, they should have evidence on their file about selling themselves – whether it was in the school amateur dramatic society or debating society, collecting money for charity or raising money for their own personal needs.

Empathy and social skills can be taught – up to a point – but one needs the basic material, found in various 'people persons', those who can understand human nature and know how to take the role of the other. Find yourself a group of empathic, hungry, resilient salespeople and your chances of success multiply enormously, but this particular combination is not common. The empathic are often not resilient and vice versa. Sales staff can be trained and may have allowable weaknesses but one needs the 'raw material' to begin with to really ensure success.

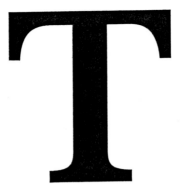

Teaching thinking

Can you teach someone who is tone-deaf to be an opera singer? Or someone who has poor hand–eye co-ordination to be a tennis international? The answer is, alas, no. You may train them, with considerable effort and motivation on their part, to be average, but never outstanding.

Intelligence is a predictor in most professions. Sales seem to be the exception, where studies show a negative correlation. Self-evidently, the more complex and cerebral the job, the more intelligence makes a difference. Even then, it accounts for only 0–20% of the variance. Consultants who regularly assess top management teams get used to the finding that the CEO is often one of the least intelligent members – certainly above the national average, but not a lot. Motivation, cunning, courage, ambition, and yes, even luck, do play their part.

One might not be able to improve intelligence much, although practice at tests has shown to improve test scores by 5–10 points. Certainly, studies on older people, including those called élite survivors, who do impressive creative, analytic and pioneering work into their eighties, even nineties, show 'if you don't use it, you lose it'. Tedious, routine, unchallenging jobs 'dull the mind, inhibit the thinking'. The brain needs exercise, and it needs capacity.

Don't despair – aspects of brain functions can be learned. Thinking styles and techniques may be taught. Various gurus have made their name through popular books that attempt to help people to think better. Most people know about Edward de Bono, with his ideas on lateral thinking, escaping from fixed patterns of behaviour, challenging assumptions, generating alternatives, jumping to new ideas and seeking to find entry points so that one can move forward.

Others believe the answer lies in mind mapping or similar faddish techniques.

Certainly, people have preferred different learning and thinking styles. These styles suit different problems and different jobs better than others. Indeed, it is the aim of recruitment and selection to fit the person with appropriate ability and style (way of seeing, analysing and discussing problems) to the job. Some people are more rigid in style, less flexible in their preferences. Others can, and do, switch style regularly, as adolescents experiment with and vary their handwriting. Style can be taught. It is unlikely to change innate preference unless done early enough. One can even change hand preference (usually from left to right, sinister to dexter) if done rigorously at an early age.

But the older one is, the more set in one's ways, the less the brain's muscle has been flexed and the less brain power and capacity one has in the first place, the less you can teach people to think. It's dreadfully politically incorrect, but it's true: 'you can't teach an old dog new tricks'.

Teamwork

Nearly all of us work with other people. Most of us are interdependent in the sense that we have to help, support and reward each other at work. No one can whistle a symphony; it takes the team effort of an orchestra to play it. Whether we call them groups, sections, squads or teams, most of us realize how much our productivity and satisfaction is due to them. This pretty obvious point is now the latest management obsession.

Management science, if there can be such a thing, is notoriously faddish. Not long ago it was strategic planning that was the key to organizational success. Then it had to do with organization structure. After that the gurus said that once the corporate culture (another oxymoron) was right, Eldorado was just around the corner!

All these solve-all solutions have now reached their sell-by date but there is, fortunately, a new solution to all the hard-pressed manager's needs. So business sections of bookshops bulge with books, nearly always written by people called 'Chuck', 'Randy' or 'Ed', on teams and teamwork. They rejoice under crypto-sporting titles such as *Team-Power*, or *How to be a Team Player; Winning Big*. Their message is simple: the power of the waterfall is nothing but a lot of drips working together. No matter how great a warrior he might be, a chief cannot do battle without his Indians.

What supporters of the team concept argue is this: bearing in mind that management is the art of getting things done through people, you need to let your people know what your goals are – what you want to accomplish, why you want to accomplish it, how they will benefit from it and the role they will play in accomplishing it. This is another way of saying that the members of the management team must be able to identify themselves individually with the company's overall goals. No chief executive, no top management group ever reached these goals by themselves. Unless the entire management team is aboard, the company will never get there.

What has caused this explosion in restating the obvious? The answer is partly in the American fearful obsession with the Japanese, who are still perceived by the Pearl Harbour generation as mindless but highly disciplined killers. The postwar Japanese miracle has puzzled the Americans – indeed, it has terrified them. What is the Japanese secret of success? The answer is teamwork.

The Japanese came from a collectivistic culture and hence naturally do things in groups or teams. We, in the Anglo-Saxon world, come from an individual culture that selects for, rewards and values individual effort. No matter how much teamwork achieves in our culture, the results tend to be identified with a single name. We therefore have to endure various mildly humiliating training courses (many in the great outdoors) to encourage teamwork because it is not natural to us. Although it is true that no member of a boat crew is praised for the individuality of rowing, this is an exception to the rule. The Japanese don't feel obligated to attend individualism courses to learn how to 'become their own person', 'do things their own way'.

Individualism in our culture runs deep. We are, however, loyal to some groups: usually those we have been forced to join, or with whom we have endured hardship and difficulty. The family, school, classmates and fellow military conscripts do often command our loyalty. But because we don't have jobs for life and find it easier to get promotion by moving between organizations, we rarely stay long enough in a team to be really part of it.

The life of a team goes through various stages: forming (the getting together); storming (arguing over who does what, who is leader, etc); norming (the acceptable explicit and implicit rules); performing (actually working well after the early stages have occurred). Teams also go through mourning when they break up. But all this takes time, and many of us never really stay long enough in a particular team to appreciate its worth.

How seriously do companies who have swallowed the team solution really take the idea? Yes, they do talk it up; go on endless (and expensive) courses; even partly restructure sections into 'new teams'. Yet very, very few reward the team rather than the individual. Most performance management systems (the euphemism for 'how pay is determined') are explicitly geared to the individual. Yes, teamwork in the sense of contribution to the team may be a criterion that is rated, but it is usually only one of many. Also, we rarely hire people with a team in mind or indeed hire the whole team.

Michael Winner got it right when he said: 'Team effort is a lot of people doing what I say.'

The team work philosophy of co-operation, interdependence and group loyalty is counter-cultural. Our business heroes are for the most part egocentric, rugged individuals, not team players. Teamwork may be a really good idea, but don't bluff yourself either that it is a total solution or that a couple of fuzzy warm courses will do the trick.

Telecentres

It is not until comparatively recently that recruiters and selectors began to systematically look for telephone-based customer skills in their staff. When goods were ordered and complaints made by letter, the skill of drafting sensitive, firm and clear documents was obviously valued. The widespread use of telephone sales has changed that; as have customer expectations of how they should be dealt with.

People who know they can phone high street fashion shops until 11pm, as well as computer companies until 9pm, have come to expect that they can generally do business 'over the phone'. And they may be angry if they discover that they cannot use electronic media and have to resort to the pejoratively termed 'snail mail'. Companies that boast how quick, reliable and effective it is to order from them can easily be seriously handicapped by either not providing a full telephone answering service, or inadequately training frontline telestaff.

The spread of access to the telephone, and the comparative reduction in the cost of a call, as well as the huge improvements in technology have meant a rapid growth in telemarketing and telesales. The boom in communication technology, mobile phones and free phone numbers has also contributed to the change in buying patterns.

The financial sector (banks, building societies, insurance companies), the transport sector (airlines, railways), the leisure industry (various holiday companies) and the ever-present mail order companies (small and large, general and specialist), have responded to telephone trends by building more call centres. Call centres can be designed and staffed to handle every type of telephone business or enquiry. Customers now want and expect them to be open 24 hours a day, seven days a week.

Telephoning allows call centres to be located anywhere: in areas where wages and related costs are lower. The Americans favour Ireland, with its well-educated, low-wage, English-speaking workforce, for establishing telemarketing centres. There is no doubt a substantial EU subsidy for locating there.

Managers of call centres try to make processing costs as cheap as possible. Most attempt to do this through technology such as the use of telephone management systems, workflow systems, profit/service data systems for the employee, and database management software. Conferences on these topics abound but the emphasis is on almost entirely technological and engineering solutions.

The human factor related to call centre staff remains neglected. Customers are interested in the price and quality of the service they receive from the person they speak to. They like clear, jolly, patient, understanding people on the other end. Most don't like the 'hard sell', the under-trained novice, the incomprehensible and inarticulate person. Defining customer service on the telephone, face-to-face, or even by letter, is difficult to do. Services are intangible because they are about performance rather than product. Also, most services cannot be counted, measured, inventoried or verified in advance of sales to ensure quality. Further, the product and the service are often inseparable because both are involved in the contact between customer and service provider.

Customers are becoming more demanding of what they want from service providers. They can, and do, specify all sorts of qualities, such as:

- Reliability – consisting of performance and dependability.
- Responsiveness – obvious willingness and readiness to provide a service.
- Competence – having comprehensive knowledge and skills to deliver the service.
- Access – the approachability and the general ease of contact with staff.

- Courtesy – explicit politeness, respect, consideration and friendliness.
- Communication – keeping customers informed in a language they can understand, and listening to them.
- Understanding – making an effort to understand the customer's needs.

Reading the increasing number of (printed) advertisements for telephone personnel, one could easily believe it is the best job in the world. It's fun, exciting, easy, done from near home, working in and with a supportive team, and the potential for making a good living is high.

Yet, if you can get hold of them, it appears that the data on call centre personnel tell another story. Job turnover and absenteeism are high, as are customer complaints. Little attention has been paid to the recruitment, selection and training for this frankly unusual and specialized job. How can recruitment be done in line with business needs? What is the demographic and psychological profile of the ideal employee? What sort of training do call staff need initially and then later in the job? Are the incentives appropriate to the personality types employed?

The problem with recruitment and selection of call staff is that one has a conundrum on one's hands. One wants extroverts rather than introverts because they are more sociable, lively and interpersonally skilled than introverts. But extroverts also like variety, and sitting all day answering the phone is tedious. Extroverts trade off speed for accuracy and may answer more calls, but take down wrong information. Extroverts are certainly more sensitive to promise of reward rather than threat of punishment but if these rewards are difficult to achieve because of the number and type of callers, they can become dispirited. They can also be erratic, particularly if a little unstable, and the last thing the customer wants is an irascible, capricious telesales person who having been rattled by the previous customer takes it out on him!

More importantly, what specific skills do managers need to get the best out of their staff, in the short, medium and long term? How can one create, maintain and manage a high-performing team over time? Technology is available to everyone; management and skills are not. It is the one area where real added value and higher return on investment can be made.

Managing call-centre teams is equally complex. Call centres are unusual places to work. The open plan office with dim light and hundreds of people speaking at once is not everyone's idea of a pleasant working environment. Visits to the toilet and the canteen may be the major form of exercise for some staff. And they can get, quite understandably, pretty rattled and snappy after dealing with dim, demanding, rude, inarticulate or naïve callers. But they need to be recruited and retained in larger numbers. Recruiting the wrong types and giving them little or inadequate training is likely to lead to poor sales and disgruntled customers.

The practice of buying products and services over the phone is on the increase. Shopping via the Internet will be next, but for the masses this may be some years away. Until then, the special nature of the people suited to the job, and effective at doing it, not to mention those who manage them, remains less well understood.

Time-filling strategies

All employees have a vested interest in pointing out how overstretched and overstressed they are. They hope that acknowledgement of this fact will lead to more money, more staff, possibly both . . . and less work. However, this dissimulation can lead to another rarely discussed source of stress: boredom stress or the tedium of underemployment.

The underemployed can be both a nuisance and a serious problem for those people working at capacity. Particularly if they are at managerial grades, underemployed bosses can seriously threaten the profitability of the organization. They call pointless meetings, which are the most favoured strategy of the timewaster. They may send long and tedious e-mails; trap an audience in the canteen; invent peculiar rituals and harass the quietly hard-working people in the organization. The worst possible combination is the relatively dim, neurotic attention-seeker in the role of the underemployed manager.

Having fought so long and so hard for promotion into some of these managerial jobs, it can come as some surprise that there is relatively little to do. What may be worse is that these managers are on display and have to look busy. So we have the scenario of the bored bureaucrat bewildering the business and the busy.

Boredom arises from a number of sources. Some jobs are inherently tedious. Consider the 'guards', attendants or whatever their job title is, at the British Museum. They are there to watch the public; to look out for picture-touchers, thieves and those occasional madmen who destroy works of art. Their coping strategy with this terrifying ennui appears to be hypnotizing themselves into a different brain-state of half-wakefulness. To semi-doze through the day is a safe strategy to cope with boredom.

Another source of boredom is repetition. This arises from having to do the same simple task over and over again. This was true of many jobs in the manufacturing industry but is less and less true as machines take over repetitious tasks for which they are ideally designed. The favoured technique of the mesmerized bored is to break or sabotage the machine. Luddism today is as much to do with the dull weariness of jobs as it was to do with saving them in the past.

Other jobs are boring because they are essentially monitoring jobs. Pilots are required to monitor computers; so are security camera or customs X-ray staff, but because they have to be alert their jobs are regularly rotated. Some monitor machines, others monitor people. The favourite trick of the bored people monitor is to stop and frustrate the public. Often people they are jealous of, rather than suspicious of, are the prime distracters of professional people monitors. Drive a smart car and traffic wardens, car-park attendants, and speed cops stop and interrogate the driver and carefully examine the vehicle. They like to humiliate the rich and powerful. It is such an amusement to render the mighty frustrated; a good scheme to alleviate boredom.

Certainly being ignored is a psychological cause of boredom. Hence the manifold use of 'attention-seeking strategies' by those who feel they are overlooked, marginalized or sidetracked. Often the 'safety and security' chappies feel undervalued. However, they soon realize their power to disrupt the diligent and pull the dutiful down a peg. Doors can be randomly locked and unlocked, entry codes changed at whim and private spaces inspected in the name of safety. It is the favourite way in which obsessives can become noticed. After all, who can argue against the cause of safety and security?

The meeting must remain the favoured device for the bored, stimulation-starved, underemployed manager. Shadowing studies of real managers show many spend as much as two-thirds of their time in meetings. Some meetings are genuinely used to canvass and share opinions; others really are called to make decisions but often they are called to diffuse responsibility by making collective decisions on risky topics.

If managers tried as hard to avoid meetings as they do in-house training courses, confidence that they are not underemployed would increase. Nearly everyone claims to dislike meetings and find them wasting time – but don't you believe them. Without meetings the average middle-aged boss or middle manager would be lost and, alas, the meeting-phobic often lose out on gossip and political intrigue. The world, as Woody Allen shrewdly observed, is run by those who turn up to meetings.

Time types

Time contractor and time estimator are very different creatures. When contractors say we meet at the restaurant at 8pm they mean (agree, contract, expect) 8pm. Estimators mean that 8pm is an estimated time of arrival and there is no reason to get upset if they arrive at 8.25 because that's about 8pm, which was a good estimate.

Worse than the estimator is the procrastinator. In some settings, procrastination has been learnt because, paradoxically, it has been rewarded rather than punished. Some researchers have noticed that procrastinators tend to be perfectionists, rather neurotic individuals, and assume that this may be the cause. Moralists point out that conscientiousness is associated with timely performance, not evil procrastination, so feel happy about condemning the latter (see procrastination).

Tips

The tip is the ultimate performance-related pay. It illustrates some of the problems of the meritocratic, equitable concept of reward related to output. Studies in America have shown that the number and size of tips is a function of all sorts of things associated with the waiter. Believe it or not, each of the following factors has been demonstrated to affect tipping:

- whether the waiter/waitress touches the customer;
- what they wear;
- whether the waiter/waitress has flowers in her hair;
- whether the waiter/waitress is physically attractive;
- whether he/she introduces him/herself by name, squats at equal eye-height during initial visit to the table and, of course, visits the table more often.

Tips also vary according to the characteristics of the customer. Tips are larger when customers are male, paying by credit card and patronize the restaurant regularly. Other factors to do with neither customer nor waiter make a difference, such as whether it is a sunny or cloudy day.

It seems reasonable that good food and prompt service are associated with higher tips, even though the quality, preparation and speed of food delivery is not within the control of the waiter. One does not, it seems, act completely fairly and simply reward the server on the basis of service. Certainly tip size is increased by friendly service, good suggestions, fine food, prompt delivery of the main course and the bill. But tipping also depends upon factors beyond the waiter's control and even almost at random. The mood of the cook, the price of the fresh produce of the day, and the avarice of the restaurant shareholders may affect the waiter's or waitress's tip as much as his/her behaviour and attitude.

This illustrates clearly one problem with performance-related pay. Performance is not always under one's total control. Most people are inter-dependent with others whose performance also affects one's own. Geo-political economic factors (which affect the real value of the pound in your pocket), often beyond one's ken, and certainly beyond one's control, can and do affect performance.

Training: is it measurable?

If you (unwisely) listen too carefully to shadow Cabinet Ministers, you may come to believe that money invested in training is the longed-for solution to all our economic woes. Hundreds of thousands would be taken off social security, and be more employable in this brave new world of 'knowledge' workers.

The same solution trips off the tongue of human resources managers and, not surprisingly, training consultants. That now-recognized error of over downsizing has made most people work faster, harder and smarter, but many argue that they need to be trained to do so. 'Training', we are told, 'is not a cost, but an investment, an enablement, indeed a necessity.' The restructuring of business and the introduction of more information technology mean that people need to broaden their skills base and learn new things. The KAISEN principle of continuous learning means, of course, continuous training.

Some organizations start their own training 'universities', like Motorola University, which has a budget of $120 million annually. There is also the famous Hamburger University where McDonald's processes 3000 store managers a year. We may be spending about £500 million a year, but figures are hard to judge.

Is the investment worth it? Does training affect the bottom line? Or is it a voguish, feel-good, PR exercise in pouring money down the drain? There are only four questions to ask and four things to measure:

1. The first is *participant reaction to training*. Measures of trainee satisfaction through post-course 'happy sheets' is cheap, easy and relatively straightforward. But make sure you, and not the teachers, choose the questions you would like the course participants to answer. Trainers can easily bias the questions to their known strengths (see Entertrainers).

2. Second, there is *learning*, which is the difference between pre- and post-course knowledge and skills. Again, this is not too difficult to measure, although there are two important caveats. It is easy to make the pre-test very difficult and the post-test very easy so that it looks as if the trainee has learnt a great deal. Also learning, unless practised and reinforced rather than punished, is all-too-soon forgotten.

3. Third, there is *behavioural change*, which is what the trainees do differently. This can take months to measure, and for most involves considerable effort. It is, in fact, best judged or rated by others – preferably by subordinates of the trainees.

4. Fourth, there are the elusive results from the bottom line. All sorts of things can be measured – sales or productivity up; rejects, absenteeism or customer complaints down.

So many directors have given up asking for proof that any, or all, training has an impact on revenue or costs. Most find it acceptable to measure training effectiveness when the programmes are translated into action. So measuring end-user or customer satisfaction is a popular and useful measure of training but it is only one and also could be the result of many factors other than training.

One reason why the grey gremlins of the bottom line have forsaken results-orientated proof that training works is that training is different now because work is different. Training is now as much about ideas as skills. It calls on new disciplines and today's training can often mean retraining and untraining. On-the-job training, distributed over time, rather than massed training, is popular. Employees now train each other, passing the baton and taking responsibility for doing it well, and training is now more high-tech. Indeed, one can take home a CD-Rom and, like Open University students, be trained in one's own home. Training can also form part of the total annual check-up and data may be used in assessment for promotion or a succession planning exercise.

But does the rigorous, measurable financial accountability of training lose its relevance? Will it do for overbearing, over-confident CEOs simply to assert 'I know that training works'? Is the feeling that morale has improved, or that communication is more open and honest after a series of courses, good enough?

Whilst it is true that training, like advertising, is very difficult to measure, it should not prevent the sceptic or cynic having a go. Trainers always stress the importance of feedback, so try giving them a bit of the tough bottom-line behavioural variety.

The trick is to try and measure a 'basket of currencies'. Many of the measurable outcomes at work are influenced by a host of different factors as well as training. Some seem more sensitive to training than others, but much depends upon the particular sector, the stage in the economic cycle etc. So numerous pre- and post-training measures need to be considered. It is, of course, important to have the trainers themselves discuss and agree these bottom-line measures.

Training does not work for all business problems, quite simply because it is an inappropriate response to a particular issue. There are inevitably good and bad trainers, good and bad courses and good and bad trainees. It is essential to monitor and evaluate the contribution of training, just like any other facet of the organization.

To have blind faith in 'trainer blarney' is to court disaster. If feedback is essential to development, get some feedback on the corporate effectiveness of training in your organization.

TV ads

It is an interesting exercise, while watching commercial television, to try to ascertain who the audience is. Without looking at those bland and unreliable viewing figures, it seems possible to deduce who the advertising companies believe is watching each programme. One does this, of course, by looking at what is advertised before, during and after the programme and how many advertisements there are. From this you can infer, comparatively at any rate, how many people are watching (more adverts mean more people) and something about their demographic breakdown. Household detergents for housewives; toys for children; cars for adults; fast food for teenagers . . . that sort of thing. It all helps to provoke good arguments among co-watchers of mundane or slow programmes, where the commercials provide an enjoyable break from the tedium.

Who, one wonders, is watching at 4am? There are advertisements for recordings of singers from past ages. Are other viewers a mixture of oldies, who are notorious early risers? There are also, curiously, advertisements for fast foods. Are these aimed at shift workers wanting a quick snack when they arrive home? Airlines are often advertised – are they after the jet-lagged viewer? Even some sort of tarot card service received an airing the other morning. Does this mean either psychics or the astrologically inclined are early risers? Why are banking services or sanitary towels advertised at 5.30am? Except, of course, that the slots are much cheaper at that time.

Understanding potential problems

Anyone who tells you they have a foolproof method of selection is either a liar or a fraud. The divorce statistics alone attest to the failure of individuals after quite considerable investment and thought to select the right person.

One can look for warning signals, however. The problem, of course, lies in the fact that interviewees are on their best behaviour. They all fudge, dissimulate and charm. They put their best foot forward, cover up personality and CV blemishes and try to present themselves in the best possible light.

How then does one detect the person who later proves to be the employee from hell: the hypochondriacal, complaining, underperformer? One method is to look for traits and behaviour patterns that have a clearly pathological dimension. The declaration 'I am firm; he is stubborn; they are bloody-minded' is well known. The idea is that many behaviour traits have both a positive and negative dimension to them. Too much or too little of an attribute can be a warning signal. Or rather the unacceptable side of everyday, quite acceptable even desirable behaviours, can signal the potential problem employee. Consider the following:

- The bold and the narcissistic. Outdoor training is partly used to encourage the average neo-pusillanimous manager to be brave and bold. Boldness is a function of confidence. It can also be an indication of narcissism, a common and deeply undesirable trait in senior executives. Narcissists are demanding, opinionated and quite unwilling to learn from their mistakes. Dangerously and morbidly obsessed, they need to be carefully screened out.

- The diligent and the compulsive. To have diligent support staff is a sheer joy. Unusually conscientious, orderly, attentive to detail they are always thought of as organized and hard working. But the over-zealous can easily be obsessionals characterized by being critical, picky and stubborn. Some compulsives find delegation impossible by trying to do too much themselves and not being able to prioritize.

- The dutiful and the dependent. Those who want to please others, to co-operate and maintain harmony are often rated as pleasant, agreeable and compliant. They do terribly well in interviews. But the excessively dutiful may be far too reluctant to make decisions on their own and they may not stand up for their subordinates. If you want someone independent, not bothered by negative feedback and willing to challenge the decision of bosses, beware the over-dutiful.

- The sceptical and the paranoid. The British rather admire scepticism (not to be confused with cynicism). They are often shrewd and difficult to fool, but too much scepticism leads to a perpetual concern with mistrusting others and always finding fault. Some may retaliate when they feel they have been wronged, which can be very bad news in the office.

- The imaginative and the schizotypal. Creativity is in: being imaginative and innovative is highly prized. Imaginative employees are unusual, colourful and entertaining, but they can also be cold, unreliable and totally impractical. Unconventional and eccentric in their dress maybe, but often very creative people are extremely immodest, egocentric and very uncooperative.

- The excitable and the unstable. It is fine to have enthusiasts – those who develop strong and oft-expressed enthusiasm for people, projects, departments; even the company as a whole – but the excitable are often moody, unable to stand pressure well, and very unpredictable. The over-excitable are quite simply unstable – they let little things bother them, become easily annoyed and change jobs frequently.

- The leisurely and the passive aggressive. To work at one's own pace and to one's own standard of performance, resisting others who try to hurry one is all very well but the leisurely become resentful and irritated when asked to increase the speed or quality of work. They often mask this by being outwardly pleasant and sociable yet passive aggressive individuals are nearly always stubborn, chronic procrastinators, and are often reluctant to be part of a team.

- The reserved and the uncommunicative. Quietly efficient employees who do not call attention to themselves and who prefer to work alone are fine but in extreme cases they can be withdrawn and uncommunicative, indifferent to others' needs, and rather unconcerned about the impression they make on others. They tend not to show public support for their employers and don't like talking to strangers. A nightmare in a customer service role.

- The mischievous and the anti-social. The excitement-seeking, non-conforming, mischievous employee is often thought of as charming, friendly and fun loving. They brighten the working day, are particularly appealing to the young, and often make a favourable impression. But after a very short time, others find them difficult to work with because they test the limits; they ignore committees and they take ill-advised risks. Often they are motivated by pure pleasure and are unwilling and unable to fully evaluate the consequences of their actions.

The moral of the story is this: for most human characteristics there is a optimal amount – neither too much nor too little. The downside of any work-desirable trait like diligence or imagination is often very unpleasant. What one sees at the interview and on the CV is nearly always, and quite obviously, the desirable end of the continuum. It therefore behoves the shrewd interviewer to look more carefully for other clues that may signal rather too much of a good thing.

Upward ratings

In most organizations, people are appraised by their superiors, who may or may not know them very well. It is possible and healthy, if somewhat unusual, to be rated and given feedback not top-down from superiors but bottom-up, from subordinates, who know and experience the consequences of management style best.

Upward feedback is in. Instead of being rated by the single person you report to, you are rated by all those staff who report to you. The appraisal boot, so to speak, is on the other foot. Of course, employees have always judged/rated their boss informally and constantly (mainly through gossip!) but this method attempts to make the implicit explicit. It has clear advantages. First, subordinates tend to know their superior more than superiors know their subordinates. They see their bosses almost daily and know their moods, foibles and preferences; they know their adequacies, skills, strengths, limitations and things that they do and do not like doing. Anyone who has been managed by a number of bosses knows their idiosyncrasies of day-to-day management of tasks, individuals and groups. Being at the sharp end of their policies and preferences, subordinates are in a privileged position to judge them.

Second, because all subordinates rate their manager from a statistical point of view, these ratings tend to be more reliable – and the more subordinates who apply ratings the better. Instead of the quirks and biases of individual managers' ratings (some being over-lenient, others strict, some showing favouritism), the various ratings of the employees can be checked for their agreement in the ratings, and then converted so that (hopefully) they can be averaged into a representative fair view.

Third, subordinates' ratings have more impact because it is more unusual to receive ratings by subordinates than by superiors. It is also surprising to bosses because, despite frequent protestations to the contrary, information flows down organizations more often, smoothly and comfortably than it flows up. So when it flows up, it is quantitatively and qualitatively different.

There are a few drawbacks to this method. Some employees might hold back from giving their frank and fair appraisal of their boss for fear of reprisals. They may also be unused to giving negative or positive feedback.

On the other hand, an anonymous rating might lead some employees to be extremely vindictive to a boss who, in the best interests of the company, is pushing his/her staff to do better. Individuals who attempt to 'knife' their superior could easily be detected, however, because their ratings would be significantly different from (and much more negative than) those of their peers.

Upward feedback can be used for personal development, training or actual merit appraisal. It is particularly useful for managers who do not elicit the views of their staff. Upward feedback may also help significantly in the two-way communication up and down organizations. It provides data on how subordinates are being managed. Assuming they are both accurate and honest, this may be a useful way for them to reflect on how they are being managed. Try to rate the way you are managed.

1. Do you know the extent of your authority in carrying out your major responsibilities?
a) I do not know what my authority is
b) I am not sure of my responsibilities
c) I am not sure of a few responsibilities
d) I have a reasonable idea about what authority I can exercise
e) I have a definite idea about what authority I can exercise

2. Are you informed of the objectives and strategy (vision and mission) of your entire department?
a) I am not informed
b) I am rarely informed
c) I have some idea of what is going on in the department
d) I have a pretty good idea of what is going on
e) I am well informed on most departmental activities and objectives

3. Does your boss give you the information you need to do the job?
a) He/she often withholds important information
b) Sometimes he/she withholds important information
c) I have to ask for information
d) He/she usually tells me what I need to know
e) He/she always tells me what I need to know

4. How significant does your work seem to your overall department's effort?
a) My work seems unnecessary much of the time
b) While my work is necessary, it doesn't seem significant in the light of the overall departmental objectives
c) My work makes some contribution to overall departmental objectives
d) I get involved in a number of significant assignments
e) Most of my work adds significantly to overall departmental objectives

8. Does your boss seem to understand your needs and wants?
a) He/she does not understand my needs at all
b) He/she probably understands some of my needs
c) He/she seems to sense my needs but doesn't do anything about them
d) He/she understands some of my needs and makes some effort to provide an environment to meet them
e) He/she always seems to understand my needs and is able to provide an environment to satisfy them

9. Do you believe you get the credit you deserve on your performance?
a) I almost never get credit
b) I usually do not get the credit I deserve
c) Sometimes
d) I usually get the credit I deserve
e) I always get the credit I deserve

10. Does your boss give you feedback on your performance?
a) He/she never discusses what he/she thinks of my performance
b) He/she is rarely complete in telling me what he/she thinks
c) He/she tends to be general in telling me what he/she thinks
d) He/she is fairly complete but avoids some issues
e) He/she fully discusses my performance

11. Do you participate in planning and owning your own work?
a) No participation. I am told what to do
b) I participate to a certain extent but only on minor details
c) Occasionally I have a significant input on planning my work
d) I have a fair amount of participation regarding how things are to be done
e) I participate a great deal, both in planning and carrying out the plans

5. Does your boss respond to questions that affect you quickly and openly?
a) He/she always puts things off
b) He/she avoids a reply if he/she can
c) It depends how he/she feels
d) It takes a while, but I usually get an answer
e) He/she answers the request immediately or within the next day

6. Does the boss really listen to your point of view?
a) He/she avoids discussing things if he/she can
b) He/she avoids discussing things
c) He/she listens but nothing ever comes of it
d) He/she listens and sometimes he/she will change her mind
e) He/she listens and makes changes when appropriate

7. How fair is your boss in handling disciplinary matters?
a) He/she is not at all fair
b) He/she gets emotionally involved and is frequently unfair
c) He/she is generally fair but occasionally reacts before he/she gets all the facts
d) He/she is consistent and fair most of the time
e) He/she is always fair

12. How often does your boss offer suggestions on how to improve your performance?
a) He/she never gives me any suggestions
b) He/she rarely offers me suggestions
c) Occasionally he/she will give me some general suggestions
d) He/she usually offers suggestions when it seems appropriate
e) He/she always offers suggestions and constructive criticism when it seems appropriate

13. To what degree does your supervisor help you in your job?
a) I do it all on my own
b) He/she provides little help
c) He/she provides some help
d) He/she provides a great deal of help
e) He/she goes out of his/her way to help me

Give yourself 5 for e; 4 for d; 3 for c; 2 for b; and 1 for a. Total your scores.

Score 55–65: You have a great boss and a good job. Stick at it.

Score 40–54: Perhaps you need to give your boss some explicit feedback.

Score 25–39: Your boss is hopeless, but can you educate him/her? If you can do so, try; if not, start looking for another job.

Score 24 or under: Quit now, you are being terribly managed.

Verbification

Americans like turning nouns into verbs. Thus one 'deplanes' instead of disembarking and one can, indeed must, autocondimentate one's food. But they have an even worse habit and that is to combine words to fudge. Thus one has 'edutainment' and 'infomercials'. The concept of the 'infomercial' is more sinister. This is presumably the commercial that actually provides (useful, truthful) information rather than a series of slick, hopefully memorable but meaningless images. The phrase 'tax avoison' is a mix of 'evasion' and 'avoidance'.

Why not have fun devising a series of new words which marry concepts which go together particularly in the world of management? So we could have 'succman' for 'succession management', 'justman' for 'just in time management'.

The trouble with the word 'management' is that politically correct feminists will object to the word because of the first syllable. These are the type who want to call seminars 'ovulars' and history 'herstory'. So management becomes 'femagement' or 'personagement'. Perhaps we should stop focusing on the naïve beliefs that language shapes and reflects attitudes that in turn change behaviour. For 50 years psychologists have found a very weak association.

Vitae

Are CVs or résumés, or 'vitas' as the Americans so nicely abbreviate them, works of pure fiction or accurate history? Are they at all useful for recruitment or selection? Are they prone to errors of omission or commission?

Curriculum vitae consultants/writers have led to 'vita inflation'. Many have been put through the plastic surgeon, the trick-photographer, the 'faction writer'. As a result they may be completely worthless as accurate portrayals of an individual life.

The American influence of 'talking up' nearly all personal achievements means that selectors have to be pretty subtle when reading between the lines. Likewise, ordinary people are now offered the benefits of CV consultants to improve the way they come across. No life is too ordinary, no work-history too boring, and no pastimes too menial to be considered unworthy of the image treatment.

The task of the CV consultants is 'impression management', which 'attempts to change, alter and shape the impression that others receive'. Given that we put in so much effort at the job interview, it makes sense to spend as much, if not more, time and money on the CV – which in itself may determine whether we ever get to the interview at all. As a consequence of the professional treatment, the most dreary and ordinary individual with a frankly mediocre, even failed, work history can look like a potential success. Whilst this may be good for the job hunter, CVmanship certainly presents a problem for the selection and recruitment specialist. There are three important clues in the modern CV. First, what is left out. Beware the CV that ignores or fudges chronicity: people may prefer to ignore long periods on the dole, a failed early career, an unwelcome start at one level. All sorts of important information may be omitted in the interests of the applicant. Selectors should perhaps have a checklist of information they really need and obtain it from the applicant if the CV does not provide it.

Second there are the grand generalizations. 'My department had a $2 million budget' does not mean 'I was in charge of it'; 'co-ordinated and facilitated staffing issues' could mean anything.

Third, there is the verifiability of the information. The more difficult it appears to check, the more probable it is a fudge. Beware the colonial experience where applicants held impressive-sounding jobs, even if they were genuine, in some far-flung outpost where their skin colour and ability to speak English ensured them senior positions. A name and address of the organizations on the CV certainly helps a great deal.

The paradox of CVmanship is that there may well be an inverse relationship between the CV and the person behind it. Over-egging the pudding – bound glossy brochures with career histories spanning several pages – screams the cumulative attempts of desperate outplacement consultants. The greater the flourish, the more the prizes, the quicker the promotion – the more ordinary the individual. Less is more.

W

Word rationing

It is a long time since anybody in this country experienced food or petrol rationing. Some even look back nostalgically to the bureaucratic world of food stamps and ration books that attempted to ensure that scarce and premium goods were equitably distributed.

In the airhead world of cyberbabble, computer-speak and consultant jargon perhaps the concept of word rationing may be useful. The idea is fairly simple. Every employee is given a ration of overused, abused or meaningless words per month. Thus you may have four 'empowerment', five 'paradigms', three 're-engineering' and six 'diversity'. You may use them when and where you like: a memo, a seminar, an official report; even a casual conversation. Once they have been used up, however, that's it until your next ration. Of course black-marketeers exist (called management gurus) who flog these words, but they should be resisted and abusers of the system fined for ration abuse.

The metric of incomprehensible, jargonistic, gobbledegook is the fog test. How does it work? Find a passage of about 100 words ending in a full stop. Find the average sentence length by dividing the number of sentences by 100. Excluding proper nouns, very common words (such as 'photocopying') and verbs with added endings, count all long, three-syllable words. Add sentence length and long word score together and then multiply by 0.4.

Using this metric, a typical Wordsworth poem scores about 6, and a passage of Kingsley Amis about 11. *Times* leaders tend to be a bit foggy, rising to 15, but there is nothing like an EU directive, insurance policy form or computer manual for a real pea souper. But let's not assume because there is fog across the Channel that all Europe is isolated. We have heard of 'Jobsworth' awards given to pedantic and unhelpful people not prepared to out themselves out because 'It's not worth me job, mate'. How about a 'foghorn' prize for those detecting the densest fog?

There is no excuse for obscure, jargon-filled, company memos. Plain English is the best medium of communication. Remember always to eschew obfuscation.

Workplace deviants

It is bad enough having lazy, unreliable, hypochondriac work peers and subordinates; it is much worse having really deceitful deviants. We are not talking about the frequently absent, temper-tantrum prone, mildly insubordinate worker, but the lying, thieving, psychopath from hell.

What is, and what causes, workplace deviancy? How can one spot, deselect and sack these people who generate substantial direct and indirect costs for their employers? First, what are we talking about? The workplace deviant is likely to engage in acts of theft, serious drug and alcohol abuse, lying and deceit, insubordination, vandalism, sabotage, chronic absenteeism and even assault. The files of workplace deviants are likely to contain numerous warning letters and threatened suspensions, grievance dispute records, worker compensation claims and accident reports. Some workplace deviants steal because of temporary life pressures – because of gambling losses, substance abuse or some other secret problem.

Consider two common and problematical issues: theft and lying. In some organizations, there is the possibly justified assumption that everyone is stealing. It becomes an opportunistic norm known by the technical term 'shrinkage'. It is a grey area with varying degrees of localized tolerance, even acceptance.

In most organizations, there is a balance of encouraging and inhibiting factors that determine levels and types of theft. Some organizations seek out personality types that may lie but are likely to be good at the job. Many have been arrested in their moral development, which can be tested by simple moral reasoning tasks. They also tend to have poor ego strength and can't resist easy temptation. They seem vulnerable to group norms and appear not to have that internal quiet voice of conscience. We know that the workplace deviant is likely to score very low on three related concepts of prudence, integrity and conscientiousness. These are not difficult to measure and there are various questionnaires which do just that. However, it should be admitted that they are fairly transparent and the lying workplace deviant can easily spot the 'correct' desirable answers. So the best solution is to get the potential employees' nominated (or better still, not nominated) former employers and colleagues to complete these questionnaires for him or her. Many of them have probably been victims of the workplace deviant and their ratings of his/her imprudence, lack of integrity and conscientiousness should be highly predictive. The many hurt and angry people left in the wake of workplace deviants means there is likely to be no shortage of those willing to tell the truth about them.

Group norms are a powerful force – rules about what it is acceptable to steal, how much, and under what conditions. These rules can be quite elaborate. Certain types of food may be stolen by restaurant staff, whereas in other organizations, there is open talk about 'taxing' wealthy clients – i.e. stealing from them. Some supervisors turn a blind eye to stealing and pilfering, seeing it as a part of the invisible wage structure. The practice of permitting theft as a 'side payment' is often considered quicker, easier and more direct than getting promotion approved.

Open, non-bureaucratic organizations tend to have less theft than rigid, over-administered organizations. Thieves, for that is what they are, may have a whole series of rationalization techniques for their clearly unacceptable behaviour:

- Minimization – 'it's only a pen; the company can afford it and won't miss it'.
- Externalization – 'the boss made me do it; I was framed'.
- Normalization – 'everyone does it; this is what we do round here'.
- Superordination – 'they owed me; it's only fair repayment'.

Organizations try to deal with these problems by doing such things as public shaming of the culprits (i.e. newspapers naming people who have been tried and convicted for such offences as drunk driving), or having corporate hotlines (for whistle blowers). Others try to target and assist those with temporary serious problems or to rotate group membership to break stealing norms. And, of course, most fundamentally, selecting out those prone to lying, stealing or sabotage.

It is important, indeed necessary, to take an organizational, as well as an individual, perspective. Lying, deceit and subterfuge are characteristics of some organizations more than others because of the nature of jobs and organizations. Consider the following, quite reasonable, hypotheses:

- The more skilled the job holder, the less he/she will be likely to cheat
- Flexibility in time keeping will be negatively associated with lying.
- Higher performance expectations on the part of the boss or company will be associated with more lying.
- People having more than one formal role will be more likely to try to deceive.
- People with considerable demands (i.e. parental) outside the organization are likely to be more deceitful.
- People reporting to more than one boss are more likely to be deceitful.

Each of these hypotheses has received empirical support. What they suggest is that certain job factors are implicated in workplace deviants by bosses. Cheats at work gravitate to, and operate in, different organizations. An anthropologist has described them in terms of four animal types:

- *Hawks:* individualistic entrepreneurs, small businessmen, fairground buskers, taxi owner-drivers and wheeler-dealer 'Mr Fixits'. The people involved all possessed a high degree of autonomy from group control and job definition and this meant that they could bend the rules to suit themselves. These are not high taxpayers!
- *Wolves* operate in 'wolf packs'. They pilfer according to agreed rules and through a well-defined division of labour. Like a wolf pack, they possess a group hierarchical structure, with a leader giving orders and with informal rules that control the behaviour of members through sanctions. Gangs of dockers, teams of miners, refuse collection gangs and airline crews fall into this category.
- *Vultures* operate on their own when they steal, but need the support of a group in order to do it. They are typically in jobs that involve a large amount of moving around and where performance success depends, to a certain degree, on an individual's flair and ability. Many forms of selling jobs come into this category. Hence travelling salesmen, waiters and driver-deliverers operate vulture fiddles. Some even boast of their behaviour.
- *Donkeys:* people who are constrained by their jobs and are isolated from other workers. Transport workers, machine-

minders and supermarket cashiers are all in donkey occupations. Donkeys can either be very powerful or powerless; they are powerless if they passively accept the constraints placed upon them but powerful if they exert power through rejecting constraints, breaking the rules and thus causing temporary disruptions.

Where there is a lack of fit between people's jobs and their cosmology (ideas, values, attitudes appropriate to them), they react in various ways. They could resign (withdrawing mentally from this personal conflict); they could experience a nervous breakdown; or they could experience a sense of alienation. Such alienation in the organization is often manifest in above-average absenteeism, employee turnover, sabotage and fiddling. Thus, fiddling represents only one of a number of possible responses by an individual to a situation of work alienation. Further, the fiddles of donkeys are not motivated primarily by the desire for monetary gain. Instead, the organizing and operating of the fiddles provide these workers with some degree of individuality and an element of creativity that is missing from their jobs.

It is easy, but erroneous, to blame all workplace deviance, like theft and sabotage, on particular individuals. It is true that there are clearly psychopathic people at work. But organizations, by their structure, their norms and their explicit systems, can help prevent, as well as detect, deviants. It is perhaps worth finding out how your organization explicitly and implicitly condones or condemns workplace deviancy before trying to hunt down the odd pathological worker.